London Corinthian Sailing Club

Centenary History

1984-1994

by

John Herbert

First published in Great Britain in 1994

Copyright © John Herbert

All rights reserved. No part of this publication may be reproduced, stored in a retrieval system, or transmitted, in any form or my any means, electronic, mechanical, photocopying, recording or otherwise, without the prior permission of the Copyright owner.

ISBN 0 947828 22 2

Typeset in New Times Roman 12pt
by
Wilton 65, Bishop Wilton, York. YO4 1RY

Printed by Antony Rowe Ltd.

Portrait of Sir Alan Herbert, C.H. in his World War II uniform of a Petty Officer in the Royal Naval Auxiliary Patrol Service. A Club member since 1923, he was President from 1943 until 1971.
Painted by Ruskin Spear R.A., in 1972 from a photograph.

My hand is on the tiller, my boat is on the wing:
Obey me, Wind and Water, for here I am a King!
But teach me all the virtues that men must have afloat,
For we are proud, but humble, who go about by boat.
So when, at Heaven's harbour, I hear St Peter's hail
I may cry back "FROM HAMMERSMITH! A FRIEND! BROUGHT UP IN SAIL!"

A. P. Herbert
1960

Acknowledgements

This Centenary History of the London Corinthian Sailing Club could not have been written without the assistance and advice of a large number of people to whom I am deeply grateful. The Club minutes were an obvious source from which to start and those from 1894 until 1940 are in the safe custody of the Hammersmith and Fulham Borough Archives and Local History Collections. I am indebted to Mr. Jerome Farrell, the chief archivist, and his efficient staff who not only provided me with the minutes, but also gave me access to microfilms and microfiche of local newspapers, street directories, history books and photographs on 19th and early 20th century Hammersmith and the riverside.

Chapter 1 deals with the International Fourteen which the Club adopted very soon after the rules had been accepted by the I.Y.R.U. Tommy Vaughan has been the official historian for years. His latest history has been invaluable and it would have been impossibile to do justice to the subject without being allowed to draw on it and also to talk to Tommy many times.

Jack Holt has been enormously helpful about the riverside in the '20's. Long before joining the Club in 1931, he had a tiny yard near the old Club where he first repaired boats, then began making them - including *Ace*, his first Fourteen. Charles Currey, to whom I remember being dangerously close on a wild spinnaker reach into Chichester Harbour during a Royal Bermuda, has also been immensely patient, informative and full of typically humourous anecdotes regarding the post-war development of hot-moulded dinghies which was pioneered by Faireys.

Many members and some non-members have provided written contributions, given tape-recorded interviews, tolerated innumerable telephone calls or lent books and photographs: Dr. Michael Gilkes, Dr. Olaf Bradbury, Sir Simeon Bull, Jeremy Pudney, Tony Newman, David Widdowson, John Salt, Chris Newnes, Michael Peacock, Dr. Tom Trevelyan, Group-Captain C.G. Plowman, Secretary of Itchenor Sailing Club, Michael Ewart-Smith, Captain Colin Marr, R.N.(Retd), Keith Goulborn, Ray Rouse, the one and only 'Robo,' Jeremy Sibthorpe, Julian Pearson; all helped on Fourteens. The Firefly class has been covered by Gavin Robertson, Mike Cook, Peter Hinton and Tony Robinson, our Commodore. The Swordfish by Tom Fielding and Peter Strauss. The Enterprises by Bill Simpson. The O.K.s by James Bridge-Butler and the Lasers by Nick Paine, Hugh Kemlo, Robin Johnson and Una-Jane Hodgson. Paul Williamson spent weeks, if not months, going through all the race records, and producing a synopsis showing the growth and decline of the various classes and the outstanding helmsmen.

Then there are the brave ones who race across oceans or Round Britain or even the world: Mike Dunham and Jono Callow (many thanks to the R.O.R.C. for their help regarding their Seamanship Trophy, originally awarded to Mike Dunham) Laurel Holland; Ann Fraser; Peter Hopps and James Chrismas. I am very pleased to have been able to include a large passage from *Woman of Steel* and my thanks to Vivien Cherry and Keith Wheatley. Then there are the equally stalwart J.O.G. racers, Tony Short, Lydia Jackson and Sally Dixon (as then); lastly those who enjoy long-range cruising.

Many others have helped on all manner of subjects: Don Storrar and Dudley Vaughan on the work involved when the Club took over Linden House - furnishing it and sorting out the domestic problems; Johnnie Evans on looking after pontoons and the rescue launch; Tom Hill on ramps, pontoons, and piles; Phil McDanell and David Widdowson on the variety of problems of being a Vice-Commodore, and Jonathan Clarke, on being an R.Y.A. Coach. The history would not be complete without a photograph of the late Wally See, which his son Alan lent me.

Then there have been all those in the background (or at the bar) who have given me enormously useful information - like the late Jack Usher, till recently the sage of Hammersmith; 50 years with the Borough Council and secretary to 20 Mayors. God bless him. Sally and Christopher Buckley who supplied me with methodically kept files and have answered a vast number of questions. Patrick Goodison, my neighbour, who turns out to have thought of the first Thames Tideway Race. Mirando Kemlo deserves a medal for reading dusty minute files, and gathering information for me on a variety of subjects, including taking a tape-recording from her husband. She's been wonderful. Alex Allan for confirmation about what went on at laying-up suppers. The Royal College of Music for information on Gustav Holst's composition for full orchestra - *Hammersmith*. My good friend Mary Miller has burned the midnight oil tearing my manuscript to bits and giving it respectability. A marvellous and invaluable editor.

Last but not least there is Mark O'Connor, without whose tuition and encouragement this work would not have gone to the publisher. In March 1993, my word-processor gave up the ghost and I had to buy another one, and then learn how to use it. Without Mark I would never have done it. At embarrassingly late hours I used to ring him to tell him something had happened to the machine; although exhausted from a day's work, he would walk across Ravenscourt Park and sort me and the word-processor out. What a friend.

Thank you all very much.

Bibliography

The International Fourteen, 1928-1989, Handbook and History by T.J. Vaughan. Published by the International Fourteen Foot Dinghy Class Association of Great Britain, 1989.

A History of Hammersmith 'based upon that of Thomas Faulkner in 1839.' Edited for the Hammersmith Local History Group by Philip D. Whitting, 1965

Minute by Minute. The Story of the Royal Yachting Association (1875-1982) by Gordon Fairley Published by the R.Y.A., 1983.

Dinghy Team Racing by Eric Twiname, Published by Adlard Coles, 1971

Woman of Steel by Vivien Cherry with Keith Wheatley. Published by Adlard Coles Nautical, London, 1993.

The Parmelia Race, 1979. The Log of Seltrust Endeavour. Loaned by Mike Dunham and 'Jono' Callow.

CONTENTS

Acknowledgements
Bibliography
Introduction by Dr. Tom Trevelyan
President of the International Fourteen World Association

Chapter		Page
1	Fifty Years of Sailing International Fourteens	1
2	How the Club was Founded	37
3	Hammersmith and the River in 1894	46
4	A Club of Our Own, 1897-1918	53
5	1918-1938	72
6	World War Two and Post-War Scene	91
7	Fireflies	112
8	Memories of the Old Club	124
9	The Swordfish Class	132
10	The Enterprise Class	137
11	Linden House and the Move	150
12	The O.K. Class	167
13	The Laser Class	172
14	Linden House, 1961 - 1994	184
15	Ocean - Going Corinthians	208

APPENDICES

A.	Synopsis of Race Results	255
B.	List of Commodores	279
C.	Members who have subscribed to the Centenary	280
D.	Major Trophy Winners	282

ILLUSTRATIONS

Portrait of Sir Alan Herbert, C.H.   Frontispiece
Poem by A.P. Herbert, from the President's Trophy

PLATES, between pages 136-137

I	Black Lion Stairs
II	One of the Club founders, off Black Lion Stairs
III	The entrance to the old Club
	A contempory photograph of the old Club
IV	19th Century formula for a measurement certificate
V	A group of members with their ladies
	The Creek, circa 1914-1924
VI	The saloon of the old Club
VII	The great flood of January 1928
VIII	A.P.H.'s canal barge *The Ark*
	A Club race in 1939
IX	The 1938 Shackleton
	A little trouble at the gybe mark
X	Doodlebug devastation
	The old Club during the mid 1950's
XI	Tea on the hard wall
	Firefly fleet late 1950's
XII	One of the Swordfish Open Meetings
	The 1960 race for Fireflies
XIII	Wally See presenting Jane Bluff with his cup
	'Goodbye' to the old Club in 1962
XIV	A.P.H. presenting the Shackleton Cup in 1962
	The 1967 Shackleton Trophy
XV	The start of a Club Enterprise race
	One of the O.K. Open meetings
XVI	Gil Winfield in the rescue launch
	The 1962 Tideway Race
XVII	Jack Holt presenting Enterprise 15,000
	Enterprises donated by the Sports Council in 1993
XVIII	Tony Robinson setting a good example
	Other members of the working party
XIX	'King' Kemlo, 13th March 1994
	The Centenary Year lunch
XX	Peter Mack in *Distress*
	Similar conditions in 1982. Jeremy Sibthorpe in *Rampant*

Introduction

by
Dr. Tom Trevelyan
President
of the
International Fourteen World Association

I started sailing Fourteens because 'Robo' conned me into it. ('Robo' is John Roberson. Today to the amazement of his many friends he is a respected yachting journalist in Australia, but in the early 1970's he was something of a maverick although a very good dinghy sailor). I'd joined the Club in 1973, feeling pretty miserable after a broken marriage and to help get it out of my system sailed O.K.s. After a year Robo over a beer suggested we share a Fourteen next season. It was a 'dog' - an old one with dubious spars and creaky fittings. We could never have won a start, let alone a race. The boat's name was *Stint*.

For me she was the key to heaven.

We took her to Graffham for our first anxiety-ridden Open Meeting. Robo was at the helm and my job was to stand on the edge and pull the sails up and down and in and out. I was flabbergasted. I had never been so fast in a boat since I crossed the Atlantic in the *Queen Mary*. Was I really allowed to do it? With Robo I learned the fun that comes from loving a wonderful boat. We met Pudney, a godlike figure who won every race he cared to enter and who, one glorious day, LENT US HIS SPINNAKER POLE. It was like being knighted - 'Arise, Sir Thomas, and be grateful. I award you the Order of the Pole.' We duly lost it overboard, and I can still picture the cheque for £11.68p that I with trembling hands wrote out and gave to the great man.

In 1974 we went to Falmouth for the P.O.W. This was a revelation. You could take these boats, powerful, barely controllable, open and possessed of the most outrageously large spinnakers, out to sea. I was terrified. Then you started on a line full of menacing sailors who appeared to know what they were doing, and had to find a way through them (there were 66 entries) to the windward mark. My heart was in my mouth. On rounding the buoy onto the reach my world fell apart. We took off in a cloud of spray, the jib tearing my arms out of their sockets. Waves appeared in front, threatened the bow and rushed underneath with terrifying speed. Something awful was sure to happen.

It did. We reached the gybe mark and I realised I was going to have to hoist the kite. You had to come in at just the right moment, catching the boat as she rolled to windward, stand up by the mast to push out the pole while the boat lurched sickeningly from side to side, and then pull like a madman on the halyard. The effect was like an afterburner on a jet fighter. I threw myself out over the side and gripped the sheet like a vice, while the centreboard started to hum, then sing as the speed reached Mach 1.

If this was Fourteen sailing it was a damn good cure for broken marriages. I was hooked. I lived for each weekend. Tuesday nights at the L.C.S.C. became a Mecca where I could worship my new God. Drinking appeared to be an essential part of the process and that was fine with me. Thus I spent five happy years. The London Corinthian was my second home. I made friends I will keep till I die. From there I was asked in 1977 to join the Fourteen Association Committee, an impossibly high honour, I thought. I am still attending today. Development, progress and change are part of the wonder of the boat. A pinnacle of development was reached in the early '80's. We were bumping up against the stops of possible performance and were soon to realise we had to change or die.

But before those momentous decisions were faced the boats had reached a high art form. My boat *Brown Trousers* (1094) was conceived at the Club over many winter beers. She had the lines of Ray Rouse's first design, a Will McCutcheon shell and was then built by Ed Warwick in a mushroom hut in Hampshire. She was a beauty; completed to a unique interior design and glued and coated throughout in epoxy.

Steve Wilton was my crew and I shall never forget the Shackleton Trophy in 1981. There was far too much wind, but we knew we had to hoist the kite or lose. We shot down past Chiswick Eyot. Off the Club some serious waves could be seen and after them the downstream pontoon lay in our path. It was going to be a gybe and we were out of control. I had that sickening certainty in my gut that this one would end in disaster. I sat like a rock in the port corner, white knuckles on the gunwale and the tiller, my bum glued to the seat, while Steve bobbed from side to side to balance the swerves and surges as we blew down the gusts and burst through the waves. The pontoon was looming fast and I was putting off the moment of decision. Too late, too late. I shouted for the gybe; Steve stood up and moved forward, fiddled for what seemed an eternity with the pole, the boom crashed over and we fell into Father Thames, chastened but happy. What a ride!

* * *

Cover illustration shows Dr. Tom Trevelyan and Steve Wilton sailing Brown Trousers in the 1982 Shackleton Race.
Wind: Force 6-7
From the photograph by Martin Dixon
(by courtesy of *Yachts and Yachting*).

Chapter 1

Fifty Years of Sailing International Fourteens
At The London Corinthian Sailing Club
and
Open Meetings

Tom has expressed vividly the exhilaration of sailing an International Fourteen and the challenge involved in controlling one in heavy weather, which has been a characteristic of them from the earliest days of the class. Only Uffa Fox, though, would dream of sailing one across the Channel to race against the French and sail back again. That was in 1928 in *Avenger* (135), the first really planing dinghy with a good windward performance and perhaps the most famous dinghy of all. We have to go back all that way to start the story of Fourteens sailing on Hammersmith and Chiswick Reaches.

The first Fourteen was an amalgam of a large number of dinghies of that length which were racing in different parts of the country as early as the turn of the century. The two classes that played the greatest part were the West of England Conference dinghy and the Norfolk dinghy - both 14ft long and undecked. One of the W.E.C. dinghy builders was Morgan Giles, who played a vital part in the development of the class, and had a yard for some years just east of Hammersmith Bridge. In the early 1900's the Boat Racing Association came into being in an attempt to promote a National class and adopted a 14ft half-decked class based on the W.E.C. dinghy. Up till then the control of racing was local and often jealously guarded. In 1911 Morgan Giles wagered £50 on a race between a W.E.C. dinghy and a Norfolk dinghy, which had a balanced lug. The contest took place on the Broads, which was a keen 14 ft sailing area - Stewart Morris's father Harold was among the enthusiasts - and Giles won four races out of five. After the First World War the Boat Racing Association was merged with the Yacht Racing Association, and within a few months rules for a National 14ft dinghy were published, having been drawn up by Morgan Giles. The Y.R.A. believed there was need to bring the many local classes together and convened a meeting of interested parties. One of them Leslie Lewis, a noted half-rater sailor from the Trent, claimed that a 14 ft dinghy could be equally at home on sea or inland and that it would be to everyone's advantage to have all 14 ft dinghies adhering to one set of rules. As a result the Small Boat Committee was set up, which in turn became the Y.R.A. Dinghy Committee, with Sir John Beale as its first chairman.

In the same year the Island Sailing Club, which had been formed many years before to encourage open boat racing, asked Charles Nicholson to design an open 14ft dinghy. The result was a fleet of tough clinker-built boats, rather similar to the R.N.S.A. dinghy, except that they had a short bowsprit; each boat costing about £35. Morgan Giles challenged the I.S.C. to a race against one of his U-bowed dinghies and won. This prompted Uffa Fox to reply by designing his first dinghy, *Ariel*, which beat Giles's boat.

Further impetus towards an agreed set of rules was provided in 1926 by the Trent Sailing Club which challenged the Royal Norfolk and Suffolk Yacht Club to a three-boat team race in Fourteens. This resulted in the famous challenge cup which is raced for to this day. In the same year the Prince of Wales was on a Royal Tour in Canada and was taken for a sail in a Canadian Fourteen. He enjoyed it so much that he presented a Trophy for the National 14 ft Class. The Prince of Wales's Cup was contested for the first time at Cowes in 1927.

In November the Yacht Racing Association proposed to apply to the International Yacht Racing Union for international status for the British Fourteen. The rules were modified so that the rig would be 125 sq. ft and the weight reduced to 225 lbs. The height of the sail plan was set at 22 ft 6in above gunwale level but the mast could be made in any way. Inside ballast was forbidden. Sir William Burton submitted these rules on 15th-16th October 1928 - 'not without opposition,' Tommy Vaughan writes. 'Then, as now, different countries had their own ideas about which class to encourage, and at the time many felt the Fourteen was far too small.' The rules of the class remained basically unchanged until the 1970's, thus demonstrating their soundness.

For the researcher the minutes of Club meetings make fairly tedious reading, however just occasionally they are enriched by an historic decision. Thus it was that on 5th March 1929, just six months' after the I.Y.R.U.'s ruling, the London Corinthian Sailing Club Management Committee resolved unanimously 'to inaugurate the International 14ft dinghy as a class boat for the Club and to endeavour thereby to create a general enthusiasm and more satisfactory results than have hitherto been obtained by handicapping.' Preference for pontoon space was to be given to the owners of Fourteens. The quarterly general meeting showed quite a lot of interest in the adoption of the class and 'as a result several boats were ordered and the number of members increased, so that the Fourteens became a most important adjunct of the Club.' The Club had certainly been quick off the mark and early the following year approached the Y.R.A. for a date to be fixed for an Open Meeting.

It was decided to name the trophy after Sir Ernest Shackleton, the famous explorer who went on three expeditions to Antarctica, the first with Captain Scott in the *Discovery*. A tall cup was fashioned out of the wood of the *Discovery*. Apart from the fact that Shackleton was a very gallant explorer who on his second expedition reached within 97 miles of the South Pole, and was knighted on his return, there is no explanation in the Club records about why the Club chose to name the International Fourteen dinghy trophy after him. He had died in 1922. Undoubtedly his feats of endurance and leadership captured the popular imagination. In particular his enforced escape from Antarctica with five others, after the base ship had been crushed in the ice, and his 800-mile sail to South Georgia in a whaler will never be forgotten. After his arrival there he led four relief expeditions before finally succeeding in rescuing his men.

The present Lord Shackleton cannot throw any light on the choice. He replied to my letter that his mother had been asked by the Club if the cup could be named in memory of her late husband and if she would present it to the winner of the first race on 13th May 1934. 'I well remember the Shackleton Trophy.... and attending it with my mother. Peter Scott competed for it (sic) and, as a family, we were rather pleased about this. It was quite a notable event.' However since receiving that letter, Jack Holt, in one of the many telephone conversations I have had with him over this book, told me that Percy Chandler, his business partner, was responsible for the suggestion that the trophy should be called after Sir Ernest, if not for the actual approach to Lady Shackleton.

Sadly, however, and rather typically, there is no real Club record of the first race except that Stewart Morris won it in *R.I.P.* (267). Considering that it was an historic day, not only for the Club but also for dinghy racing in general, as Lord Shackleton points out, it seems extraordinary that none of the Club officers made sure that there was an account of the race. The Race Records, infuriatingly, were only begun after a long break the following year, and not even Richard Tilbury, who wrote the Club's history up till 1935, had the wit to mention it. In every other respect the race was very efficiently run: advertisements were taken in newspapers and invitations were sent to the Flag Officers of many clubs and to the Press; Sir George Bull even went to the length of arranging replicas of the cup on the same lines as for the P.O.W.

Club entries included: Percy Chandler, 2nd in *Ace* (228) who was crewed by Jack Holt. *Ace* was the first Fourteen built by Jack and cost £150. Then came Sir George Bull in *Anthea*, a Morgan Giles design with a 32 lb plate; and Teddy Mitchell in *Anne* (56), a very early boat as her number implies with bamboo spars and a gunter rig, but was 'a delightful boat to sail' according to Jack Holt, who in the '20's crewed for Teddy and did any repairs that were necessary. There were probably more Club entries, although Jack feels that to get three Fourteens from one club in those early years was 'fabulous.'

The following year the Chandler-Holt partnership won the Shackleton, sailing *Ace* again against undoubtedly stiff competition which included Peter Scott. It is obvious that from the start the event was one of great interest to the class because there were twenty entries which was good considering it had only been in existence for six years. After the war the number of Club Fourteens increased so much that the Commodore had a special pontoon constructed to lie alongside the wall to carry six to eight of them. It cost £175.

After 1935, except in 1954 and 1956, when Stewart Morris was the winner, the Shackleton was won virtually without a break until 1960 by Bruce Wolfe, from Upper Thames. In that year to the astonishment of all the visiting pundits from Itchenor, Upper Thames and elsewhere, Chris Buckley came first helming *Boanerges* (661) with her owner Tony Newman as crew. He was the first member of the Club to win the Shackleton since Percy Chandler. "Who's that good helmsman of yours who won?" was the question in the changing room. "Oh, just one of our better Enterprise sailors!" came the reply. I've always said Chris Buckley could get into any dinghy and very often win regardless of whether he'd been sailing her a lot recently. Bruce-Wolfe was second.

Although its got nothing to do with Hammersmith, I can't let those early years of the class go by without lifting from Tommy Vaughan's history of the Fourteens the story he tells from Uffa's *Sailing, Seamanship and Yacht Construction* of how *R.I.P.*, an unusual name for a boat, came to be built. Stewart had won not only the first Shackleton in her, but more to the point the 1932 and 1933 P.O.W.s. 'When I met Harold Morris (Stewart's father) at the Easter All-in-Meet at the Tamesis Club in 1930,' wrote Uffa,' he told me of his aches and pains, and agreed to my suggestion that he was only walking about to save funeral expenses. I said: "Why not have a new dinghy built; she'll finish you off and you can be buried in her?" The idea tickled him so much that he ordered and named *R.I.P.* right away, and throughout her designing and building we wrote letters describing her successful race against *Charon* across the Styx and his astonishment at being beaten for the first time on his own waters.' *R.I.P.* was on the same lines as *Avenger*, which had a fine bow, with prominent V sections steadily developing into a very flat floor.

Dr. Olaf Bradbury, who was originally destined for the R.N. and was in the same term at Osborne and later Dartmouth as Sir George Bull, must be the oldest Commodore alive today if not the oldest member. 'George introduced me to the Club in 1936,' he told me. I was lucky enough to find Percy Chandler wanting to sell *Ace* and I bought her for £100. It was enormous fun. After 22 ft Montague whalers in the Navy it was like riding a thoroughbred instead of a carthorse. She had a very large plate which was so heavy that one man could hardly lift it up although there was a rotary drum to help do this. I was lucky enough to pick up Steve Bassett as a crew.

Ace was a beauty and went to windward very well. I remember Steve often saying by the time we'd got to Barnes, 'I've had it.' She would plane, but you had to get the crew in the right place. We did quite well and won the first winter series in 1936. I wore old grey flannel trousers, two or three jerseys, a tweed coat and a trilby hat. The changing room was a general free for all after every race; everyone wanting to get into that wonderful bar which was always full. The class didn't increase much until after the war.

During the war I had laid *Ace* up in Jack Holt's yard (previously Morgan Giles's). Miraculously she escaped any damage from the bombing and we completely re-rigged her. It was October 1946 and the start of the Winter Series and I was desperately keen to take part. To my horror a few days before the first race Steve went down with flu. I remember well wandering round the bar after most people had got afloat looking for a crew. The only person there was a gentleman in his mid-fifties wearing a nice suit and good shoes - a most improbable sailor - but almost on bended knee I asked him to crew me and he agreed. His name was Procter (it must have been Francis Procter, the Secretary, and father of Winifred, who later sailed a Fourteen for years) and he agreed.

We got off all right. He'd never sailed a Fourteen before, but although there was a good stiff breeze all went well on the beat up to the Barnes mark which we rounded and started the long run back. Then came the moment when we would have to gybe. I told him exactly what to do, and that if we didn't work together getting the boom over - there were no 'kickers' in those days - there'd be trouble. The critical moment arrived. I pulled the helm up and he got the boom half over - then he funked it and let it go back onto the same side. *Ace* heeled right over and in we went. The stern sank and *Ace* floated bows up. Then the thought suddenly struck me, that in our refit Steve and I had thrown away the rubber buoyancy bags, normally kept amidships, as they had perished during the war, and I'd forgotten to replace them. So *Ace* only had her copper bow buoyancy tank.

Procter very quickly turned blue from his immersion. Nobody ever wore life jackets and there was no rescue boat. Mercifully your father was afloat in *Water Gipsy* and was promptly on the spot. Together we hauled Procter out and he was taken below and brought round with a tot or two. Fortunately he suffered no ill effects, or I might have been in dire trouble. That was the only time I was in the drink.'

Bradbury was Commodore for 1947 and 1948 and in that year was the first winner of what was originally called The President's Trophy for Fourteens and Swordfish which was presented by A.P.H. It was a silver tray with a poem engraved on it which you will read about later.

By 1948 there were 15 owners of Fourteens. Apart from those already mentioned, with the year when they joined the Club in brackets, there were Elsie and Joe Bloor (1939), *Filister*; Winifred Procter (1937) *Dauntless*; F.J. Snary (1946) *Lorelei*; Squadron-Leader T.A. Charlesworth (1939) *Aquilon*; R. Jorgenson (1940) *Dania*; Don Storrar (1948) *Viking*; 'Storm' Roberts (1945) *Pheon*; Dr. Mike Gilkes (1943) *Nimbus*; F.W. Herbert (1935) Shadow, and Mike Cook, a very distinguished Firefly sailor who did not join the Club till 1953, but in 1948 bought *Verve*. This was the only Fourteen Uffa Fox built in 1947 and cost Mike £275 including sails. (Uffa had lost a lot of money before the war when he built 40 boats in one year and sold them for £185 each). Lastly there were Anthony Lousada and I who bought *Dark Wind* (445) for £300. I had half that in the Post Office Savings Bank and asked my father to stake me the rest but for some strange reason he wouldn't - I don't know why because generally he was generous to everyone. I was very keen to have a Fourteen and mentioned it to Anthony, my brother-in-law, who was delighted to come to my rescue. This was a happy partnership and not only lasted some years, but involved two other boats. I was always somewhat embarrassed financially that I hardly owned an inch of either of them.

Dark Wind had been designed by T.A. Charlesworth - a member of the Club who had made Squadron-Leader in the war. Although I knew him and his daughter well at the old Club, I never realised he was a designer until I talked to Simeon Bull when researching this book. *Dark Wind*'s first owner was R.R. Allen, a member of Itchenor, whom I later often saw when I was down there at Open Meetings. He'd advertised the boat and Anthony and I saw her at a boat-builder's at Watford. We were entranced by her pretty lines, but her sides were two thicknesses of tongue and grooved longitudinal planking which in time became somewhat corrugated. This explained Simeon's somewhat disparaging remarks about Charlesworth as a designer and the Watford body-builder as a second rate 'furniture builder.'

In this way I started sailing a Fourteen and quickly found that I had to unlearn a lot of the things my father had told me when at about the age of 10 he took me out on the Thames in his lugsail *The Bee*. He had firmly inculcated into me that one should put the centreboard down before gybing. I found, like many others, that gybing, certainly in a strong wind and particularly in a Fourteen is more likely to be successful if the plate is lifted half up. Sailing *Dark Wind* was very exciting compared to *The Bee*, although we very quickly found that she leaked badly in spite of the sheet of oiled canvas in between the wood planks, adding substance to Simeon's remarks.

We soon learned what a wonderful reach Hammersmith is for sailing a performance dinghy, but I am leaving it to pundits like Pudney, Trevelyan, Goulborn, Robo and others to give their views about sailing a Fourteen on Hammersmith and Chiswick Reaches with the splendid variety of courses offered by the complete 'S' shape between Hammersmith Bridge and Barnes. In 1953 Anthony Lousada presented the *Dark Wind* Trophy, a beautiful Swedish silver beaker for which various types of dinghies could compete on a handicap basis during the Winter season. One day he was out before the start with someone else as crew, as I was abroad, when he saw a man jump off Hammersmith bridge; "Doctor needed," Anthony shouted. Mike Gilkes was quickly on hand in *Friar Tuck* and managed with his crew's help to drag the man on board and sail for Wally See's. Meanwhile the race had started - no thought of a postponement - and Anthony won. Needless to say Mike protested to the committee and the race was abandoned.

We did have one moment of glory. This was in our third Fourteen, *Water Music* (678), a Mark 1V Proctor built by Faireys. It was the 1959 Jos Collins and it blew very hard. There was a turnout of thirty one boats. Coming up to Barnes for the second time, there was only Bruce-Wolfe and ourselves - everyone else had 'gone in.' Bruce-Wolfe sailing *Mayfly* rounded the top mark and bore away towards the Middlesex shore where he would have to gybe. We were about 100 yards behind him - I was helming. Unfortunately for Bruce-Wolfe his 'kicker' parted on the gybe - so strong was the wind - and he went in. We managed to gybe successfully and sailed home, the first Club members ever to win the Jos Collins. The next day, for the Shackleton, conditions were almost the same and Bruce-Wolfe won, but we weren't far behind him, finishing third.

By 1960 there were another seventeen boats. Among members, mentioned in order of their joining the Club: L.C. Grand, known, I gather, at Eton by his chums as 'Elsie,' because of his initials; Simeon Bull, Sir Duncan Oppenheim, J.T. Fathi, Bruce Fraser, John Underwood, Tony Simpson, Pat 'Dr. Who' Troughton, Tony Newman, Dr. Paul Smart, Arthur Prince, Jack Shiells, R.J. Ogle, and Hugh Kemlo. Such numbers made great sailing and the spirit of the day is portrayed well by Simeon's appearance aged 19 at the 1953 P.O.W. at Lowestoft. He had had a good introduction to dinghy sailing at Eton, where he had been Captain of Sailing. His father records in his diary: 'Rather against my better judgement I agreed to lend Simeon *Serapis* for the P.O.W.'

Simeon was quite frank about how it was done. 'I had no knowledge of how to sail a Fourteen but I managed to bounce my father into lending me *Serapis* through Stewart Morris. I'd never met him, but he knew that my father wouldn't go to Lowestoft and he managed to persuade him that the boat and I would be safe because he could provide me with an expert crew - the South African Snipe champion.' "How did you do?" I asked. "Well it was blowing old boots the whole week. My South African crew lasted until Tuesday, after which he was taken to hospital suffering from exposure - you know what it's like at Lowestoft. I can't remember who crewed for me the rest of the week, but I think we were 12th in the big race."

1960 was my introduction to a wet and windy P.O.W. week at Falmouth in my own boat, *Little Billee* (724), a Proctor V, built by Souter's. As Tommy Vaughan recounts John Prentice should be remembered for his sponsorship of the Proctor V which led to a rapid build-up of the class in the U.K, and indirectly to the beginning of the boom in America and Canada. Johnnie had commissioned Ian Proctor to design him a boat and was looking round for a builder. He approached Souters, who agreed to build it, but to bring the job down to an economic price, suggested an order for a batch to cover the cost of the mould. Johnnie placed the order and then set about getting rid of his surplus boats. I bought one of them as having left Fleet Street I was a little better off. I think the price was £520. She was beautifully made, the gunwales of spruce and the triple-skinned hull of Honduras mahogany. To me, working at Christie's, she looked like a piece of French furniture.

The Mark Vs had a stormy introduction but proved their undoubted potential at the 1960 P.O.W. week at Falmouth, writes Tommy Vaughan. I was lucky in having found a wonderful crew - Chris Newnes - a partnership which survived seven years before he was seduced quite naturally into the big time league of sailing with my nephew, Jeremy Pudney and later such luminaries as Johnson Wooderson and Mike Peacock. But in 1960 we were, like Tom Trevelyan later, completely green to sailing in a regatta against the likes of Stewart Morris, Brigadier R.H. Farrant, George Bennion, Richard Ewart-Smith and Will and John McCann, all from Itchenor. Then there were Ian Cox, John Prentice, E. Bruce-Wolfe, Dr. G. Gilbert Scott, Robin Stevenson, Robin Webb, Sam Waters and many others. We were going to do battle with all the hotshots. Other Corinthians were Simeon Bull, Arthur Prince and Jack Shiells.

You must excuse this bout of nostalgia: in those days everything was so different, particularly if you were a new boy. To show you how new I was for some unexplained reason I had ordered blue sails. I still can't remember why, because obviously they would stick out like a sore thumb at the start - 'don't worry, John, you were never that near the line' Chris Newnes reminded me when I asked him about the sails. Added to which people took Chris aside and said: 'why does your skipper want to look like an Enterprise?' (No offence meant Bill, Hugh and others).

It didn't matter it was all so exciting. We left the dinghy-park at about 10 and often didn't get back till late in the afternoon, absolutely knackered. There were no wet-suits. We wore a pair of shorts - a shirt and two jerseys underneath which I wore a corset as I had had a slipped disc - and an anorak incorporating a life-jacket. We also took a suit of heavy weather sails, which we stuffed in little cubbyholes each side of the mast, in case when we got out to the start line we found it was blowing hard. Falmouth was where in 1938 Peter Scott and John Winter had introduced an unofficial form of trapeze, but there were no trapezes in 1960 or even 'ladies'-aids' - handles the crew could hold when sitting out which came in about five years later.

The first day it blew 42 knots and the race was held in the harbour where I found an ebb tide created worse conditions than those in the open bay. We went in on the last round and had considerable difficulty righting the boat, so we retired. Sam Waters, who I believe had a heart attack before taking up Fourteens, being a brilliant seaman was 1st over the line. As always the first three - or is it six- had to produce their sails, and Sam was protested out by the well-known American helmsman, George Moffat, because he'd used a National Twelve sail with only three batten pockets. Well, rules, I suppose, are rules, but I thought it very unsportsmanlike after such an horrendous race. Sam was a much-loved figure, and if there weren't any signs of wind at the Itchenor Opens, he'd go to the end of the jetty and throw a coin in and shout 'Black Pig,' a legend going back to the days of the wreckers on the Cornish coasts.

All the other races during the week were held out in the bay which meant about a two-mile sail to the start. The winds continued fresh so we were generally soaked by the time we got there. However after the terror of trying to get a good start, we set off on the first beat. We normally felt quite happy as the boat was footing well. Then we came to the windward mark and for the first-time we experienced the ecstasy of turning onto the reaching leg, the boat taking off on a wild plane; playing the main sheet all the time - in out, in out - but luffing up to pass a boat and the surge as one bore away; spray coming aboard solid into one's face all the time, and the self-bailers gurgling away.

Chris reminds me that in one race he had to climb the mast because the spinnaker halyard had an Inglefield clip on the end, and this had caught round the jumper wires. Nobody would be such a fool as to use such a set-up today, and I soon dispensed with it. Chris was so game; He seemed to regard it as the most natural thing in the world to climb the mast during a race. The boat was at an alarming angle, charging down the reach, with me holding the jib sheet as well as the main. Somehow Chris unhitched the clip and made it fast to the spinnaker head in time to do the hoist. At the end of each race there was the long sail back, and having put the boat to bed and had a shower in someone else's B and B, we retired to a nearby cafe for a huge fry-up with many others. Oh, the joy of relaxing under such conditions and looking forward to the evening beer-up!

I had taken a room in one of the granite cottages climbing up the hill behind the Royal Cornwall. I remember so well, every morning a chink in the curtains would show the clouds scudding across the sky. "Oh, John, I don't think I can take another day with a wind like that." But he did. On the big race day, Thursday, we were out in good time. Eileen Ramsay was there with her camera and her photographs show all the mainsails flapping wildly. Suddenly our main started coming down. I nearly wept. The halyard shackle had broken (in those days we used brass!) Jack Shiells from the Club, planed past in *Serapis*, crewed by Alan Pedersen, and shouted "capsize her, John." In those days we all carried knives on lanyards and generally had two or three spare shackles on the lanyard. We turned the boat over; Chris swam out, pulled the main up to the top of the mast and shackled one of my spares onto the halyard. He then swam back and together we righted the boat, hauled up the sail, put the self-bailers down and quickly planed her dry. What a relief, but what a way to start a 15-mile race.

Well, we didn't do so badly, blue sails and all. Out of the sixty two starters we were 11th in the P.O.W. and 14th overall. Stewart was 1st; George Moffat, 2nd; Bruce-Wolfe, 3rd; Johnnie Prentice, 4th; Sam Waters, 5th and Guthrie Penman, 6th. It was an unforgettable baptism, although the euphoria of sailing a Fourteen increased once the trapeze came in, particularly three-sail reaching across Chichester Harbour, the boat dancing from wave to wave. I've always said sailing a Fourteen in a blow is nearly as good as sex, and sometimes better.'

One of the Club members who arrived in the mid '50's was Tony Newman of the Foreign Service. He'd just returned, I think from Beirut, where in those happy days he was able to ski some mornings and sail a 505 in the evening. He sold his Mercedes and bought a Fourteen: 'So I started to learn how to sail a Fourteen and find my way round the river, both fairly difficult at times.' Tony, a highly intelligent man was also no slouch when it came to sailing, although when Mike Gilkes lent him his boat *Truculent* for the 1956 P.O.W. at Torquay, he says: 'The sailing was exciting but I found how much I had to learn about sailing on the sea.' Didn't we all? In 1962, he had *Sagapo* (771) built, but was prevented from going to Weymouth for the P.O.W., so he lent her to Captain Bill Humphrey, R.N., of Hayling Island Sailing Club, along with Eve France his gallant crew. What is more she won the Morgan-Giles Cup for the first lady to finish, and was the first member of the Club to gain that honour.

'In the early '60's,' Tony writes, 'Fourteens really flourished at the Club and the class was numerous and very competent. In 1965 the Club team won the Walker Team Trophy to the astonishment of both Itchenor Sailing Club and the Oxford and Cambridge Sailing Society. At the time the Society were undoubtedly good, winning just about every team race and Itchenor were usually second. The Club team was: Jack Shiells (captain), Jeremy Pudney, James Vernon and me. It was a very windy day and we had to work very hard to win, but our win was only made possible by a brilliantly daring piece of tactics by Jeremy.' The incident was so improbable that Eric Twiname mentions it in his book *Dinghy Team Racing*. Having referred to the ploy of the leading boat sailing off in the wrong direction or for the wrong mark, Twiname writes: 'A variant of the same tactics was used by Jeremy Pudney in an International Fourteen race. Instead of sailing off in the wrong direction he rounded the first mark the wrong way and each member of the opposing teams followed - as did chaos when they attempted to unwind.' Of course Jack, Tony and James rounded the mark correctly, hoisted their spinnakers and were off and won.

The Walker Team Trophy was presented to Itchenor Sailing Club in 1964 by the United States International 14ft Association at the instance of Stuart Walker. Stu, a doctor by profession was one of America's greatest dinghy enthusiasts and the author of a number of books on sailing them. The Trophy is a silver shield in the shape of the United Kingdom mounted on mahogany. To quote Tommy Vaughan: 'Stu Walker.... rebuilt and inspired the American Fourteen foot fleet during the '50's and '60's.... He was the dynamo of the American fleet.' I presume Stu had thought of presenting a Trophy to the Mecca (at least in the south of England) of Fourteen sailing out of affection. It may appear I am wandering a bit from home waters, but in winning the Trophy the Club showed it was beginning to get some helmsmen who had to be reckoned with. Nor was it the last win. The Club also won the Walker Team Trophy in 1968, 1971, 1973, 1981, 1982 and 1985.

Tony Newman concludes : 'I think the '60's saw a considerable change in the Club's attitude to Fourteen sailing. As more and more people went off in the summer to Itchenor and elsewhere on the circuit - although they returned for the Club's Open Meetings - so the interest in the winter season increased and the Winter Series produced large entries and really splendid racing.' Between 1960 and 1970 there were another 13 owners of Fourteens; notably Jeremy Pudney, Keith Goulborn, John Hart, John Geoffrey, John and Jeremy Vines, Ray and Shirley Rouse, Tony Robinson, Robo, Alex Edwards, Clem Noel, John Pullinger and P. Hallett. There were others who were winter members only, such as Don Lucas, and were very welcome. In the Winter Series in the late '60's the Club had a larger fleet than Itchenor had in summer.

Jeremy taught himself to sail in his early 'teens on the somewhat unlikely waters (for a future world champion) of a Sevenoaks gravel pit. 'Rich men's sons had Fireflies, but being the son of a poet I was lucky to get a Fleetwind,' Jeremy told me. 'We were completely self-taught and tried to keep up with the Fireflies; I think the competitive instinct was born there and in some ways it helps to make you a good sailor. Next came Cadets at Greshams, where I became close friends with John and Jeremy Vines. We raced on The Broads every week. I loved it, because it also meant not having to play cricket, which I hated. There we also learnt the elements of team racing. Every year there was the Cadet championship at Burnham on Crouch where there were sometimes 100 boats and this became my Mecca. One day, to my astonishment, I found I was leading the fleet, but I didn't know the course as I never expected to be in that situation, but somehow managed to win. This fed the competitive spirit and the desire to win.

I joined the Club in 1955 to sail Fireflies which was a highly competitive experience against the likes of Peter Hinton, Jeremy Vines, Mike Cook and Mike Collyer to name just a few. A lot of us did the racing circuit, but came back to the Club in the winter. That of course was the old Club which in spite of the discomfort of the changing room had all the charm of what a sailing club should be.' The race records between 1955 and 1961 mention Jeremy as 'doing well' or 'prominent' in the Firefly races. In 1962 he joined the Fourteens: 'I bought Brian Saffery-Cooper's old boat and called it *Bashful*, because knowing I was joining the elite class and being bashful by nature, I thought it was a suitable name.

Initially after the Firefly which was more manoeuvrable I found the Fourteen a little cumbersome, but then one began to appreciate the power of the boat and the excitement of managing the sail area (although considerably less than today). Hammersmith Reach with its famous wind against tide was enough to frighten any newcomer to Fourteens, with their tendency to nosedive, and must be one of the best places to get a sense of seamanship. We had the beginnings of an extremely competitive fleet. If you were to do any good you needed a high standard of short tacking up to Barnes, avoiding the rowers, watching out for the gusts coming through the trees, and being careful not to gybe too early anywhere near the barges off Lep. The characteristics of the reach at that time made it a very good training ground.'

The barges near Lep (where the mock Georgian houses are now) were a really dangerous hazard, particularly on a spring flood tide. The gybe mark was meant to be laid opposite the western end of Chiswick Eyot, but sometimes the anchor dragged or it was laid too near. One person who knows what it's like to be keel-hauled is Simeon Bull. He and his regular crew, David Shelley, were sailing *Serapis* on a windy day and came to the gybe mark; went in and on a sluicing tide were swept straight under the swim head of one of the barges. 'The buoy had been laid too close and we ended going right under the barge and coming out the other end. That was very frightening. Sort of thing that sticks in the mind,' Simeon concluded with what seemed considerable sang-froid. The same thing nearly happened to Ray Rouse, another of the Fourteen stars to emerge from the Club. Crewed by his gallant wife, Shirley, in the early '70's they capsized at the gybe mark. 'Having been swept under the bow of one of the barges, we somehow managed to scramble round the side of the brute, and popped round the stern to the relief of the rest of the fleet who were convinced that we'd been keel-hauled the full length of the barge.'

Jeremy Pudney describes his feelings at some of his first Open Meetings when top-flight helmsmen like Stewart Morris, Bruce Banks, Bruce-Wolfe, and Mike Peacock came to do battle. 'You knew they were miles beyond your own standards at that time, but there was always the chance that knowing the river you might use it to your own advantage. Then there were pleasant memories of the circuit and getting more experience racing against the hot-shots. Of course winning the Walker Trophy for the first time in 1965 was a tremendous thing. For a river club to pull that off against a heavily-loaded Itchenor team consisting of Morris, Peacock and others on their own water and the stalwarts of the Oxford and Cambridge Society was a splendid achievement not only for the individuals but also for the team. I remember we were all very proud. There was also the excitement of returning for the winter series at the Club where by the mid-'60's, (as Tony Newman has said) there was a highly competitive fleet.'

It was in 1965 in the Club newsletter, which had come

out the year for the first time the year before, that Jeremy was asked for a contribution on Fourteens. Notwithstanding his earlier quite genuine feelings that Hammersmith and Chiswick Reaches were excellent for learning to sail a Fourteen, with which Michael Peacock agrees, Jeremy wrote: 'It does seem worth mentioning that one of the possible reasons for the Club's Fourteen members' inability to quite make the top flight in Open events is, I feel, due to the restrictions placed on us by old Father Thames. It is well nigh impossible to tune an International Fourteen with any degree of accuracy except on open water and this, in turn, accounts for the increasing tendency of the Fourteens to sneak off to the open seas at the earliest opportunity, leaving the Thames to the critical blue-sail brigade.'

This was long before there was any development in the class, and Jeremy had only just begun to show those at Itchenor what he could do. What he said was undoubtedly true. For many of us the sheer ecstasy of sailing a Fourteen, certainly when there was any wind, was enough; many of us didn't bother to be competitive enough or really learn to tune our boats. We tried as hard as we could to get the boat footing fast, but that wasn't enough. We weren't taking it seriously enough, or if we were trying to we weren't succeeding. In retrospect if I had had a few years in Fireflies doing the circuit and team racing (if considered good enough) I would have been a better Fourteen sailor. But time was not on my side.

I asked Jeremy how long it was before he was snapping at Stewart's stern. 'One of my first P.O.W.s was in 1964 at Lowestoft where I came 4th in one of the races much to my own and everyone else's astonishment. It was in my old boat and with old sails, but it was very windy and purely a question of seamanship. Gradually after that I began to get close to Stewart, particularly after getting my new boat *Fanciful* in 1966 - so-called because I thought there might be a chance of beating some of the great names in her. Things came to a head when Stewart had me banned from sailing at Itchenor because he maintained the interior of my boat was illegal. I had joined the rear tanks together and was accused of having a deck. Stewart protested me and got Itchenor to refuse my entry; I was of course sailing as a member of the London Corinthian. At great expense which I couldn't afford I got the local shipwrights to alter the sternsheets, but I insisted that Stewart's protest go to the R.Y.A., and they threw it out.' The Fourteen committee had had the same view as Tommy Vaughan points out.

'The fact that he paid attention to the layout of my boat was a sign that he was worried about me getting close to him. Later on he accused me of holding him back because I was covering him. He eventually got through, but was very abusive afterwards. The next day when it was windy we were racing neck and neck and at the last gybe he capsized and I won sweet revenge. But naturally I had a great respect for him. However unlike most newcomers I never got a word of advice or help from him.' Some people may think - *'Nil nisi bonum sed mortuis est'* - that it's in somewhat bad taste of me to have asked Jeremy such a question. But as an ex-journalist I don't think histories are worthy of the name unless they give the full story.

Stewart's attitude was quite natural - he had won twelve P.O.W.s by that time. He was 'the grand old man of Fourteens' and will always be revered as such among those who sailed Fourteens all over the world. But it didn't make him any less human. It was quite natural for him to feel 'who the hell is this whippersnapper?' If it had been Mike Peacock or Richard Ewart-Smith I think he would have felt differently. They'd been longer in 'the club' - and the Fourteens are a club, I always felt, when I was sailing one, regardless of where you come in the fleet and for that reason a very nice one. Leaving that aside, the incident underlines how brilliant Jeremy was as a Fourteen helmsman after only four years in the class.

What I have just said underlines Keith Goulborn's initial reaction to Fourteens. Keith had joined the Club in 1955, the same year as Jeremy, but he was only 11, crewing for his father in his Firefly and gaining undoubtedly valuable experience. But his first recollection was of having to wait outside on the hard of the old Club for hours eating crisps, because he was too young to go into the bar; the second was 'the disgusting arrogance of the Fourteen owners who acted as if they owned the river.' In 1969, a somewhat unlikely figure, John Salt, persuaded Keith to enter for the Jos Collins and Shackleton Open Meetings, borrowing David Widdowson's Fourteen *Shearwater* (683), an Austin Farrar design.' Once round the Barnes mark John put up the spinnaker and I was quite astonished at the boat's power. Although we didn't sail the boat very well we came 3rd, which I was quite pleased about.

I realised then that most Fourteen sailors didn't sail their boats at all well when conditions were light. They sat on their gunwales, as Robo used to say years later, like lumps of owl shit, waiting for the wind to blow. On Hammersmith Reaches, Firefly sailors had learned to make the most of every little puff of wind to drive the boat along when it was light, and every bit was a bonus. Most of the other Fourteen helmsmen did very little when it was light. On Sunday for the Shackleton, the wind had changed direction so it was a beat against the tide. Having for some years crewed Fireflies I thought that I had forgotten more about beating against the tide than most Corinthian Fourteen sailors would ever learn. I know it sounds arrogant, but the fact was that we won, and won handsomely. Looking back on it a 3rd and a 1st was pretty good.' An example of what Jeremy had said of taking advantage of local knowledge and being competitive.

I don't know about the arrogance, but what Keith said about many of us doing little in light airs may well have been right. Undoubtedly his approach was very dedicated and it was his willingness to put more effort into the whole business of preparing for a race, to knowing the tides and watching for wind shifts at Open Meetings which later made him another outstanding helmsman. 'A.P.H. gave away the prizes and I remember being somewhat overawed by the likes of Stewart Morris, Bruce-Wolfe, Ian Cox and Pudney and receiving the Trophy amongst the great and the good,' Keith told me, 'and it seemed to me the message was clear: sell the Firefly and get a Fourteen. So I bought *Dismay* (883) from Ian Cox. Designed and built by Souters, she was four years old - a bit tatty - but a good strong boat and she gave me four years' good sailing, finally selling her in the States in '73.' It didn't take him long to become U.K. team material.

I had ten winters at the Club - I did the circuit in the summer and they were pretty happy times whatever the weather. There are lots of memories. I won the President's Trophy inscribed with that wonderful poem four or five times.' Right in front of the Club he demonstrated a superb piece of seamanship: lying first ahead of Kemlo, the downhaul on his rudder slipped, and his rudder came off; he gybed the boat immediately and came round just near the rudder; picked it up, put it back on his transom, tacked across the river and was still ahead of Kemlo. "That gave me immense pleasure," he said.

There was great rivalry between Keith and Robo and Hugh Kemlo and Robin Dent. On the whole they shared the honours fairly evenly, but there was one Jos Collins-Shackleton weekend when Hugh had won the Jos Collins. Robo tells how the next day they trailed Hugh round the whole course. They were coming up towards the last mark by Hammersmith bridge and as Hugh approached the mark Robo shouted something.

Hugh turned round and said: "What was that?" and went straight into the mark.'

Robo, however, gives Hugh full marks quite rightly as he has probably won more prizes at the Club in Fourteens, Enterprises and Lasers than any other member. 'Hugh is an intuitive helmsman and very competitive' he told me. So was Keith, winning seven P.O.W. silver replicas (these are given to the first six in the Prince of Wales Cup Race itself).

I asked Robo what it was like crewing for Pudney: 'Very demanding. Jeremy was racing directly he left the dock; going flat out. There was no question of getting one's breath before the start after inspecting the line for the wind. We normally did quite a large bit of the course before the start. To me helmsmen are either 'footers or pointers;' Jeremy always 'footed.' You were never allowed to cleat the jib (as so many of us helmsmen did); he told me to play the jib all the time, while he watched every wave. Terrific concentration and wonderful helming, but it was absolutely exhausting for the crew as there was no rest.

Jeremy's tactics were always right. I remember a time when I was crewing for Keith and we were lying second in the Itchenor Gallon to Richard Ewart-Smith and 'Notty' (Robin Nott has been an owner now for many years, but before buying a boat I reckon he was the fastest crew in the fleet in spite of being 6ft 4ins - 'don't say ready about - just say go.') It was the extra 'hitch' from Ellanore over to S.W. Pilsey, and we were catching them. Keith was obviously wondering whether to go to windward and risk being luffed or try to go through their lee. I suddenly noticed that Notty, as was his wont, was lying right out, hands behind his neck and jib firmly cleated. I shouted to Keith, "Look at Notty, try freeing off and go through their lee." We freed off, bore away and drove the boat fast and to their surprise popped up ahead of them and went on to win. That's exactly what Jeremy would have done instinctively.'

If asked what races he remembers most, Jeremy immediately said the Cowes P.O.W. in 1967. None of us who took part in it will ever forget it as the *Queen Mary* sailed right through the course on the first round. The Canadian, Ian Bruce, had taken the lead immediately and had no trouble. Five boats nipped ahead of the great bows including Jeremy and Mike Peacock. 'This was one of my most exciting races,' Jeremy told me, 'I was racing in *Fanciful* against Mike, one of the most brilliant helmsmen in any conditions - in *Buccaneer*. We swopped places on every single round, I beating him upwind; he beating me downwind. On the last downwind reaching leg he again beat me but in those days you used to have to fix the spinnaker up before hoisting. I arranged to have this done on the final reach, so I got a quicker hoist and rolled over him, after the most exhausting and exhilarating race; in some ways even more exhilarating than when I won the P.O.W. at Falmouth in 1970.' The year before he had been in the British team that went to Canada. Mike Peacock was captain and the others members of the team were Ken Merron and Johnson Wooderson. The British team won all nine races against strong teams from America's west and east coasts and from Canada. Jeremy Pudney, using a trapeze, then went on to win the Canadian World Championships against 55 other boats.

There was a tremendous camaraderie in the Club among the Fourteens during the '60's-'70's afloat and ashore. The stories are endless. Annick Bull crewing for Simeon during the winter got fed up with being verbally abused. "Simeon George Bull, if you don't stop shouting at me I'm leaving you." Simeon was unperturbed. When the next blast of invective hit the bows, Annick got up and dived overboard. Unfortunately she swam to the Surrey bank. By the time she got back to the Club she was suffering from near hypothermia. They were by no means the only husband and wife crew to shout at each other, but they went on twice as long, as Annick would break into French when English vituperation had not brought results, but Simeon was equal to that.

Don Lucas from Upper Thames, one of the winter members I have already mentioned, had a boat called *Pink Panther* and a nice girl crew, Liz Squibb. It was one of those infamous south-westerly days when to use Robo's words 'the wind was blowing the oysters off the rocks' and they were running down the river. Don decided it was time to take the spinnaker down, and Liz busied herself with her head face downwards near the mast. Nothing happened. "Get the bloody thing down," Don screamed. "Don't shout at me, Don come and do it yourself. Its jammed." So with the boat still careering downstream they exchanged positions. Liz sat in the stern holding onto the tiller with both hands, knuckles white, completely unaware that an eight was resting dead ahead. Don had his head still buried in the bottom of the boat, when *Pink Panther* went straight down the port side of the eight, cutting off four oars.

Robo, whose memory seems extraordinarily clear, recalls another incident involving an eight. For once there was a light westerly and the Enterprise fleet was running down the Barnes shore. An eight came up fast on the last boat and the cox obviously smaller than most, steered the eight straight into an Enterprise, so that the first three feet of the eight's stem came through the transom flap. The eight swung round, the stem snapped off and she started sinking. Six of the crew jumped overboard and the boat was rowed back by the stroke and the next man with the broken bows in the air. The extraordinary thing was that two or three members of the Club took the broken stem round to all the rowing clubs and nobody reported having an accident. It was therefore mounted by Johnnie Evans as a drinking trophy.

In Keith's early days, when John Salt was still crewing him, there was the occasion one gusty day when they were tearing down the river in *Dismay*, John playing the spinnaker. Suddenly the boat started rolling violently. This reminded Keith of his days in Fireflies, which I gather are notorious under such conditions, and he decided it was time to bail out, because they were obviously going to go in. When he came to the surface the boat was still charging down the river, John quite oblivious that he was alone. Keith shouted and John turned round and saw the situation; 'I remember his little fat face went completely white, and the boat did then go over. I swam to the Surrey shore, ran along the bank, dived in and swam to the boat which we righted quite easily. It wasn't till some weeks later that John told me he couldn't swim, and he was quite frightened of capsizing.'

Robo remembers especially one of his winter races with Keith: 'Keith was evidently getting very hot, not that I was aware of it - he was wearing the first type of wet suit any of us ever had which were like armour. On top he had a shorty oilskin. Just as we were passing the Club he stood up, put the tiller between his legs and started pulling the oilskin over his head. Simultaneously the clever telescopic tiller, which Ian Cox had made for the boat, backed into itself so no one was steering the boat. Just then a gust came and the boat took off. I did not know why, but she suddenly luffed up and capsized. I went over the dry side, and while sitting on the hull heard a squawking sound and looked over the side and saw Keith with his hands coming out of his oilskin but his head inside. I pulled the oilskin off and we got the boat up and still won the race.'

Other people too have memories. Commander Michael Higham, R.N. was kind enough to remind me of how he came to sail a Fourteen for the first time. Osbert Lancaster could have made a cartoon out of it, I think. 'In 1967 or so I was in the Club one Saturday standing humbly near some of the Fourteen people (I think my 'owner' had just sold his Enterprise - anyway I was out of a crewing job). Something like the following conversation took place. "Sailing tomorrow, Maurice?" "I can't. I haven't got a boat." "Dean (presumably Robert who one year was part of a potential U.K. America's Cup challenger) will lend you his boat. Dean, lend Maurice your boat." "Gladly." "Thank you, Dean, but I've no crew." "Higham will crew for you. Higham, crew for Maurice tomorrow." (Higham quietly aside to 'X') "Who is this fellow Maurice - can he sail." (X) "It's Stewart Morris." I crewed and so my first sail in a Fourteen was with Stewart Morris. I started with (I hope hidden) anxieties, but he was kindness itself. His orders were gently phrased '.... and meanwhile, Michael, if with your sixteenth hand you would....' We talked (it wasn't a very windy day) and he told me of how he'd lost points in the Med Fleet by putting an Admiral out of a race ('Got him on starboard') and I gained points by reporting that the bearing of an opponent, wooded by the foot of the jib, was 'drawing aft,' which reminded him of the days when he was a Fighter Direction Officer. I certainly enjoyed the day, and I hope he did.'

Laying-up suppers and other social events often became as lively as the sailing. There was generally a lot of bun throwing which annoyed whoever was Commodore. Robo was naturally blamed for starting the unseemly behaviour. He always replied: 'Come and sit next to me and you'll see, you're wrong. I only retaliate when buns are thrown at me.' A memorable occasion was when Bob Fisher got to his feet, (it was probably when he was Rear-Commodore Sailing in the '70's) and 'was rabbiting on,' according to Robo, 'about nothing and we were all getting rather bored. Alex Allan, an old friend of mine, surreptitiously put a spare plate of spaghetti bolognaise on Bob's seat, on which he eventually sat down. When Bob realised what had happened his face turned to thunder, but he realised that to lose his temper would make everyone laugh all the more, so he picked up the plate and emptied what wasn't on his backside over Alex's head. Wisely, because of the nature of the event Alex hadn't brought his car, so he got some odd looks in the Underground because of the spaghetti caught in his curly hair.' To be fair to Bob Fisher, David Widdowson reminds me that together they started the Tuesday evening Club get-togethers, which are still a great success.

Between 1970 and 1980 there were eight more Fourteen owners or permanent crews of Fourteens: Philip McDanell, A.J. Dixon, Robin Johnson, Dan Owen, Tom Trevelyan, Adam Hogg, Jeremy Sibthorpe and Julian Pearson. 1970 also marked the end of an era. Stewart Morris decided to sell *Encore*; but he was pleased to be asked to become President of the class. International agreement was reached at last on one trapeze which was used for the Falmouth P.O.W. Jeremy had already joined Itchenor, although remaining a member of the Club for the winter series: 'One had got to the stage, once one began to get to the top of the fleet, when one had to sail where the 'top cats' were, although I continued sailing on the river in the winter. There was that marvellous feeling as a basic L.C.S.C. member of beginning to do a little better on the open circuit and representing the Club, which was nice.'

This is no place to discuss in detail how the Fourteen developed into the amazing machine it is today, but it must be mentioned as not only Jeremy Pudney but Tom Trevelyan, Ray Rouse, Jeremy Sibthorpe and other members of the Club have played a great part over nearly 30 years and are continuing to do so. There was tremendous resistance to change in the mid-'60's-'70's because of the dominant position of the U.K. association. However the Americans and Canadians were producing much better sailors, and felt 'why should the Brits be running the show?' The stewardship of the class had allowed it to become moribund and insular. 'Having a marketing background,' Jeremy told me, 'I and many others felt we had to bring the Fourteen up to date. We had to make it a state of the art boat, in the same way as it was when it first became an international class. What you dearly loved sailing at the London Corinthian would disappear off the scene unless every form of influence and persuasion were used to update the product.'

As a result of this the World Association was formed in the '60's to be a forum for what was hoped would be amicable discussions between the three countries on development, but the discussions were far from amicable at times, in spite of the 'calm and impartial' chairmanship of Johnnie Prentice at the beginning. For many years Jeremy Pudney was involved with the W.A. representing the U.K. association, but later he became World President at various times and has now been World Secretary for a number of years. Some readers may feel they've heard the name Pudney enough, but I'm afraid it's fully justified and the Club should be very proud of him.

Tommy Vaughan writes: 'Among the many famous names in the class, that of Jeremy Pudney is one that deserves special comment for the efforts he has devoted to Fourteens. To many around the world he is 'Mr. Fourteen.' The class was fortunate to have someone whose job took him to most corners of the globe, so that he acted as a roving ambassador and diplomat for the class. Certainly the Fourteen we sail today is, in no small way, the result of his single-minded enthusiasm, not least his encouragement of designers and builders, having commissioned no less than seventeen Fourteens between 1961 and 1988.'

Let us hear a word from Jeremy: 'The class has developed in a most extraordinary way. You could say that of all the people who take up sailing I have been one of the most fortunate to have gone through a period of so much development in the same boat. This is possibly why I'm still sailing. I started my sailing career at a relatively young age before the days of wet-suits, crewing my beloved uncle in corduroys; I've experienced all the excitement of rig development, single trapezes, a revised sail plan, weight reduction, double trapezes, fully-battened mainsails and asymmetrical spinnakers, and seen the image of the class grow in that period; I've enjoyed every new challenge, and of course relished arranging purely for my own benefit the use of asymmetrical spinnakers so that I could cope with the demands of the boat at the ripe old age of 55. There are very few people who see their own class develop in that way in the period of a sailing career, and I don't think there are any of us who have been involved in those 30 years of the class' development, from 1962 to 1993 who haven't found them satisfying and challenging and it all began at the London Corinthian.'

To begin with the result of development was a decline in P.O.W. turnouts in '84,'85 and '86, but after that the class rebuilt itself with its new image attracting younger sailors not only in this country, America and Canada, but also in the last few years in Germany, Denmark, Italy, Switzerland and Austria, all because of the new image of the Fourteen. In fact even some time before the introduction of most of the major changes, Jeremy on his frequent business trips to the Far East had intrigued the Japanese with his accounts of the thrills to be got from sailing a Fourteen and a number of Japanese dinghy sailors came to the P.O.W. at Pevensey Bay in 1983, when I was one of a number who lent them boats. In 1986, thanks to £14,000 sponsorship by Kleinwort Benson, the International Team Racing and World Championship was held in the Pacific and Lake Inawashiro respectively. The U.K. team was led by Jeremy Sibthorpe, who originally joined the Club as a winter member in 1974 to sail Enterprises.

The developments to the Fourteen class inevitably led to a gradual drop in turnouts at the Club, although Open Meetings during the '70's were well supported. Initially it wasn't so much the higher 'I' rig or the first trapeze in the early '70's, but the emergence of the Queen Mary and Datchet reservoirs which added more competitive water to sail on. This gradually drew Club Fourteens away during winter weekends and indeed I went to Queen Mary myself in the early '80's but found it a very bleak place in winter although it had all the water Fourteens wanted. In the early '70's Tom Trevelyan, who was Rear Commodore Sailing, was chairman of a sub-committee, consisting of Robo, James Bridge-Butler and others, to advise on whether to start a branch at Queen Mary, following an approach from there, which was supported by Jeremy Pudney. Datchet was also visited. 'We rejected the idea,' says Tom, 'as we were not in the business of running a watersports centre for the Water Board.'

In spite of the shadow of Queen Mary hanging over the Club, the Fourteen class was still very much alive on the river and for Open Meetings there were splendid turnouts. There were also a number of memorable parties. In 1973 Shirley Rouse presented Ray with a brand new Phil Morrison, built by Laurie Smart, and appropriately named *Heartbeat*. At Torquay that year Shirley won the Morgan Giles Trophy for the first lady home in the P.O.W. race. Later on there was Robo's stag party before he married Fanny, a splendid girl and excellent sailor. Unmentionable things happened at that party which not even I am prepared to put on paper.

Back to sailing. In 1975 Ray, being a master of many crafts, designed his first Rouse Fourteen and called her *Seabeat*. Shirley released him from his obligation to her so that Tom Trevelyan could take her place as crew. Together Ray and Tom made the U.K. team and helped to win the International Team Racing series at Hayling. Earlier in the year Ray had represented the U.K. on the sub-committee redrafting the rules which were later accepted by the I.Y.R.U. The year was the 50th anniversary of the first P.O.W. Ray, crewed by Chris McLaughlin, another Club member, won the big race and as a bonus became only the third person to win the P.O.W. in a boat of his own design, following Uffa Fox and Charles Currey. Illustrious company indeed for a member of a river club!

In 1977 Tom Trevelyan bought a Kirby IV and with Robo as crew was 4th in the P.O.W. (Keith Goulborn was 3rd). In 1979 Tom bought a Rouse 1 and named it *Brown Trousers* which is where we started. Jeremy Sibthorpe also remembers that Shackleton. Jeremy started sailing, like many other members of the Club, at Strand on the Green. 'The highlight of 1964 was the visit to London Corinthian for the West London Hospital Trophy. I was then sailing a Heron. I was totally awe-inspired by the Fourteens and their majestic power and speed, and knew from the age of 11 that I had to have one.' He joined the Club in 1974, originally as a winter member to sail Enterprises and became class captain in 1979. In 1980 curiously enough he borrowed for the Shackleton Trophy, a good old boat of mine; an Opus II called *Firebird* and came second beating Jeremy Pudney. 'I was hooked and immediately bought *Perseverance* (1041), a Kirby V and became Fourteen class captain. My main objective was to beat that wily old master Hugh Kemlo. It wasn't easy then and isn't easy now.

My best race ever at Hammersmith was the Shackleton Trophy in October 1981. It was blowing Force 7 from the south-west; there were three-foot waves breaking over the Club pontoons and white horses everywhere. My vivid memory is of 90 per cent of the fleet capsizing 10 yards after leaving the pontoon. Halfway through the race the mad Dr. Trevelyan (funny he should describe him thus because when I asked Robo what Tom was like as a helmsman he said 'a lunatic') in *Brown Trousers* put up his spinnaker having rounded the Barnes mark and shouted at me very loudly "get out of the f——— way" as he virtually took off - I was still beating up. We overtook a cyclist who was peddling along the towpath as hard as he could as we were on a white knuckle run - both hands on the tiller. Hugh Kemlo sailed a very conservative course and didn't capsize. Most people capsized at least six times. Sadly my tiller extension broke twenty yards from the finish when we were in 2nd place.'

Club turnouts began to drop rapidly in the mid '80's, but that didn't stop the Club winning the Walker Trophy in 1982 and 1983 again against Itchenor and the Oxford and Cambridge Sailing Society; the Club team being Jeremy Sibthorpe as captain; Jeremy Pudney; Keith Goulborn and Tom Trevelyan. Looking at the P.O.W. results from 1985, one can see that the fully-developed Fourteen had brought a new generation into the class. However in 1986 Jeremy Sibthorpe went to the P.O.W. at Lowestoft. There was a fleet of 48, considerably less than 'the old days' and it was significant that two-thirds of the boats were less than two years' old. Jeremy finished 5th in the big race and got his replica and also the tie that goes with it. 'I reckon it cost me £40,000.'

In 1987, owing to Kleinwort Benson's generous sponsorship, the U.K. team led by Jeremy, who was crewed by Bruce Grant - one of the most experienced in the class, went to Japan for the first team racing and World Championship ever to be held there. A handy typhoon provided the conditions the U.K. enjoy and the team won the series with fourteen wins, sailing in the Pacific with 30 ft waves 100 ft apart, against teams from Japan, the east and west coasts of the U.S.A., Canada, Australia and New Zealand. There was an entry of eighty for the Worlds which were held at Lake Inawashiro, and the British once again were unbeatable taking 1st, 2nd, 3rd and 4th places.

The only possible adverse comment on what must have been an amazing and most enjoyable sailing experience was that the western participants must have lost a great deal of weight, because apart from the energy they expended sailing many of them found the diet not only difficult to eat physically, but hardly to their liking. Jeremy Sibthorpe said breakfast was raw eggs and seaweed eaten with chopsticks; lunch the same; and dinner: 'have you ever tried eating raw squid?' A worse experience perhaps for Jeremy was the Worlds at Torquay in 1991 when he found himself battling to make a good start with a hundred and fifty other boats.

Julian Pearson, who became a member in 1978 has not yet been mentioned. I raced a Fourteen against his parents for many years before meeting him. He then began to hitch a lift to Itchenor and P.O.W.s. His parents had, I think, by then given up racing and Julian appeared to be very impoverished. His sartorial appearance then and even at times now is one of garments patched or full of holes. This did not make any difference to his popularity. At Itchenor I think he often kipped down in the bar, until everyone had gone to bed and then tried, to the Secretary's fury, to find an empty bunk in one of the dormitories. At P.O.W.s he often slept on the beach under a boat cover.

For all that he became a remarkable Fourteen helmsman or crew, and took part in the 1989 San Francisco Worlds. With the Golden Gate bridge as a backdrop, San Francisco must be one of the most wonderful harbours to sail in; it is also, it appears, one of the most demanding. It nearly always blows hard and there is generally a strong tide, requiring exhausting short tacking, which comes easily to London Corinthian members. Keith Goulborn and Robo were nearly always first to the windward mark, but after that found the wind and wave conditions impossible. Jeremy Sibthorpe describes it as the most 'awe-inspiringly windy venue to sail in. At the Golden Gate the wind may be Force 4, but by the time you get near Alcatraz prison island, it has funnelled up to Force 6 owing to the shape of the harbour. They call the area the 'washing machine' because the tide goes one way and the wind another. You don't want to capsize there because of the ferries, the odd whale and being washed up on Alcatraz.' In spite of such impossible 'hairy' conditions Julian helmed his boat into 8th place against a hundred and fifteen entries. A magnificent bit of sailing.

Last year Julian was selected for one of the U.K. teams against Canada and the U.S.A. In the World Championships which followed at Kingston, Julian crewed Jeremy Pudney and they came 11th out of eighty eight boats. A great effort by both of them. Julian and Martin Dixon now appear to be the Club's sole Fourteeners, although even they have forsaken the river. Thus ends my account of what is actually more than 50 years' sailing Fourteens on Hammersmith and Chiswick reaches. It is sad that we see those wonderful boats no longer, but as Stu Walker said: 'a development class has got to develop' and the Club's members have played a significant part in that, and spawned also many outstanding helmsmen and crews.

For the winners, the silverware is obviously highly satisfying, but the trophies also reflect the sailing skills, tactics and seamanship which were developed originally on Hammersmith and Chiswick Reaches and in recent years have been exercised in America, Canada, Japan, and many countries in Europe apart from many parts of our country. Nothing can take that away from the London Corinthian Sailing Club whatever the circumstances it finds itself in.

Chapter 2

How the Club was Founded

Most of today's oldest members have always been led to believe that the decision to found the Club was made over several pints of beer in the Black Lion pub. I regret to say, having dredged through all the minutes that there is no written evidence of any such convivial occasion. It could still be true, however, as there were moorings off 'Black Lion Stairs' (known for at least the last 80 years as Bell Steps). Sailing was a popular pastime on the upper reaches of the tideway even in the 18th century, although like Ratty we might regard it today as 'messing about in boats' rather than serious sailing. This doubtless sounds patronising and is only excused by contemporary photographs of the boats in question and their owners often smoking or 'chewing' a pipe and wearing caps.

The boats were of a weird and wonderful variety: dipping lugsail dinghies of up to 14 ft long; 'half-raters' similar to those sailed at Upper Thames and 18 ft waterline keel boats, some with mizzen masts and others with booms which extended almost 6ft aft of their transom and these obviously needed 'legs' to remain upright in the mud at low tide (the mud sometimes had an almost red colour from the worms which lived there and were much liked by the daice, sticklebacks and even larger fish which could often be seen until the mid-30's).

What could be more natural than for those who met regularly going to and from their boats at 'the Stairs' to get together in the Black Lion and discuss following the example of Ranelagh (1889) in Putney Reach and indeed the London Sailing Club and Eyot Sailing Club in Hammersmith Reach? Having come to this daring decision our eleven enthusiasts or 'gentlemen,' as the first minute describes them, evidently thought that they should invest the occasion with some formality and dissociate themselves from the beery atmosphere of a pub.

It was decided therefore to meet on 20th October 1894, at 327 Kennington Road, S.E., the home of W.E. Burgess, soon to become Treasurer. A south-east London venue may seem surprising as all but four of the gentlemen lived locally. Cars were in their infancy; the days of horse-drawn trams were over but the District Line, or Underground, had been extended to Hammersmith, and from Westminster it was quite easy to get to Kennington.

The Club was to be called the Corinthian Sailing Club; its objects were to encourage the building, sailing and racing of sailing boats. Black Lion Stairs were to be the Club's 'Station' (sic) even though it is impossible once the tide is up to see either east or west from 'the Stairs,' only straight across the river. Strengthening the traditional association with the Black Lion was the decision that the Club's burgee would be a black lion rampant on a red background. The course would be from 'Black Lion Stairs' to St. Ann's Tower and back, twice. St. Ann's Tower, was a private house with a tower which no longer exists in 'St. Ann's Road' behind Barnes River Police Station; in fact very near where our turning mark has been for so many years.

The annual subscription was to be 10/6d, (in today's money £27.10) to be due on 1st January and to be paid by 31st. March. Everyone joining after 31st March would have to pay an entrance fee of 2/6d (£6.10). I am indebted to Lloyd's Bank Economic Unit for the conversion rate of the 1900 pound in today's terms. Suffice it to say that the pound in 1894 would be worth only 1.9p today, and that every sum in the minutes has to be multiplied by 52.6. It is immediately evident not only from contemporary photographs of the members but from the value of the pound, that the age composition of the Club was vastly different from that of most clubs today. From the start the Club struggled against financial problems (don't we still) even though the members, if not men of substance, were from the professional or business classes; not teenagers or young people in their first jobs as many are today.

Mr. D. White, who lived in Stockwell Green, was elected to be the first Commodore and served in that office for seven years, steering the Club through many problems. At the first meeting all the other officers necessary to run the Club were elected and an initial set of rules worked out, including 'lifebelts or jackets to be worn or within reach.' The other rules were on the same lines as those of today, although one somewhat unusual one was 'that the entrance fee for a race shall be settled at the time the date is fixed and that on no occasion shall it exceed 2/6d' (£6.10 - quite a lot of money). I shall not mention all the officers' names, but there is a list of Commodores in Appendix B at the back. With respect to handicapping 'the Y.R.A. Code of rating and sailing rules shall be accepted for match sailing.' This vexed problem, which was never really solved till the introduction of the Portsmouth yardstick in 1958, will be dealt with later.

It was obvious that the immediate need was to find proper riverside premises where members could not only discuss the future but keep their sailing gear. Bearing in mind Mr. Burgess's address in south-east London, it says much for the enthusiasm of the original members who had already been joined by nine more that they were willing to meet there again. However by December 1895 a temporary solution had been found: Mr. Bell, of 19 Lower Mall, agreed to rent the Club his front room for £5 (£13.30) a year including coal, gaslight, table and chairs and undertook to build lockers.

Further rules were made providing that: officers should

be elected every January for a year; strangers should not be admitted without being signed in by a member; auditors must be appointed; races to be held twice a month with Club funds allocated as prizes, the entrance fee to be 1/- (£2.10) and each owner to provide an efficient lifebelt for his crew and the O.O.D. to see that this was carried out; starting signals would be a five and one minute gun or whistle followed by the start a minute later; a scale of time allowances to be put in the rule book and of course Club badges for Flag Officers; members must agree to be bound by the rules.

It was at the second meeting that Mr. Lucas D'Oyley Carte of the opera company was elected a member and his brother Rupert shortly afterwards. It was agreed also to make Mr. E.B. Cole the first Honorary Member. Mr. Cole was a boatbuilder whose yard, close to The Dove pub, went back to 1801. His son Frank, 40 years later in 1936, built the *Water Gipsy* for my father who was then President of the Club. Equally memorable for me as a boy of 10 was Frank teaching me how to scull over the stern of a dinghy, a very valuable skill on the tideway in those days although hardly necessary now.

The Club could hardly consider itself to be well-known, but it was determined to be recognised as an established part of the river scene. In July 1895, a letter was written to the Thames Conservancy (the Port of London Authority was not made responsible for the administration of the port until 1909) to protest at a proposed new regulation that all sailing boats should give way to rowing boats. The Club's views were made public in a letter to *The Daily Telegraph*. We are not told whether the Thames Conservancy ever replied to this letter, and the problem has continued, but on the whole it has been resolved by the good sense of both sailors and rowers without recourse to regulations.

Collisions still occur occasionally and certainly did in the '20's when the boats were less manoeuvrable than the modern class dinghy. A.P.H., who was made a member in 1923, told me when he was first trying to teach me to sail that the only race he ever won in his dipping lugsail, *The Bee*, was because a racing sculler rammed and deeply penetrated the stem of the boat ahead of him. 'Mr. S. Byles, who was winning, had to be towed to the bank where the sculler was extracted like a reluctant tooth. Meanwhile I heartlessly sailed on and was victorious.' Mr. Byles, whose boat was called *Why Not*, must have been exceptionally annoyed, as he very often won, and certainly didn't expect to be beaten by *The Bee*.

The Club was in good heart despite its letter having been ignored and at the end of 1895 held their first annual dinner at Mr. Tom Sullivan's 'Rutland Hotel;' the pub is of course still there. Twenty-five members sat down to dinner and it was 'an excellent repast.' The convenient if not perfect arrangement for meeting at 19 Lower Mall did not last long. Early in 1896 the Club found itself homeless once again. According to the minutes Mr. Bell told the Club he was going to give up his tenancy of 19 Lower Mall which in fact he did. (It soon became the headquarters of the Furnivall Sculling Club). However the late Bob Salt, who joined the Club in 1927 and was Commodore in 1973 and 1974, and a good friend of many of us, told me that there had been 'words' between the Secretary and Mr. Bell's wife.

The Club was forced back into holding its monthly meetings at Kennington Road and in July actually on Black Lion Stairs - what the passing public thought of this gathering of middle-aged gentlemen sitting on the stone steps, I can't imagine, but I hope it was a warm evening. However the premises problem did not stop Club races during the spring and summer and a workable set of rules and a racing calendar were printed.

Two of the most important rules were: boats could not race without a certificate from the official measurer, who inspected them at Black Lion Stairs and O.O.D.s who failed to turn up for duty or find a substitute were to be fined 2/6d (£6.10) - I wonder what members would think of such a rule being introduced today? In addition permission was given by the West Middlesex Water Company to paint a white perpendicular mark on the Barnes reservoir fence opposite 'the Stairs' to establish an accurate start and finishing line.

The Club was homeless, but meetings were held at The Lowndes Arms, a pub off Eaton Square, which belonged to one of the members and was obviously more convenient than Kennington. The Club appears to have made its presence felt on the tideway because The Thames (Western) Improvement Committee sought their help in trying to get the Thames Conservancy to build a half-tide lock at Putney, like the one at Richmond. This would have been nice for the Club as it would probably have made it possible to sail at all states of the tide; but it would not have been popular with commercial traffic which would be delayed if they were catching the first of the flood or equally if when going downstream they were late on the ebb. Nevertheless the Commodore and Vice-Commodore represented the Club when the half-tide lock at Putney was discussed.

The possibility of such a scheme was raised many times in the next 30 years, and most strongly by The Thames Barrage Association in 1935. They forwarded to Parliament professional plans for a barrage which would not only be a flood barrier, but incorporate a number of locks of different sizes. This would have created a tideless Thames and made sailing possible at all times; perhaps more important it would have enabled ships alongside wharves to unload their cargoes and depart without having to wait for another tide and consequently pay harbour dues or 'demurrage.' Because of the tide and demurrage and in particular the restrictive practices of the unions after the last war, London became the most expensive port in the country, and gradually lost all its trade except at Tilbury. The barrage would have been sited where the flood barrier is today, west of the entrance to the Royal Docks system. Parliament and, in particular Sir John Simon, refused on defence grounds even to debate the matter.

Early in the autumn of 1896, the London Sailing Club, Lower Mall, (the kink in the river wall towards the eastern end of Furnival Gardens marks the site today), announced that they were moving to Erith (and later to Burnham on Crouch) and wanted to let the club premises for £80 a year (£4,208) or sell the lease for £400 (£21,040). These terms were beyond the means of the Club and the London Sailing Club did not respond to haggling about the rent. Having decided that 'the Club was not justified in committing itself' to the London Sailing Club's terms, a sub-committee was formed to search for alternative moorings and a room was found the other side of The Creek, 100 yards to the west of the London Sailing Club's premises. The historical significance of The Creek is described in full in the next chapter.

Approaches were made to the famous binder and printer, T.J. Cobden-Sanderson, who, as the English Heritage plaque proclaims, lived two doors away from The Dove public house. The suggestion was for moorings to be laid in front of Mr. Sanderson's house and for the Club to rent a room in The Dove. However Mr. Sanderson didn't like the idea. Eventually in January 1897, at the annual meeting held at The Lowndes Arms, Mr. H. Lewis, the Vice-Commodore, offered to buy the London Sailing Club's lease and let it to the Club for three years at a rent of £40 or £45, with an option to renew at the same terms provided there were guarantors. Mr. Lewis very generously did not ask for any money from the guarantors, only their signatures on the lease. By 25th March the lease was signed and the committee decided to incorporate 'London' into the Club's name. In this way the London Corinthian Sailing Club was born and the members were able to watch the 1897 Oxford and Cambridge Boat Race from their own premises.

However before that event the members decided quite understandably that the signing of the lease was a cause for celebration. A caretaker, it seems, had been engaged as a steward at 10/- a week (£26) and he was sent out to buy '1 dozen Scotch whisky, 1 dozen Irish, three bottles of claret, 1 bottle of brandy half a gross of Bass, 1 dozen Guinness, two dozen ginger beer, 100 Rosa Castilla cigars, 100 cigarettes and half a pound of tobacco.' He was also told to buy packs of playing cards, dominoes and draughts. It's quite an interesting order and one hopes a good time was had by all. The steward was later allowed to charge members 6d a sitting for cards and 3d for dominoes and draughts, and he was requested to make a list of his charges for refreshments 'other than drinks,' such as tea, chops and steaks.

I find the picture of our earliest members sitting down to play dominoes with a large Scotch nearby rather endearing, and it bears out what I said earlier about the age composition. From the first it was obvious that members decided that the Club was going to be a place not only to sail from but for convivial evenings, albeit without their wives. The question of ladies being full members, with voting rights and a voice in the running of the Club was a long-drawn out matter. It's interesting sociologically that it was not until 1961 that 'the admission of lady members as being in accord with ideas of today' was accepted. This sounds extraordinary to us now, particularly as the issue was raised repeatedly.

In the earliest years, as with men's clubs today, the

members did not want their cosy drinking snuggery - and the old Club bar was exactly that - invaded. However it would be wrong to think male members were completely anti-women. The question of ladies becoming members was first raised only a few months after the 1897 Boat Race, when the minutes read: 'Gentlemen intimated that they would gladly welcome the presence of ladies as guests of members but preferred not to elect them as members.'

Two years later, in 1899, the first lady members were elected on the understanding that they could not hold office, propose or second any resolution or vote or take any part in the running of the Club. In 1905 the subject came up again, and it was decided that lady members could have the same privileges as full members but only until 7 pm and not on Race days or other 'special occasions.' I will leave the 'women's membership' saga there for the moment, except to say once again that it was obvious that the male members wanted the Club to be an oasis where they could enjoy their pink gins in peace.

It is time to turn to what Hammersmith and the riverside was like at the turn of the last century.

Chapter 3

Hammersmith and the River in 1894

Hammersmith as a Borough and the river as a commercial waterway were obviously very different 100 years ago from what they are today. In 1801 Hammersmith was a rural village renowned for its orchards and market gardens. The population was 5,600 and the Broadway was the village green. By 1900 the population was 112,000.

In order to understand what the Club's environment was like in 1894, both along the riverside and on the tideway, it is necessary to dip into the history of the Borough and the Port of London. Hammersmith goes back to Domesday Book times. The derivation of the name is obscure, but Hamer's Hythe - 'hythe' is old English for haven or harbour as in Rotherhithe and Greenhithe - is given as a possible choice. Hamer's is obviously the genitive of a personal name which appears in The Domesday Book, and there are even maps showing 'The Island of Hame;' this of course is Chiswick Eyot, but in those days it stretched much further east into Hammersmith.

One thing is certain. The hythe was The Creek, approximately 100 yards west, as I have already said, of the Club's earliest premises on the western edge of what is now Furnivall Gardens, close to where Cole's Boatyard used to be. This was the cradle of early riverside life at Hammersmith. Even in 1915, when the then L.C.C. did a survey of London, there was a village of white-washed cottages and a general shop known as 'Noah's Ark' near 'The High Bridge' over The Creek. This was where four bridle paths met: one from Upper Mall; a second stretching south from King Street; a third was from the direction of the Broadway and lastly one led to the Club's old premises and Lower Mall. Near the entrance to The Creek were more cottages, while further along the riverside became more commercial; with wharves and small engineering businesses. Years later these included such firms as Julius Sax, electrical engineers, next door to the Club, while on the other side of the path were the Tilbury Motor Body works. In fact the whole of what is now Furnivall Gardens was a mixture of cottages and commerce.

The Creek was fed by Stamford Brook, but filled up naturally with every tide and stretched nearly as far as where the cinema is today. It was an ideal place for a settlement, enabling craft to unload their catches of fish, which were plentiful up to 150 years ago, and other cargoes from the wharves down river and equally to transport bricks - one of the 'hamlet's' earliest industries - to the City wharves.

By the middle of the 19th century dumb lighters and even Thames barges were bringing their cargoes into The Creek and continued to do so until 1930: screened shingle and cement for Sankey's - builder's merchants; hops for the malthouses of Cromwell's brewery and many other cargoes for the different wharfingers. The arch-shaped High Bridge, or 'Bridge of Sighs,' as it was sometimes called, joined Upper Mall to 'Middle Mall' and the bridle path to the Club. In order to get under the bridge the Thames barges had to drop their masts, which was nothing unusual for those wonderful craft, and push their way up The Creek. Some historians refer to the The Creek as 'a squalid slum area' and others as 'Little Wapping.' It may have been a bit scruffy but it was undoubtedly colourful and served local businesses and shopkeepers well. In 1936 it was filled in and Stamford Brook channelled through a culvert into the river.

Taking the riverside path from the High Bridge over The Creek (there is still a small rise in the path where it stood) one came to a passage with tall and somewhat forbidding walls of grey brick each side. Immediately on the right was the Club, while on the other side of the passage were The Phoenix Lead Mills, owned by F.A. Clark and Son, who also owned the land the Club stood on and the wharf immediately to the east of the Club. Barges tied up here in the early days with raw material for the works. Many years later when the Club's pontoons were full up, 'Clark's' grudgingly allowed boats to be accommodated there.

If the Creek was full of character and activity, so was Lower Mall from the Club's premises to Hammersmith Bridge. It was all very different from the broad and in my opinion somewhat antiseptic walk, beloved of planners, which extends eastwards today from Furnivall Gardens. The Friends' Meeting House and the Vicarage were there of course, and then in contrast businesses such as the Blenheim Engineering Works and Patent Impervious Stone; the raw material being unloaded at the Rutland Wharf.

Next door to Rutland Wharf was the Furnival Sculling Club. There is a certain charm about how this club was founded. Dr. F.J. Furnivall (1825-1910) was a distinguished scholar and critic of Chaucer and Shakespeare. When working at The British Museum he used to lunch at an A.B.C. (I think the initials stood for the Aerated Bread Company, which has long since been absorbed or gone bust). He became interested in the teashop girls' welfare, and in 1896 founded the Hammersmith Sculling Club for Girls and Men, often spending his Sundays with them on the river. Dr. Furnivall would have revelled in the all-year round activity at the Auriol and West End Rowing Clubs and in his own creation, which rightly still bears his name.

Next to the sculling club was the West End Boat House and yard belonging to Mr. John Biffen, the well-known maker of oars, or 'blades' as they were called. Like the Cole family, there were many Biffens. This is where Jack Holt began; he had a tiny part of the Biffen yard. I remember being taken there as a small boy and shown the first International Fourteen Jack was building. Before setting himself up on the Putney Embankment he moved just beyond Hammersmith Bridge to the yard vacated by Morgan Giles, as mentioned in Chapter 1.

After the West End Boat House, Lower Mall was pretty well as it is today including the West End Amateur Rowing Association and the Rutland Hotel (although it is no longer an hotel). Behind the Rutland was George Sims's boatyard which even after the last war made the eights for the Oxford crew. Next door to The Rutland was The Anchor Boat House, belonging to another member of the Biffen family, and then The Blue Anchor, my favourite pub apart from The Dove, on this part of the riverside. It may have been the splendid view of Hammersmith Bridge from the The Blue Anchor's bow window that inspired Gustav Holst to write his score for *Hammersmith*, a prelude and scherzo for full orchestra, in 1931. Holst lived from 1908 to 1913 in a house east of Barnes bridge and the Royal College of Music tell me that his prelude on Hammersmith definitely refers to the river, and the scherzo to the bustle of the Broadway and the markets nearby. Regency or 'gentlemen's houses,' as they were called in their day, concluded Lower Mall and were a contrast to the noise of hammers and the bustle of its working area. Digby Mansions was obviously built later.

On the tideway it was as interesting then as it is dull today, *pace* the rowers and our own sailing races. Until about 1950 the Port of London was still the greatest port in the world. The Upper and Lower Pool and the wharves on both sides of the river all the way down to Tilbury, let alone those in the great dock systems, were crowded with ships unloading cargoes of every conceivable kind. It is certain that there was a lot of smoke and dirt in The Pool and downstream from the coal-burning ships about the time the Club was founded. There were also Thames spritsail barges tacking up the river on the tide, their sails full-bellied with wind and silent save for the ear-tingling rattle of ropes moving through blocks as the skipper put his barge about, which took at least a minute. It was a dramatic sight and of great significance to the City. It is portrayed magnificently by William Wyllie's great oil *Toil, Glitter, Grime and Wealth on a Flowing Tide* which is in the Tate Gallery. One could still see the occasional barge sailing commercially on the tideway after the war.

And what, I can hear you say has this got to do with the London Corinthian? I admit to having always been mesmerised, like Holst, by the lure of London River. It was a thrilling sight to be sailing in the Greenwich Races before and after the war because of the activity in the Pool of London and downstream. But more to the point members of the Club had to keep a watchful eye on tugs, barges and even bigger vessels not only in the early years but till quite recently. It must not be forgotten that the Port of London originally extended as far as Teddington and even in the '60's small Dutch cargo ships, steamed past the Club to a non-union dock at Isleworth. Day or night you could always hear them coming with their 'tut tutter, tut tutter.'

Every tide brought a procession of tugs, each one towing as many as six lighters, on their way to the Creek in the early years of the Club, and later the wharves at Lep, west of the Eyot, or even to those at Vitamins Ltd, which were next door to The Ship, where Lord Napier Place stands today. As you will read later it was this traffic which for many years caused great problems to the boats moored fore and aft in three rows off the Club.

Living on the riverside I often heard the throb of the diesels at night when I was cosy in bed and the tugs were taking advantage of how the tide served. It was a wonderful sound. If you were wise you also learned the meaning of the blasts on their sirens: four long blasts followed by one meant the tug would be turning round to starboard into the tide to 'drop' a barge off at Vitamins or Lep. If you were tacking up river it was as well to take such manoeuvres into consideration.

As memorable as the Thames sailing barges down river were the men on the dumb lighters, who with no motive power save the tide and two great sweeps, used to bring their ungainly craft into Vitamins' wharf, or in the early years of the Club into the Creek. If they miscalculated there was no rowing back; however those men were Freemen of the River having served seven years' apprenticeship and they knew how to use the tides to the greatest advantage on every bend of the river up to Brentford.

By the time the Club was founded, Hammersmith had become not only a salubrious dormitory suburb for those who previously had lived as well as worked in the City, but offered good opportunities for prospective industrialists. One of the main reasons was the excellent communications. In 1887 the present suspension bridge had replaced an earlier one; even more important steam and Underground railways were running from the City to Hammersmith. Easy transport must have encouraged the Club's earliest members to choose Hammersmith Reach, the best sailing reach on the tideway. And for those with business in mind, the Thames then offered a cheap form of transport for raw materials from the docks and wharves down river. In addition there were plentiful supplies of gas for lighting and fresh water: the West Middlesex Water Works had bought nine acres for reservoirs in Barnes as early as 1809, and laid the first great water supply pipe under the river in 1838.

Among many businesses that recognised the services and opportunities in Hammersmith there was Mr. Robertson's lamp-making factory in Brook Green which was opened the year before the Club was founded. By 1915 this had become the Osram and Robertson Lamp Company and later still G.E.C. George Wimpey, began on their present site in The Grove as a small stonemason's yard in 1886. A completely different trade, J. Lyons and Co, moved to Cadby Hall, near Olympia, in 1894.

Thanks to the Underground, Hammersmith became well-known in 'the West End' not only for growing businesses, but also for the wide variety of entertainment in what 100 years before had been described as 'that village five miles west of us.' There was Olympia with such extravaganzas as Barnum and Bailey; The Lyric Theatre opened in 1890 and The King's in 1902; there were two music halls; the White City had exhibitions and every kind of sporting event, including the Olympic Games of 1908, and of course there was the annual Homeric struggle between Oxford and Cambridge on the tideway which as shown by Walter Greaves's *Hammersmith Bridge on Boat Race Day* in The Tate, was a tremendously popular event. And this brings me back to the site of the London Corinthian Sailing Club in 1894. What did the Club look like, and how did the members shape up to the many problems which confront every club?

Chapter 4

A Club of Our Own, 1897 - 1918.

The brick facade had a dark woebegone look save for the words 'London Sailing Club,' painted rather amateurishly in white lettering. This was quickly changed and replaced by a brass plate with the Club's new name and burgee which was fixed to the front gate. This opened onto a garden that received little attention until after the Second World War when 'boat-owning lady members,' such as Winifred Procter, Elsie Bloor and others took it in hand. The building was probably late 19th century, approximately half the width of Linden House, and had no architectural merits - and there is no reason why it should have had as it was a purpose-built sailing club.

On the right of the front door was an iron staircase to the dining room. Tucked into the corner of the building near the staircase was the 'Gents,' which with the years became embarrassingly noisy and worse still malodorous. The front door led immediately via swing doors into the saloon which measured about 18 ft by 12 ft Half the width was taken up by a curved bar, from which a door led off to the steward's living quarters.

Before the Club took possession there was a need for someone to sleep there to look after the boats and the premises. Mr. M.T. Regis, one of the founder members volunteered to do so, 'provided that the place was found to be habitable.' I never chose to penetrate what I always thought could not help but be a midden. Today the accommodation would not be legal.

Opposite the bar there was an oval bench and a few small tables, while through the glass-fronted door at the far end of the saloon one could see out onto the hard and beyond the walls of the hard, if the tide was high, three rows of boats rocking at their moorings. Tideboards were placed in the centre of the main hard wall and were obviously essential, but could be taken out when the tide permitted and members wanted to get down to their boats more easily. There was a minute changing room to the left (for men of course - there was no need then for one for ladies) and that was all. It was the size of the saloon, lit at night by gas mantles, and its proximity to the Thames that gave the Club such character. There was a lot of work to be done, but there was no doubt about the possibilities of making it into a snuggery, as well as a place to race from.

The Club's first President, Mr. (later Sir) William Bull spent an evening there in 1887 as the guest of the London Sailing Club. His diary for 20th September records: '.... Arter (the tenant by coincidence of Linden House) sent round on Sunday inviting me to dinner at the London Sailing Club; so after coming home from the City, I went round to the new clubhouse which stands just by The Creek. Although it is not so picturesque as the little wooden shanty by Biffen's (near where Alan See's is today) it is very comfortable. The principal room (above the saloon where soon there was to be a billiards table) is a large one with views of the river, charts, yachting sketches and models ornamenting the walls. Twenty-six men sat down to dinner, the majority of whom had been sailing in the Club races in the afternoon. The dinner was a good one and the men very pleasant. Afterwards songs were sung, recitations recited, and whiskey (sic) and rum consumed ad lib. Left about 12. The fellows want me to join.'

Starting a sailing club, even if in possession of the premises, is an enormous task, as we know from the change to Linden House. However there was no lack of enthusiasm and willingness on the part of elected officers and members, of which there were now thirty, to make the London Corinthian as attractive as Mr. Bull had found the London Sailing Club. The Management Committee, under the chairmanship of Mr. D. White, the Commodore met to discuss the priorities for action. There was already a rule book and a racing calendar, but these had to be revised to suit the new premises and moorings. First the Secretary had to write to the Thames Conservancy to say the Club had taken over the London Sailing Club's premises and wished to retain the latter's rights to the moorings and the concrete causeway which led down between the boats. Approval for this was taken for granted: the members were so keen to see their boats bobbing about in front of the Club that without waiting for a reply they brought their boats down from Black Lion Stairs.

They then had to be allocated moorings for which rent had to be paid: this was to be £2 for a racing season - 31st March to 31st October - and 4/- a month for the rest of the year. The Club had inherited a punt which was used by members to get out to their boats, but quite soon the habit developed of asking the steward to ferry them out, which not unnaturally quickly became a bone of contention with the steward, as you will see. When not being used the punt was moored to a ladder leading down from the hard and then later to a pontoon where it was naturally at the mercy of the wash from passing tugs, pleasure steamers and motor boats, let alone the wind and tide, and constantly being damaged by banging against the ladder. It was obviously now in need of repair, which was why the London Sailing Club had left it behind. Mr. Burgess, at whose home in Kennington, you may remember, the Club had been founded, undertook to repair the punt and also to build six new lockers for the changing room. There would be a ballot for the lockers and a charge of 5/- a year made for their hire. One of the first decisions the management committee took, although it meant dipping into the Club's slender resources, was to order a strong dinghy to be made by Mr. Maynard, of Chiswick, yet another local shipwright, for £4. A dinghy would certainly be a more practical form of transport to and from the moorings than the punt. One of the most important new rules was that each boat had to be provided with fenders so that she didn't damage her neighbours.

Bearing in mind the post-war history of the Club and the efforts to improve the social atmosphere, Commodore White and his colleagues seem to have been extraordinarily enlightened. Within a month of taking possession of the Club it was decided that Tuesdays, Thursdays, and Saturdays would be Club Nights, when all the members of the Committee were expected to turn up. In this way they hoped to increase the general attendance of members and their guests - 'provided that they signed the book' - and create a convivial atmosphere which would encourage new members.

It only took three months before the steward quite understandably complained to the Commodore about his lot. His initial pay was 10/- a week; equivalent to £6.60 or approximately half the official Income Support rate today for a man of 44, in fact hardly a living wage. As well as serving behind the bar he was expected to take members to and from their boats. 'Some gentlemen expect me even to coal their launches and no members ever give me a tip.' The Commodore took immediate action. In future each member was to pay the steward 6d a week for taking him to and from his boat, but in return the steward had to wash down the boats and bale them out. After a year the steward was given the extra chore of putting a paraffin riding light every night on one of the boats on the outside trot, underlining the danger from passing traffic.

The steward was allowed to augment his pay by charging members 6d a sitting for playing cards and 3d for dominoes and draughts. Very stupidly he was also allowed a percentage of the bar profits from sales, which inevitably led to endless deficits and new stewards. Within a year Mr. Steed, the first steward, was given a month's notice. His replacement, Mr. Browning, with a wife and son, was a great success, but died after a year. All in all the Club was unlucky with its stewards, undoubtedly partly through its own fault; it was not until 1924 that the steward received a regular wage.

The Committee very sensibly decided to print the time of high water as well as the starting time of each race in the racing calendar. To begin with the entrance fee for a race was 1/- but in 1899 it was increased to 2/6d. This had to be paid to the Secretary the day before the race. Prizes came in the form of money from entrance fees augmented by Club funds. If there were six boats in a race, the first would get half the total entrance fee, the second two-thirds of what remained and the third one-third of what was left.

I mentioned earlier that all boats had to be measured and that this would be according to the Y.R.A. code of rating at the time. To quote from the chapter on the subject in 'A Century of Sailing on the Thames' by Ingrid Holford: 'This chapter required many aspirins and much strong coffee to write, and the same prescription may be needed by the reader. Most of the early data has been gleaned from the *Manual of Yacht and Boat* sailing by Dixon Kemp, the master mind behind most of the 19th century formula.' I am indebted to Tommy Vaughan for supplying me with Xerox copies of the relevant pages of Mr. Kemp's book. It was a very complicated subject, but basically the formula for rating, certainly up till the middle '20's, can be reduced to: Sail Area (square ft.) multiplied by the Load Waterline (feet) divided by 6000. It was called the Decimal Three rule because the result of the sum had to equal ·3. The disadvantage of this system was that in heavy weather the larger boat with smaller sails won and in light conditions the reverse was true.

Under this system the Club ruled that no time allowance would be given to boats rating under ·25. That all boats rating between ·25 and ·3 would be timed as ·3 raters; that all boats rating between ·3 and ·4 would be timed as ·4 raters and that all boats rating between ·4 and ·5 would be timed as ·5 raters. A special book with each boat's handicap was kept for the Officer of the Day, who you will recall was fined if he did not turn up. For the London Corinthian the system was a perennial source of dissatisfaction because the boats were all of a different size, rig and build. From 1902 it was the practice to handicap boats according to their performance; thus the winner of the last race would be the 'scratch' boat and have a minute added to her time and if she had won the previous two races she would have two minutes. The second and third boats were handicapped proportionately. New proposals were constantly brought up at A.G.M.s, but found unlikely to be an improvement even if everyone could understand them. It was not until the Portsmouth Yardstick was introduced in 1958 that there was a satisfactory handicapping system.

In spite of the somewhat *ad hoc* handicapping, members enjoyed racing from their own Club at last and discussing problems they found with their boats in the bar afterwards. Others took their drinks to the bench and in the evenings played cards, draughts or cribbage. These pursuits were improved in September 1897, when Mr. Lewis, Vice-Commodore and the Club's landlord, offered to erect a billiards table at his own expense provided that two-thirds of the receipts went to him, and the other third to the Club. The charges for a game of billiards were 1/- for 126 up and 8d for 62 up. The billiards table was installed quite easily by taking it up the stairway from the front garden. Billiards became very popular and a year later it was decided to hold the first of many handicap matches. These eventually led, particularly in the winter months, to inter-club matches and others against the local police.

By the end of the 1898 season there were twenty one boats, and it was decided to have the first annual dinner - tickets not to exceed 3/6d - which was held in the New Year. From the start the Committee was publicity conscious and free tickets were sent to the editors of the local Press and magazines like *The Yachtsman* and *Yachting World* which were taken regularly. Everyone obviously enjoyed themselves at the dinner because there is a minute recording the 'excellent manner in which it was arranged.'

Nevertheless the problems the present membership know so well began to rear their heads: lack of response to the Club Nights, subscriptions not being paid and the changing room in a squalid state. It was unfortunate therefore that Mr. Lewis, Vice-Commodore and the Club's landlord, chose in the summer of 1899 to offer to sell to the Club the remainder of the lease together with fixtures and the billiards table, for £200; the equivalent of £10,500. Somewhat unwisely the members accepted the offer and planned to raise the money by £1 debentures to be repaid by quarterly ballot out of the difference between the ground rent and the rent then paid to Mr. Lewis. The decision to buy the lease was clearly prompted by a desire for independence and to be free of the five per cent interest Mr. Lewis was getting on his investment.

As always there were difficulties raising the money, which led to the Commodore writing a letter to every member asking him to attend the October General Meeting 'otherwise we shall probably lose the clubhouse.' Only twelve members turned up. Nevertheless the meeting endorsed the provisional acceptance of Mr. Lewis's offer, except now he was to receive £140 by Christmas and the balance within two years plus five per cent interest on the amount owing. Needless to say the Secretary, in response to a letter from Mr. Lewis's solicitors, was forced to write to those members who had promised help towards the lease to ask them to pay up. It's true only £9 was owing but that was equivalent to £473 today. The balance was never raised so the whole scheme fell through. Mr. Lewis, ever-understanding, agreed to a new tenancy agreement based on the old one of £50 a year, and making him responsible for all repairs.

Whether it was frustration over the lack of support from the members, exhaustion from being Commodore for seven years or 'in consequence of certain grievances' in committee, Mr. White announced that he would be standing down in October. Before he did so there was a special meeting to examine the Club's finances: they were not in a good state. The attempt to buy the lease had involved heavy legal expenses; many members were overdue with their subscription to the extent that the Club was having difficulty paying the rent and there was also the question of the balcony which was in a shaky state and a recurrent thorn in the side of successive committees. In 1901 a notice was put up telling members that they were not to use the supports for making fast their ropes when hauling up their boats off the hard. However in spite of its somewhat rickety appearance, it never seems to have justified the anxiety, and bore its fair share of the weight of Boat Race guests.

Before retiring Mr. White tried to rally the members at his last General Meeting as Commodore in a hard-hitting speech. 'The Club.... is in a poor state.. in debt £20. Everyone knows why.... no interest, no attendances etc. Must clear debt and start afresh.... Present members in room the machinery of the Club. To do anything we must work together. Proposal: Each member to contribute 10/-. Must make a point of seeing the remainder of the members. No point in writing; they take no notice and will not understand the state of the Club. Let them know that things will be carried out on entirely different lines. There will be sport and other advantages which if used will help the Club to make a name for itself and flourish. Must be done or Club will fail. No good raising subs: members would leave.

Next thing.... make the Club more attractive. Must be done at once. No time must be lost. Proposal: Each member present to.... attend Club nights. Bar prices to remain same for the moment. Billiards, cards etc. Try to get new members and bring friends down. Cushions must be re-covered, tables have cloths over them.... make place respectable. Hire a piano.... many members play and sing. In this way members will take the trouble to attend Club evenings.... carry on like this till Spring, then sport.

Proposal.... a special one-design dinghy class.... ten members already willing to build.... cost about £12. All can afford boats. Can always sell such a boat. As soon as sport is introduced the Club will thrive. Keen racing will arouse local interest.... more new members.... flourishing accounts in all papers.... Club must be made attractive.... changing rooms.... most important they should be kept clean. By this time Club should be able to hold its own and pay steward a better wage. Essential to keep him.... and for him to provide lunch and tea on Saturdays for members who had come some distance.... This would be a great attraction and is a most necessary item. In time when members find they can be supplied with meals, Saturdays will be a great enticement. Must be no half and half affair. Saturdays can also be ladies' days until members adjourn to the saloon about dusk. Special races for their amusement and those on river bank. Local men presenting Cups.... more publicity and renewal of interest. Keener sport.... result increased membership. Club improvements. Better and larger boats. Open races. A Regatta. Raise subscriptions.'

It was a rousing and imaginative speech which I think will interest members. Although the problems facing the Club today are in some ways different, there is a lot in Commodore White's speech that applies as much now as it has always applied. One cannot pretend it had any immediate affect, but the Club's financial situation was helped by Mr. Lewis giving the Club a gratuitous rebate of £10 off the rent the following year. Mr. White had done well and in spite of its difficulties the Club was regarded as the foremost sailing club in the vicinity. In addition to the obvious problems which faced him during his seven years as Commodore, Mr. White made a point of mentioning 'certain grievances.' These may well have been the irritations of club politics, but it's interesting that both Club officers and members at Club meetings became vociferous over quite minor matters, just as they do today.

Two issues should suffice to give you some idea of the feelings that were aroused over what may seem trivial matters to us, although they were not to the gentlemen concerned. The first row happened as early as 1896. The boat *Birdie* was disqualified from taking her prizes in two consecutive races, because her crew was a member who was alleged not to have paid his subscription. The crew had in fact paid his subscription, but had sent it to the Treasurer which seems quite logical, but it should have been sent first to the Secretary, and there was a rule to this effect. A long discussion ensued and the majority felt that *Birdie* should not be disqualified. The Secretary countered that the rules and regulations of the Club should be adhered to. However the majority of members thought it nit-picking and that the rule should be changed.

As a result, at the next meeting the Secretary, Mr. A. Daubeny, resigned over the Treasurer's attitude and the General Meeting's determination to allow *Birdie* her prizes, a violation of the Club's rules. 'I decline to act in conjunction with Mr. Burgess, the Treasurer, any longer. Not only did Mr. Daubeny resign, but Mr. Burgess did as well - from being Treasurer and

Measurer. At the next meeting the Committee reaffirmed the rule which said that subscriptions should go to the Secretary first and Mr. Daubeny agreed to take up his office again.

Another altercation occurred two years after the Club had taken possession of its premises when a Mr. Hubbard 'expressed dissent from the alteration of the price of Fremlin's beer to 4d a pint and contended that such an alteration should not have been made without its first being raised at a General Meeting.' The Commodore pointed out that under Rule 4 the change in price did not require confirmation by a General Meeting. Mr. Hubbard and one other took exception to this. After considerable discussion the alteration was held over until the next General Meeting to enable the Committee to formally report the change in the price and let the Secretary read the minutes referring to the alteration. Six months later the Committee cravenly climbed down and reduced the price of Fremlins to 3d a pint. It so happened that this coincided with Commodore White's announcement that he was standing down. Maybe it was the straw that broke the camel's back.

Eventually the financial difficulties were overcome. Apart from Mr. Lewis's generous rebate of £10 in 1901, the amalgamation of the Club with Minima, from above Teddington, gave the Club quite a boost because of the better sailing and racing available on our reach. The basis was that the members of each club could be elected to the other for 10/- a year. Looking back on this difficult period it is quite interesting that in 1889 the committee approved the purchase of a dinner service - this was just when the Secretary was getting terse letters from Mr. Lewis's solicitor about the rent; and a few years later a tea service was bought. The members evidently wanted their meals daintily served.

There was no doubt that members were getting a lot of fun out of the races. This is evident from the first book of

Racing Records, dated 1902-1909 written for some years in the most beautiful copperplate. There are eighteen boats mentioned in the handicapping lists, turnouts ranging between four and ten. The boats were all different, as I have said, and raced with time allowances varying from scratch to twenty five minutes, which were regularly adjusted during the season. Can you imagine the veiled acrimony surrounding the estimation of these handicaps by the Sailing Committee? Declarations had to be signed and there was a 2/6d fine for 'frivolous or vexatious protests.'

Unlike today the members favoured one or two 'Longs' as a course. In the Race Results members were generally referred to as 'Mr..,' although in later years there were boat-owning lady members. Many of the O.O.D.'s remarks were written in dramatic style, such as was used 26th April 1902: 'Wind very strong from N.N.E. and squally. Most of the boats sported double reefed canvas and found quite enough wind. The first four boats crossed the line practically together. *Phyllis* starting five minutes later. The strong wind carried them up to Barnes in slashing style, but the thrash back against wind and tide made things generally damp and the dust fly (sic). During the second round *Iris*'s rudder was carried away during a slammer of wind, and *May*, while finishing in good time, caught a squall close to the Surrey bank opposite The Doves and capsized. Plenty of assistance from club members. Boat towed to moorings waterlogged.'

Or on 4th October: '*Iris* crossed the line first, followed by *Hobo, Omega, Kitten* and *Tercel* last having a fine breeze from the north-east. They made good time up to the Barnes mark, but the beat back over the tide spread them out somewhat. *Iris* lost 1st place by 35 seconds to *Tercel. Kitten* was not sailing up to her usual form and came in last.' *Tercel* was scratch boat and had had four previous wins. Sometimes there were minor disasters: '*Assegai* fouled oil boat rounding buoy off Club and carried away her bowsprit.' Or in a different vein: '*Dorothy* was disqualified for having a Paid Hand on board.' There were quite a few protests and a lot of disqualifications, mostly for fouling another boat or the mark and in some case not giving up.

Sometimes the course was 'Thorneycroft Four times;' what we would call four shorts. 'Thorneycroft' was the firm of marine engineers on Church Wharf where the mock-Georgian houses stand today. It moved from Chiswick in about 1904 and eventually in 1966 amalgamated with Vospers, the well-known builders of high speed patrol boats, minesweepers and other craft. Tom Thorneycroft was one of the most successful helmsmen in the early years of International Fourteens. The first race in the Results Book had the above course: '*Iris* crossed the line first followed by *May* with *Kitten* close on her heels; working up to the buoy on the first round *May* came up on *Iris* but her sheet broke and she lost a lot of time, which practically put her out of the race. *Rocket*'s taking in a reef put her a long way behind, and she and *May* gave up, leaving *Iris* an easy winner.'

1903 was a memorable year for two reasons: there was the first inter-club race against Ranelagh and it was the beginning of the close and friendly association on and off the water which exists to this day. Eighteen boats crossed the line on July 11th, and in September the Club went to Putney for a return match. In one of the earliest races the Barnes mark dragged its anchor under Barnes bridge and the race had to be postponed. After that the Sailing Committee decided that in future there would have to be a mark boat with a member of the Committee on board during inter-club races, which meant a nice long row for one of the members. The camaraderie which grew up as a result of these inter-club races, when contestants were automatically deemed members of the Club, led to inter-club billiards and cribbage matches in the winter and resulted in just the social atmosphere members wanted. The second feature worth recording was that a concert was held after the Boat Race to which Flag Officers from local clubs and their ladies were invited. The musicians were asked to give their services free. This was a great success and became a regular event right up until the 1930's.

So great was the enthusiasm in the Club that as early as 1902 the Commodore and Vice-Commodore thought it was time it had a President, and who better than Sir Thomas Lipton? This was a fairly momentous decision for a club that was only eight years old - some might say even presumptuous. Having built up his very successful chain of grocery shops between 1865 and the turn of the century, Sir Thomas had been knighted in 1898 and made a baronet in 1902; maybe the news prompted the Commodore's letter. Sir Thomas had been blackballed by the Royal Yacht Squadron a few years earlier for being in 'trade' and he thought that if he could win the America's Cup the R.Y.S. would relent. Therefore between 1899 and 1930 he raced five of his beautiful *Shamrock* J class yachts for the America's Cup, but sadly without success. Minutes are an infuriating basis for any history as they give no detail, and in this case never even made the point that no reply was received from Sir Thomas to the Club's invitation.

In 1904, the Club had another try, this time writing to a more likely candidate - Mr. (later Sir) William Bull, Hammersmith's first M.P. Once again there is no record of any reply - until 1925. This seems most unlikely, but if the minutes are to be believed a letter from Sir William was read to the A.G.M. on 24th February 1925, in which he consented to become their President, and a letter was written thanking him. His failure to reply more promptly provoked Mr. H. V. Turner to propose and Mr. C. Danby to second at the A.G.M. in January 1906, that the posts of President and Vice-President should be abolished. It was carried 'nem con.' I do not think it is generally known that apart from eventually becoming President of the Club, Sir William Bull opened the first debate in the House of Commons this century proposing a Channel Tunnel.

The finances of the Club were obviously better in 1903 because a shed on Union Wharf nearby was rented for £20 a year for storing Club boats. The steward's wages had been raised to 12/6d a week, plus coal and gas, and he was given a pair of top boots and a smart blue jersey with the Club's name on it. But few stewards lasted more than a year which meant more work for the Secretary and was also unsettling for the members, although through the complaints book it was they who had generally been responsible for the steward's dismissal. On one occasion the Secretary refused to be party to the steward's dismissal because of the personal feelings on the part of three members. A long letter of resignation followed. When the matter was voted on there were five for retaining the steward and four against. Another storm in a teacup.

The membership began to increase in 1905. Remarkably it was agreed that ladies should have the same privileges as Full members 'until 7 p.m.' except on race days and other special occasions. I presume this meant that ladies were able to stay later than 7 pm on race days - the minute can be read two ways. There was no question, of course, of ladies having a vote or taking part in the management of the Club; they were Associate Members (B). Later in the year there was a proposal that there should be a Ladies' Race which took place on July 6th, four lady helmswomen making history on Hammersmith reach.

This was also the year of the race for the Doreen Cup, the first challenge cup ever donated to the Club. The donor insisted on remaining anonymous, leaving the Secretary to say that through the kindness of one of his friends he was able to offer a Challenge Cup to be raced for each year. Each entry for the Doreen Cup was to have sailed his boat in at least three races during the current season The winner was to receive a medal and a shield was to be made for the winner's names. These shields for the various cups were a feature of the saloon. They were made in later years by John Holt, Jack Holt's great uncle, and other local shipwrights and exist to this day. Eight boats competed in the first race, but the O.O.D. does not tell us anything of interest about it.

The Doreen Cup, inter-club races and the Club's regular races received quite a lot of publicity and attracted the interest of people walking from Hammersmith Bridge to Chiswick. This all helped to increase membership even though in 1908 the subscription had been raised to a guinea. The Club became solvent when in the following year Mr. Lewis of his own accord reduced the rent to £35 a year. However there were still four members with 'long-standing debts' and the committee was authorised to take any steps to recover the money. Today the situation is just as bad, causing the Treasurer an immense amount of extra work chasing erring members.

In 1912 the Club's membership increased largely as a result of the Committee realising the importance of publicity. The Racing Secretary was instructed to act as public relations officer for the Club; giving the results of the races to the Press. 'The name of the Club must always be kept in the forefront of local sport, which will result in more local interest and more members.' An unexpected swelling of the numbers of members came from The Aquamotus Club nearby. Although mainly a motor boat club they said they would like to amalgamate with the London Corinthian. This meant 19 more members. The motor boat owners did not enter so readily into the Club activities as they were often bound for Erith or even further downstream to Benfleet. However on rough days they were only too pleased to help as rescue boats and also tow boats back from Putney after an inter-club race with Ranelagh.

Thus the Commodore, Mr. W.G. Richardson, was able to express at the annual dinner the hope that the rising prosperity of the Club would continue and emphasised that 'the social side of the Club programme might be fostered with advantage.' He suggested an informal Club dinner to be followed by another where 'new members' might entertain their lady friends with a musical evening and light refreshments. He also suggested a billiards handicap. The Committee's recognition of the importance of the social side was very different from the attitude which existed for a time when the Club first moved to Linden House. I accept that it was the question of 'social' or non-sailing members which worried the Management Committees then, but as has been proved that far from taking over the Club, many 'social' members have made a positive contribution; not just increased the bar profits.

The death of Mr. Lewis in 1913 was a sad blow to the Club as he was not only their generous landlord but a founder member. His death naturally resulted in concern about the reaction of the superior landlord, Mr. Clarke, the owner of the lead mills behind the Club. After a considerably anxious time a 14-year lease was granted at a rent of £50 a year - more than in Mr. Lewis's time, but the Club still had its home. It also had a new neighbour - the one time H.M.S. *Stork*. Originally *The Stork* had been a 465-ton 'composite steam gunboat' (sail assisted as her two masts suggested). She could be said to be the last of the 'wooden walls' as the Navy's ships were once known. Built at Poplar in 1882, she was the last ship to be built of timber, although with an iron frame. She was originally armed with two 64 pounders and two 20 pounders, but I doubt if she saw any action. In 1887 she was converted into a survey ship. Now she was to end her days in a specially dredged berth off Upper Mall - so that she could remain afloat at all states of the tide - as a training ship for sea cadets and later for war orphans. When the boys were allowed ashore, they rowed to an iron ladder set into the wall opposite the end of Weltje Road.

The Stork and her commanding officer, Commander Grant, were welcomed by the Club, and the Commodore proposed a rowing competition against *The Stork* boys and that a special subscription list should be opened to pay for the cost. Normally, when racing, boats left *The Stork* to starboard when going up river, but one day the O.O.D. decided to set a special course. This was from the Club start, and then between *The Stork* and Upper Mall, and likewise between the Eyot and Chiswick Mall, twice round. Quite tricky bearing in mind that the boats in those days were far less manoeuvrable.

However storm clouds were gathering. With the outbreak of the First World War all racing and even messing about in boats ceased for security reasons. This naturally proved a very dull period. For once the Club had a steward, Mr. Salter, who was universally popular with the members and also honest. Unfortunately Mr. Salter was a naval reservist and was immediately called up. In 1915 his ship, H.M.S. *India* was torpedoed and with many of the ship's company he lost his life. After the war John Holt, Jack Holt's great-uncle presented the Club with a shield to commemorate all those members who lost their lives in the war. This was hung in the billiards room.

An entertainment committee was formed to help keep the Club ticking over by arranging concerts and social evenings. The only other matter of note during the war period was the somewhat unsavoury Villiers scandal. Mr. C. S. Villiers became Commodore in 1914. In 1916 the Secretary reported to the Management Committee that Mr. Villiers had £50 of Club money. He had promised to pay it before the present meeting but had failed to do so. Three months later Villiers was warned that the matter would be put in the hands of the Club's solicitors. This had no effect and Villiers was then said to be ill in hospital. Eventually the Club wrote to the House Surgeon asking him to substantiate that Villiers was too ill to take any action. Almost a year after the matter had been reported Villiers's sister wrote saying her brother had died. An unhappy end to an unpleasant matter.

To give you an idea of the strange craft on the Club moorings there is a minute dated 14th May 1918: 'All boat owners must recognise that regarding mooring fees all boats under a displacement of three tons will be charged a flat rate of 15/- a quarter and that boats of three tons and over will be specially considered by the Committee.' It is amazing to think of a three-ton boat sailing on Hammersmith Reach.

On the 15th November 1918, Mr. T. Cope Allengame, who had taken over the office of Commodore in place of Villiers, told the Club: 'In view of the cessation of hostilities the question of reverting to pre-war conditions has been discussed and full facilities will be provided for members and races arranged.' How they reacted to this note of hope will be discussed in the next chapter.

Chapter 5

1918 - 1938

In spite of the Commodore's assurance to members that the Club would now return to its pre-war footing, the immediate post-war years were disappointing for the Committee. The Club's finances were in good shape, and certain members who had lent money to the Club could be repaid. The Secretary, Frank Collis, a friendly although at times cantankerous figure, who will be remembered by some of the oldest members, suggested that subscriptions should be raised so that town members would pay £1.1.6d, country members, 15/9d, lady members, 7/6d and the entrance fee would stand at 10/6d. This was accepted without demur, but when the Sailing Committee produced a race programme and list of handicaps for the season, there was little enthusiasm among the members to take part in races.

But there were a few eager spirits with positive ideas. Mr. Baker at a meeting in May 1920, proposed a Club dinghy class; members should subscribe towards three 14ft sailing dinghies costing £40 each and the Club should purchase them when funds permitted. The Committee was in favour, but there were shouts from the back of the room 'we've got pothunters in the Club.' Turnouts continued to be bad, causing the Commodore to comment at the September meeting that he hoped the Club would rally in 1921. He made a point of saying that he 'regretted the remarks of certain members at the last meeting who had talked about 'pothunters' just because certain members had agreed to buy three dinghies. These remarks discouraged racing and he hoped the proposal would be successful.'

Later it was agreed by a narrow vote that the Club should buy the three dinghies and that a dinghy redemption fund should be set up to be paid off gradually with any surplus funds at the end of the year. But the opposition wasn't over. At a meeting shortly before Christmas, Frank Collis read a letter signed by twenty four members protesting against the motion to commandeer the balance of the Club's funds to buy the dinghies. There was a long 'discussion' - no doubt acrimonious at times - at the end of which it was decided that the motion should remain *sine die*. The end of a good idea and we have to wait until 1929 for a better one.

Ashore, the goodwill that existed amongst members before the war seems to have disappeared. There was so much antagonism between different groups that they vented their grievances in pubs rather than drink in the Club. Much of the gossip was to do with the private business of the Club. This was too much for Frank Collis, the Treasurer, whose resignation letter is worth recording as it is not only quite moving but relevant to today. 'I wish to inform you of my intention to relinquish the office of Secretary of the Club, which I have held for seven years through strenuous and difficult times. I now feel that this office has been long enough in one member's hands and that new energies would be advantageous to the Club.

I must say that I very much regret to notice the lack of enthusiasm for the main objects of the Club after the consistent efforts of the founders and their followers to maintain and encourage the scientific sport, which has proved so beneficial to the nation. I therefore sincerely trust that the members realise this fact and that every effort will be made to revive the sport which was so much appreciated by the inhabitants and visitors and incidentally encouraged members to become capable nautical men. Assuring you of my continued support.' That support was indeed given as Frank Collis was Treasurer throughout the Second World War.

Early in 1923 Wilfred Forster, the new Commodore, appealed to all concerned to bring about unity within the Club. In May a Mr. Asler said he would be pleased to negotiate conciliatory meetings as there was a general wish for reconciliation. One member who had threatened to resign because of the attitude of a group of members agreed to think again. Gradually the rumpus died down. There was a suggestion soon after this incident that there should be greater vetting of members, but sensibly it was overruled. Inevitably, as indeed today and in all clubs, members will find some people more to their liking than others.

The fact that there was a succession of dishonest stewards about this time didn't help in restoring the pre-war warmth of the snuggery. Ladies were allowed into the Club (and even children provided that parents 'restrained' them from running about in the bar); but they weren't allowed to be in the bar during opening hours either to drink or even to wait: 'Women will be served and wait for their husbands or friends in the billiards room.' So the members were as intransigent about the invasion of their snuggery as ever. However the steward problem was settled the following year (1924) when the Committee decided, as they should have done years before, to give him, and his wife if he had one, a regular and proper wage, so that he did not have to make a profit on the bar takings. The steward naturally said he would far prefer this arrangement to the old one. It was just about this time that the Commodore, Mr. W.E. Huckle, had to give members a stern warning about using the billiards table and 'evading payment.' A notice went up saying that any member 'found offending would be drastically dealt with.'

On the tideway in 1924 there appears to have been a

return to old times. Racing was flourishing once more in the Club but there are no race results until 1935 so it is difficult to make this period as lively as I would like. The presentation of a number of cups in the mid-20's attracted a large number of entrants not only from Ranelagh, but Hurlingham, Minima, Tamesis, and Twickenham sailing clubs. The West London Corinthian Sailing Club Hospital Challenge Cup, presented by a Mr. Bindoff in 1924, was open to all comers and attracted thirty entrants. The proceeds from entries were donated to the hospital. The following year the Webb Cresta Challenge Cup was presented by a member, R. Webb. After the Second World War and introduction of the Fireflies this became one of their cups, but it is not clear on what terms it was originally presented. The Commodore, R. Tilbury, decided that the racing had been so successful that Sir William Bull, now president, and Lady Bull should be invited to the 1925 annual dinner which was held at the Victoria Mansions Restaurant, SW1. One of Sir William's sons, George, later Commodore for many years and then President, was there as a newly elected a member, as also was A.P.H., who had become a member two years' earlier. Tickets cost 8/6d.

Lady Bull was asked to give away the prizes and when she had done so, Sir William announced that his wife wanted to donate a silver Challenge Bowl to be raced for only by members of the Club by all types of boat on a handicap basis. Owners of competing boats must steer their own craft. In the following year the Wilfred Forster cup was presented in his memory by his widow; he had been Commodore in 1923. After the war it was decided that the cup would be for International Fourteens and Swordfish and to belong to the winner outright if won three times in succession. Your humble author did win it outright in the '50's, but handed it back to the Club as he would otherwise have had to have presented another cup in its place and wasn't financially able to do so. In 1926 Frank Collis, who with his wife lived in Lonsdale Road, almost opposite the Barnes turning marks, presented another cup to be known as The Barnes Trophy.

A serious problem was that not only had the number of boats increased, but the P.L.A. had recently ordered the Club to take their moorings closer in by 40 ft, thus allowing only a 60 ft frontage. This meant that those members who did not race regularly were threatened with losing their moorings. It is evident that the Committee was taking its racing responsibilities seriously. The Y.R.A. was approached to give a definition of 'amateurs' with regard to sailing races. The Association's answer was long, but not without interest. 'In answer to your question the Y.R.A. has no official definition of an amateur. The general definition is: 'an amateur on a racing yacht is one who has never been paid wages to do such or similar work; beyond which there is no other disqualification.' This definition disqualifies a 'waterman.' It does not necessarily disqualify a builder or repairer of boats, but it would certainly disqualify some such persons. It seems to disqualify such persons as you contemplate who can earn a living by the waterside and who pick up a wage here or there by doing similar work to that done by amateurs on racing yachts. This subject is now greatly debated - particularly by foreign yachtsmen. The Council of this Association has received much correspondence about it, but has never passed or recorded any resolution upon the subject, beyond saying some 30 years ago 'that membership of a recognised yacht club did not necessarily of itself qualify a person as an amateur.' Yours faithfully, B. Heckstall Smith, Secretary Y.R.A.

Following this exchange of letters, which did not seem to get the Club much further in its search for a clear-cut ruling about who should be banned from racing in Club boats, it was decided in 1924, according to the minutes, that a Club Representative should be elected to the Y.R.A. There was nothing automatic about this, particularly for clubs as small as the London Corinthian. Sir Simeon Bull lent me the Y.R.A. handbook for 1930 from his late father's library. It is a fascinating record because it not only gives all the I.Y.R.U. rules for racing, rating and handicapping and many other subjects, but also illustrates the extent to which sailing in the '20's and '30's was very different socially from the way it is today.

It may sound very snobbish, but sailing - certainly racing - was a 'gentlemen's sport' in those years. This is obvious from the size of the vast majority of members' yachts, beginning with the 221-ton *Britannia* belonging to His Majesty the King and the 175-ton *Shamrock V* sailed by our old friend Sir Thomas Lipton. Underlining this point there is a nice passage on 'Handicap Racing:' '.... Racing in the smaller classes (ex-15 met, ex-12 met, etc.) were considered. The Council appointed a small sub-committee to deal with the subject.' Of the two hundred and twenty one members of the Y.R.A. in 1930 only a handful admitted to having a 14ft dinghy, although it's not absolutely clear what was their design. Only one is listed as being a 14ft National (of the pre-International rules period). Sir John Beale, who did so much for the promotion of International Fourteens, had *Windrush* a 14 ft sloop, while Morgan Giles, the designer, had *Pierette* an 11 ft aux cutter/ yawl. Strangely Uffa Fox does not appear to have had any dinghy at all then, but a 20-ton schooner *Black Rose*. It is equally surprising that Harold Morris, the father of Stewart Morris, who was an enthusiastic dinghy sailor on The Broads when lugsails were all the vogue, was not a member of the Y.R.A.

To become a member of the Y.R.A., a club 'had to be of

sufficient importance to warrant recognition' .... 'the Council from time to time revise the list of recognised yacht clubs and strike out the name of any club therefrom if in its opinion for any circumstance it shall cease to warrant recognition.' Of the hundred and sixty four clubs listed in all parts of the English-speaking world or what was once called 'the Empire,' sixty eight had the prefix Royal. Only thirty were pure sailing clubs like the London Corinthian. Their members may not have enjoyed the same financial status, but their clubs were welcome provided they 'warranted recognition.' Thus it is pleasing that the London Corinthian was immediately accepted by the Y.R.A. and puts a perspective on the standing of the Club in U.K. yachting over 60 years ago. Trent Valley, The Little Ship, Bosham, Itchenor and The Thames sailing clubs became members some 10 years later. I say 10 years, as 1924 was the date according to the minutes when the Club was recognised, but it may be wrong. I decided to check with the R.Y.A. who have the old Y.R.A. records and according to these the Club was recognised in 1919.

With racing flourishing and membership of the Y.R.A. established, we can for a moment leave the sailing scene and have a look at the Club itself. During the 1920's there was a number of improvements. Among the most important were the installation of electric light followed a few years later by a telephone to the left of the front door. Club members were very 'generous' with gifts some of which were welcome and some not, although they were always accepted 'with hearty thanks.' Mr. Tilbury donated a set of ivory billiards balls. Sir William Bull gave a unique old map of the Thames estuary; another member presented a 'tortoise stove' which was put in the billiards room, proving not quite such a popular gift as the billiards balls, as it smoked so much that a gas fire was installed in its place. A stag's head lasted only a few months in the saloon:

members found it so depressing that it too was relegated to the billiards room. An even odder present was Volume 2 of the Seamanship Manual: the donor might have proved his generosity by buying the Club Volume 1 of that important book. Even stranger than some of these gifts was the sudden statutory order in 1926 that Entertainment Tax would in future have to be paid on the proceeds raised from Boat Race tickets. In the following year the L.C.C. insisted that the black lion on the Club's flag was an heraldic device and that the Club was therefore liable for Armorial Bearing Tax, one guinea. As the tax had not been paid before the Club had to pay £7.

At the A.G.M. the vexed question of ladies' membership came up again and it was agreed that ladies could be full members 'for the purposes of sailing races, but would not be entitled to attend meetings or take any part in the management of the Club.' Curiously the ladies did not resent this discrimination which today would be dubbed male chauvinism. Some in fact were quite happy not to have anything to do with the management. It is an amazing commentary on the social times that it was not until the Club moved into Linden House that ladies 'got the vote.' However, long before that, in the late '20's and early '30's lady members earned the 'hearty thanks of the Commodore and members.' Whist drives, billiards, draughts and cribbage, were all part of the winter programme. The whist drive 'season' opened and a programme, with dates, was published and circulated. For reasons which are naturally not specified in the minutes in 1931 these were loss-making affairs and caused the Commodore of the day to raise the whole question of whist drives in general and to point out that those organised by the ladies were actually profitable. As a result the ladies took over the whole programme and were asked 'to regularise the arrangements for whist drives and hand the accounts over to the Commodore.'

A number of 'locals' were elected members about this time who will be remembered by the older members: Teddy Mitchell (1927), an architect, 9 Hammersmith Terrace; George Harris (1927) of Chiswick Mall; Stephen Bassett (1928); 'Morty' Stephenson (1929), a much-loved figure even though he didn't sail, but lived in Kelmscott House, once the home of William Morris; Frank Bluff, a fat but pleasant business man, of Strawberry House, Chiswick Mall, the same year; Bob Salt, (1930), John's father. These together with George Bull (1925), Frank Collis (1910), the famous musician Leon Goosens (1920), and no doubt A.P.H. (1923), were the snuggery's 'regulars' for a few pink gins or what ever took their fancy. Even allowing for inflation bar prices were cheap but they were raised in 1932 as follows: spirits 7d; gin and vermouth 8d; bottled beer 5d; Bass, Worthington and Guinness 7d; port and sherry 6d.

Before finishing with the 1920's, there is one more episode to be recounted. In the early hours of 13th January 1928, there was a flood. The front page lead headline of the *West London Observer* and no doubt many other papers read: 'Thames Flood Disaster' - 'Torrent Sweeps over River Banks'.... '14 Sleepers Drowned in Basements.' We have got used to storm surges coinciding with spring tides and causing floods, but this appears to be the first and worst one in our history. Hammersmith was inundated at 1 a.m., the river pouring over the embankment at Lower and Upper Malls and Hammersmith Terrace. The tide rushed up the Creek flooding the wharves on each side and the shops and houses in King Street to a depth of two feet. Among those drowned were three maids sleeping in the basements of Rivercourt House and other Upper Mall houses. More might have been drowned but for Mr. Colley, a shipwright; although his yard was in Lower Mall he lived in one of the cottages near the Creek. Using a dinghy he kept at home he paddled through The Dove's passage - the water was 14 ins deep in the 'taproom' of the pub - and on to Upper Mall waking everyone up. According to the local sage, the late Jack Usher, the P.L.A. recognised Colley's action by afterwards giving him a large bell which he could ring in the event of another flood.

Mr. Lambourne, the Club's steward, and his wife and children - God knows how they all slept and lived in such small quarters - were woken to find the water lapping their beds. Lambourne's first action was to check the moorings and the boats. Shortly after he'd done so the hard wall collapsed, as did the embankments on Lower and Upper Mall and the river walls of some of the houses in Hammersmith Terrace, because the pressure of the flood water on the land side of the embankment wall was too great. Mr. Lambourne narrowly escaped being washed away with the flood water.

What the flood did to Hammersmith Terrace was probably my earliest memory. The force of it was such that it knocked down the walls between the houses. When the tide turned, the water poured through the gaps in the river wall, leaving gardens littered with not only the normal detritus of floods, but the bricks of broken down walls, herbaceous border plants washed out of their beds, guinea pig hutches, dead gold fish from the pond and at the base of our conservatory a very small pram dinghy which my father had used to rescue floating objects of value when the flood was at its highest. There is a rather tattered photograph of the post-flood scene in front of me as I type.

The water in the basement, which was and still is the dining room, had reached within six inches of the ceiling. Later my father cut a 'high-water' notch, just as the Committee of the old Club fixed a plaque recording the high-water mark which is beside the bar today. It must have taken a considerable time for the water to drain away, presumably down the drains into the main storm pipes on Chiswick Eyot. When all of it had gone, my nanny - you didn't have to be rich in those days to employ one - was told she could take me down to the dining room.

It was not a pretty sight: three or four inches of mud and flotsam; the grandfather clock had floated away from its normal place and was horizontal in the mud; a lot of china had been washed off the dresser; and from a corner shelf various small decorations and two gold medals, presented to my father by the King for speechmaking at Winchester College, had been swept off and buried in the mud. In the general post-flood trauma these treasures were forgotten and shovelled up by the workmen employed to clear up the mess. A very personal loss for my father but at least our maids were sleeping upstairs. And as for poor Mr. Lambourne, the steward, all his clothes, bed linen and furniture were sodden with filthy water and much of his personal property ruined. I'm glad to say the Committee did not forget him, although how they arrived at the princely sum of £5.11.3d to compensate him for his loss I do not know. Since then the river walls have been raised twice, by at least four feet, and the Woolwich Barrier has been built.

It was just before the flood that the Club improvement policy got under way. The balcony was finally demolished and a new one built; the bar floor was renewed with some patent stone compound and a piano was bought for winter sing-songs. Everything was ready in time for the Boat Race and the concert which would be held afterwards to which lady members and guests were to be welcome. *Photopress, The Times, the West London Observer* and other papers were invited as usual. The Sailing Committee were very businesslike. Early in 1929 a draft programme for inter-club races was sent to Ranelagh so as to avoid any clashes. Having received confirmation regarding the dates of inter-club races, letters were sent to other clubs up and down the river with the dates of Open Meetings. Local rowing clubs were asked to speak to coxes about giving way to boats racing - which they would be able to recognise by the 'square flag' at the masthead. Finally the Club handbook not only contained members' names, addresses and telephone numbers but also the name of their boat and the time of High Water. And in the following year it had the O.O.D. list printed and this was much better observed than it is today.

George Bull, although he had not been a member very long, was already Vice-Commodore and I am sure at the Committee meeting on 5th March 1929, he was strongly in support of the motion: 'To inaugurate the International Fourteen Foot dinghy as a class boat for the Club and to endeavour to create a general enthusiasm and more satisfactory results than have hitherto been obtained by handicapping.' This was confirmed on the 9th April and as a result George Bull, Teddy Mitchell and Percy Chandler all bought Fourteens. In order to encourage others, Fourteens were given preference over moorings. The story of the International Fourteens at Hammersmith has already been told in Chapter 1, so I will say no more about those years which for those of us who raced those wonderful boats are unforgettable.

In 1931 Sir William Bull died. Lady Bull succeeded him as President and A.P.H. was made Vice-President together with Frank Collis. It was in this year too that Jack Holt, boat repairer, builder and later designer, became a member. As I mentioned in an earlier chapter, he had a small shed behind the Furnivall Sculling Club left to him by his great-uncle John Holt, who had been a Club officer for many years. From here he started his highly successful career. First it was just maintaining and repairing boats. Teddy Mitchell for whom he crewed was one his first customers. *Dorothy*, a 22 ft half-decked rater was one of Mitchell's boats and typical of many in the Club. In 1932 Jack went into partnership with Percy Chandler to promote and build boats. Chandler had a Morgan Giles Fourteen *Echo* (179), but *Ace* (228) was designed and built for him by Jack in 1934.

Handicap and inter-cup racing continued as it had done since the mid-1920's and in 1932 the office of Press Secretary was revived with the comment: 'This is an office that might with advantage be made a regular post on the Committee.' As well as the usual Press guests at the Boat Race, Movietone News was only too pleased to come and film the boats passing, just as the B.B.C. does today. Since the war, efforts have been made to get race results into the sporting and indeed national Press, as Itchenor and other sailing clubs manage to do, but these have lacked the same sense of purpose. Press attitudes also have changed and it's unrealistic to think that anything but Open Meetings will interest the national papers today. The turnout anyhow for the Club's Open meetings has declined so drastically over recent years that it's surprising if the Club were to get any publicity at all even in *Yachts and Yachting*.

1933 was the first of George Bull's 14-year stint as Commodore. He decided to give a special prize for a long distance race on 6th June presumably down to Greenwich, but as usual there are no details in the minutes. This was followed by the West London Hospital Race for which the prizes were tickets for the Gaumont Cinema, more recently the Odeon and now something else. The 'silverware' came back with the Wilfred Forster Cup. Apart from the racing, for which there were evidently satisfactory turnouts, there are three domestic matters which seem worth mentioning. Firstly Teddy Mitchell, the architect, described the Steward's quarters as 'most unsatisfactory,' which if anything was an understatement, but forced the Committee to pay for some improvements. Secondly, Richard Tilbury Junior, the Rear-Commodore, volunteered to write a history of the Club to date, which he completed in 1935, but of which the Club does not seem to have a copy; I only discovered it when researching in the Borough Archive Department near The Ark building. Thirdly and probably of more interest was the extraordinarily nice gesture by the members to the Commodore, Vice-Commodore Bob Salt, and Richard Tilbury. At the beginning of the year the three flag-officers were all bachelors for the first time in the history of the Club and all under 30. However within three months all were married, and at a supper in the autumn three handsome silver cigarette caskets engraved with the Club's burgee were bought and presented to them.

1934 was an historic year for the Club because it was the year of the first Shackleton Cup, the Club's Open Meeting for International Fourteen Foot dinghies. This has already been adequately discussed in Chapter 1. In July the Twickenham and Ranelagh Clubs were invited to take part in the Greenwich Race, with a prize for the first visiting boat. On these occasions the boats were towed back by *The Ark*, A.P.H.'s colourful ex-canal barge - she had all the traditional castles and hearts and diamonds painted on her hull - and other motor boats.

However we will pass on to 1935 as it is in that year that full racing results were recorded once again. The season ran from May to October as usual and there were twenty one races in all. There were twenty five to thirty boats in the Club, but racing turnouts, including the three Fourteens, ranged from four to 10, all on individual handicaps worked out on past performance. However for Open meetings the numbers were obviously greater: twenty one for The West London Hospital Cup. The Rear-Commodore's race that year must have been a lot of fun, even if it did prove a challenge to some. Entrants not only had to start and finish moored, but 'pick up a floating bottle bearing the name of their boat, obtain a bird's feather off Chiswick Eyot, and make an eye splice in a rope to be obtained from a man stationed in a motor boat between the Eyot and The Bull's Head, Barnes!' I wonder how many members can do an eye splice today?

1936 was equally active: thirty four races in all, turnouts being larger owing to the Brent Sailing Club joining the Club after having lost their water at the Welsh Harp - 'and proved themselves good sportsmen and company.' The Hammersmith Bridge to Greenwich was as popular as ever, the fastest time being 2.27.35 and the slowest 3.18.00. There were up to nineteen entries in Trophy races - the Doreen Cup being won by Miss Vaughan, the first lady in the history of the Club to win it.

The year was a watershed, because apart from the thirty four races during the summer, winter races were organised for the first time. This was mainly due to Dr. Olaf Bradbury who must be the oldest living member and certainly the oldest ex-Commodore, an office he took over in 1947 from George Bull. 'I remember distinctly Bassett and I in *Ace* were instrumental in starting the first winter points because we won the Trophy for the seventeen races. It was a beautiful silver-rigged mast with a gaff and the Club's burgee and they also presented me with a replica to keep. In spite of the cold nobody ever wore life jackets. We all got wet but had a jolly good drink when we got back in the bar.'

I have related more of Dr. Bradbury's Fourteen memories in Chapter 1, but what follows is a splendid personal picture of the Club at that time. 'The fleet was a motley collection of odd boats. The others went off at the same time as us and finished much later. It was all very unofficial and unorganised. The men's changing room was rather smelly and an absolute shambles of wet clothes and gym shoes; everyone dressing and undressing at the same time in that tiny room, often picking up other people's clothes by accident. The tiny and crowded bar; no women of course, but the girls used to come and crew sometimes - they had an awful little cubby-hole to change in where there was also a loo.' Dr. Bradbury mentioned women and the bar. It was in July of that year that the Secretary was 'requested to speak to those ladies and explain that the bar could be used only by gentlemen.'

'What one enjoyed,' Dr. Bradbury continued, 'was the membership, so varied and most extraordinary. It was all so gooey. Young and old, competent and incompetent, eccentric and odd characters. There was an old fellow called Mason. Nobody ever saw him do anything. If one came into the bar, whatever the time of day, he'd be there, so one would say 'Hullo Mason, have a drink.' 'No thank you, I've just finished my tea.' Nobody knew where he came from or what he did, but he'd always finished his tea. There were a lot of odd characters like that. [Author's note: Actually this is a little unfair on Mason. He may have been odd about always having had his tea, but he had done his bit for the Club having been Commodore in 1931 and 1932, long before Bradbury joined].

'At weekends parents often brought their children. On one occasion I remember a small boy fell off the pontoon into the river and all hell broke loose. His mother went into hysterics, but all was well; my wife and others fished the lad out. A less happy memory was the annual dinner and dance at The Clarendon, Hammersmith Broadway. We were all dancing away and having a splendid time when there was a call for silence. The wireless had been turned on loudly and there we sat listening somewhat stunned to hear King Edward VIII making his abdication speech. This put a dampener on the party and I think we all quickly dispersed.'

Before leaving 1936, I should mention that A.P.H. and Frank Bluff had both agreed to present prizes to replace the old L.C.S.C. Trophy and West London Hospital Cup. The L.C.S.C. Trophy was for all types of dinghy on a handicap basis and to be competed for by amateur members of a bona-fide Thames sailing club. The Frank Bluff Trophy in years to come was allocated to Enterprises, but they were not raced as a class until 1960.

The following year (1937) saw *Boss*, the first of the London Corinthian Sailing Club one designs launched - in spite of the 'pothunters' gibe of long ago. They were designed and built by Jack Holt; 16 ft long, half-decked and clinker built, rather like an enlarged 12 ft National. Jack had moved from his original tiny yard behind the Furnival Sculling Club to a derelict compound just east of Hammersmith Bridge and behind the City Barge pub. It was there that in the 1920's, before moving to Teignmouth in Devon that Morgan Giles had designed many of the prototypes for the International Fourteen. Jack, without the permission of the Council, erected a second-hand bungalow transported from Woolwich Arsenal. The Town Clerk had apoplexy but it took the Council three years to get him out. During this time Jack was building every conceivable type of boat: Board of Trade life boats, 12 Sq Metre Sharpies, launches for Imperial Airways and lastly the Club one designs, of which only four were built before the outbreak of war put paid to them. Ted King-Morgan bought *Dart*, L.C/3., and I can remember him sailing her with his beautiful and gallant wife Barbara. As keen a sailor as Barbara King-Morgan was Winifred Procter, then still in the Handicap class, but after the Second World War she was very successful in her Fourteen, *Dauntless*, which had been built by Uffa Fox in 1933.

There were now as many races as ever, but some helmsmen were evidently chancing their arm as a notice appeared in the bar 'Sailing Rules are to be more strictly enforced in future - members are getting lax in some matters.' The winter series continued, and in the evenings navigation classes were held by Dr. Bradbury, who during his time in the R.N. became as expert with a sextant as he was at firing torpedoes. According to Bradbury these classes started because his crew, Stephen Bassett, wanted to pass his Y.R.A. Yachtmaster's exam, but gradually as war clouds gathered more and more members who intended to volunteer for the R.N. joined the classes which were held in the billiards room. A photograph of some of the class was taken on A.P.H.'s new *Water Gipsy* above Barnes Bridge; no doubt the class had found it necessary for seamanship reasons to practice anchor drill and rowing to at least one of the many local hostelries.

A.P.H. had decided in 1936 that it was time for a slightly more seaworthy craft than *The Ark* and had commissioned Frank Cole to build the 39 ft *Water Gipsy* on condition it was ready for the Coronation. He presented *The Ark* subject to survey to the Club with the hope that she would be of use. I'm afraid this came into the category of gifts which the Club could have done without. The Ark - her 9 h.p. Thorneycroft handy-billy engine had been removed for installation in the *Water Gipsy* - was surveyed immediately and the hull was found to be in very bad condition and the superstructure 'quite rotten.' There was a vote that *The Ark* should be kept till the end of the year and a decision taken then. Putting off till tomorrow what should obviously be done immediately is often unwise, particularly in view of *The Ark*'s length. It's true the Committee managed to sell the boat's 'Baby-Blake' for 10/- and early in 1938 received a letter from someone who actually wanted to buy her. A few months later fate forced the Committee to take the decision they should have done earlier. *The Ark* broke away from her moorings and the pontoon on which the Fourteens were berthed was damaged by her rudder. After that she was towed down river to a breaker's yard.

1938 and 1939 saw the same enthusiasm. Bruce-Wolfe won the '38 Shackleton in a new Fourteen, *Spider* (389) against 28 others, the biggest fleet to date and an excellent reflection on the L.C.S.C. and Hammersmith Reach because there were still only four Club Fourteens. In the same year there was the London River Race: Hammersmith, Greenwich, Tower Bridge, Woolwich and back to Greenwich. The winter races started with up to seventeen which was good and included Tom Fielding for the first time in a National Twelve. In 1939 Bruce-Wolfe could only manage a 2nd out of a fleet of twenty two, the race being won by Mr. N. Moore in *Melita* (398). All the reports talk of 'spectacular Chinese gybes' because these were pre-kicking strap days. Turnouts were around ten for the winter series, a little down but they included for the first time friends to be, Joe and Elsie Bloor.

War was declared at 11.15 a.m. on Sunday, 3rd September 1939 and sailing was to suffer a brief interruption.

Chapter 6

World War Two. 1939 - 1946
and
Post-War Scene

There was a 'phoney' war period on the river as there was throughout the country and in France. War having been declared at the end of the summer of 1939, sailing did suffer, although I'm not quite clear why because there was no official or enemy interference. That came later. Sixteen members disappeared quickly into the Services. First to go was Commander Olaf Bradbury, R.N.; he had left the Royal Navy in 1933 having decided to take up medicine, but was naturally on the Emergency List having qualified as a 'Dagger' Torpedo Officer.

The Committee met to decide on the precautions to be taken against air-raids. All the Club trophies had to be put in a place of safety, so they were wrapped up and put in a disused water cistern behind the bar. This seems a somewhat bizarre decision, but was deemed to be sufficient protection from the bombs which were soon to fall not only upon the docks but upon Hammersmith. Later they were removed to the safety of the Westminster Bank. Then the all-important 'blackout' screens and curtains had to be made. The steward was to be responsible for checking the blackout each evening to make sure there were no chinks of light. It was probably matters such as these and a general feeling of 'what's going to happen next?' that caused racing to stop from 2nd September until 29th October. On that day there was the first of seven winter races, with three to seven starters.

In the spring of 1940 the United Hospitals Sailing Club from Burnham on Crouch, who were prohibited from sailing on their own water for security reasons, were accepted as wartime members, paying a subscription of 15/6d and mooring fees of 15/- a year for their six 15 ft lugsail dinghies. This was a useful development both from a financial and from a racing point of view. Your humble author also became a country member. For the summer season, engraved spoons were given as prizes for the 1st and 2nd boats (including crews) in each race. Entries went up to nine.

It was on 13th July that Commander Teynham, RN, on behalf of Admiral Dunbar-Nasmith - who had been appointed Flag-Officer Port of London and had taken over the P.L.A. building on Tower Hill as his headquarters - issued an order that 'all boats had to be removed from their moorings and sailing was not to be allowed on the river as a precaution against possible invasion of the country.' Members had to be telephoned and all helped to get the smaller boats onto Clark's wharf - as far as I can see without even asking the owner's permission - while the larger boats were taken through Barnes bridge; here the authorities evidently didn't think the Germans would find them. All the boats in the three trots in front of Hammersmith Terrace were towed away, presumably up river, although most of them seldom moved or could move from their moorings. They never came back after the war, which was a pity as they added colour and interest to the river scene. Only a fortnight after the fierce directive, Commander Teynham on Tower Hill or his Commander in Chief relented and said that sailing was permitted provided that all owners applied for permits and boats were back at their moorings 15 minutes before sunset. The rule made it necessary for a large licence number to be painted on the bows, an indignity borne with extreme reluctance by the owners of International Fourteens. 17th August was the date for the first race after the regulations came into force. Unfortunately it had to be abandoned as all but two boats sank when placed in the water - presumably they had 'opened up' while ashore. Later the Naval Control Service gave permission for 12 boats to be kept at moorings until winter set in.

That was the end of the 'phoney' war. The Blitz on London started shortly after the Battle of Britain. On the night of 12th October two bombs fell in the river just east of the Creek and the blast damaged the Club and some of the boats. The Rear-Commodore Sailing wrote somewhat despondently in the results book: 'so ever since that night no official races have been held, but a few members have gone cruising now and then. Those sailing members who remain are bravely trying to carry on despite old Hitler.' Many members know nothing about the Blitz as they had probably not been born. They may think the Rear-Commodore's minute the kind of remark the heroic Captain Mainwaring of 'Dad's Army' fame might have made. Churchill's 'Britain can Take it' was not just part of his bulldog spirit propaganda. The Blitz was very unpleasant and the courage shown not only by the emergency services but by men and women all over the country was considerable. In many areas such as the docks in London and other strategic targets throughout Britain there was terrible destruction. Hammersmith had its share of mines and bombs, and the noise and blast when they went off were very frightening.

I remember one night in 1941 getting under the kitchen table with my mother during one particularly bad raid, before going back to quieter nights at school. My mother was having a night off from being an ambulance driver. Hammersmith Terrace, without any exaggeration, was rocked to its foundations, all the windows were blown out and bomb splinters came into the ground floor. Those on leave from the Services were quite often glad to go back to their camps which were normally away from obvious targets. For the steward alone in the Club, a small and by no stretch of the imagination a strongly built building, it must have been terrifying. Fortunately Clark's Lead Mills, across the footpath, recognised the situation and invited him to use their air-raid shelter.

In spite of the damage and the problems rationing imposed it was decided to hold a lunch party on 2nd November - we are not told whether it was to restore morale but it was evidently a great success. Thirty-seven members turned up together with five from Minima Yacht Club and there was even a profit of seven shillings. Not surprisingly the Blitz caused a considerable drop in bar takings, members preferring to be in their homes during the air-raids. Committee meetings were held at weekends in daylight, although some Officers objected for a time about their being held on Sundays. The damage to the Club was assessed at £100, of which £6.11.11d was bar stock. This was reported to Clark's, the landlord who wrote to the War Damage Commission, but the repairs took two years to complete.

The following year a new lease was due to be signed. I haven't mentioned this normally daunting subject for some time because ever since the death in 1913 of Mr. Clark, his Trustees had acted most reasonably, granting the Club two 14-year leases in succession at a rent of £50 a year. This time they weren't quite so friendly saying that they 'were prepared to let the Club remain on the site until three months after the signing of peace at a rent of £60 a year, but that they would not agree to another lease.'

The Rear-Commodore Sailing needn't have been so gloomy because in the following year normal racing was resumed. One new member to brave the waters and who became very popular was Miss Kathleen Hobling or 'Hobbie' as she came to be known. She had a Norwegian pram (lugsail) named *Goblin*; another was Tom Fielding, an army signals officer, who was stationed for a time nearby in General Alan Brook's headquarters in the old St. Paul's School building. Tom had become a member that year (1941), and raced with Guy Bellairs, a telecommunications wizard in the War Office, in his Fourteen. Later he bought one of the United Hospital dinghies for £10 and made a mainsail out of a parachute. 'They were terrible boats when running and sometimes submarined unless you sat right aft on the transom. I remember well seeing 'Storm' Roberts 'going down.'

Then there were those on leave like Joe Bloor who was in the R.N.V.R.. 'When he was on leave, we always sailed,' Elsie his wife recalls. 'Francis Procter, Winifred's father, lent us a lugsail dinghy which was part of the Handicap fleet. We sailed in old clothes and plimpsolls - unheard of footwear nowadays and we had no jamming cleats and no life jackets. Dinghy sailors today are pampered. I eventually developed corns on my hands. The only problem in my early days was that I found getting to the river via the bar very intimidating. It was filled with elderly gentlemen drinking, like Winifred's father, who couldn't have been sweeter, Dr. Bradbury, Morton Stevenson, Frank Bluff, George Bull, A.P.H. and others. Ladies were not welcome in the bar, in fact forbidden, and few actually sailed. Our changing room was an outside lavatory - very inconvenient at times. Winifred Procter, being a boat owner, was allowed to have a locker in the gentlemen's changing room. She caused consternation one day when she went to her locker and found Ted King-Morgan 'starkers.' Nothing daunted she marched in, got her gear and was out again without batting an eyelid.'

At the suggestion of Jack Holt, who had moved his premises down to The Embankment, Putney, there was an inter-club race on our water with Ranelagh, which he had now joined. Ten boats crossed the line and the race was won by Jack's ebullient partner, Beecher Moore. The next year there was another visit by Ranelagh and the visitors included Ian Proctor in a National Twelve. Racing was healthy again with turnouts of up to eleven boats and for Open and Trophy races there were as many as twenty three starters. The prizes were now book tokens. At the suggestion of the Hammersmith Regatta Committee, the West London Hospital Race was revived as an Open race although no cup was presented. Ranelagh, Twickenham and other clubs were invited and the entrance fees went to the hospital. In September A.P.H. suggested a pursuit race - the first ever to be held - with twelve boats being divided into four starts according to potential speed.

A.P.H had gained a title of which he was very proud: Petty-Officer A.P. Herbert (with two 'good conduct stripes') because the *Water Gipsy* had been taken over by the Royal Naval Auxiliary Patrol Service, having first joined the River Emergency Service, a kind of nautical Civil Defence. She was now flying the White Ensign but when it came to the evacuation of the British Expeditionary Force from the beaches of Dunkirk, the *Water Gipsy* was not allowed to go, although she would have been perfect for ferrying soldiers off the beaches as she only drew 2ft 6ins. Instead she was ordered to remain behind and 'guard London.' Petty-Officer Herbert and his crew of three - Petty-Officer Eddie Elsbury, Leading Seaman Tom Cheeseman and Stoker Fred O'Connor - were kitted out at Chatham Barracks and the *Water Gipsy* was armed with a Lewis Gun and a Hotchkiss; cutlasses of the Hornblower variety were in racks above the bunks, and of course there were rifles and hand grenades as well.

In five years the *Water Gipsy* steamed over 50,000 miles. Her patrol was from Westminster down to Holehaven on Canvey Island, Sea Reach, and sometimes to Southend, with an assortment of cargo: mail, hydrogen cylinders (for the barrage balloons flying from dumb lighters in Sea Reach), ammunition, drums of diesel and petrol, cutlasses, buoys, rum and a variety of other essentials such as toilet paper. Everything had to be lashed down on the long roof of her cabin to prevent it from rolling overboard. Later on she had other duties, such as teaching Wrens seamanship and boathandling; (many 'liberty' boats in Plymouth, Portsmouth and on the Clyde were handled most efficiently by Wren crews and they also always seemed to be the prettiest ones).

The *Water Gipsy* suffered many bomb splinters and had some miraculous escapes, but the most noteworthy and for once most comical was that on the 15th September 1940 - the day the R.A.F. shot down fifty six German aircraft - when she was up at Hammersmith having been given the previous night off. About midday the sirens went and *Water Gipsy*'s crew got the anchor up and set off down river, but on passing the Club Petty-Officer Herbert thought it only right to go ashore and have a gin and a gossip (his crew had been made honorary members for the duration). The tide wasn't up to the Club's walls, but there was a red buoy with the Club's red burgee on it. Everything seemed very quiet, even allowing for the air-raid, and nobody came out to salute the White Ensign. Then from astern came a lot of shouting, and there stood Frank Cole in his boatyard. A protracted conversation ensued, the Petty-Officer being unable to hear what Frank was saying with the engines going. Able-Seaman Longstaff - he'd just joined the boat - was in the bows and said: 'It sounds like 'Just where you are.' Then the penny dropped - the empty Club and Frank Cole's shouts. Water Gipsy had tied up to a buoy marking a suspected land mine. A quick departure was made.

Mines were one of the most deadly of the German weapons. When they landed on property they caused huge destruction and if they landed anywhere in the river, they could easily drift under wharves. Often they had a delayed action fuse and blew up without warning as happened when the *Water Gipsy* was at Holehaven. A huge tanker which had survived the dangerous Atlantic crossing had just finished tying up when she blew up and set ablaze, endangering the wharf and storage tanks. Mine-sweeping extended from the mouth of the Thames up to Hammersmith. So serious was the danger, that in 1941 *Water Gipsy* was given a new job: organising minewatching exercises. Sometimes there were inspiring sights, such as the motor gun boats and motor torpedo boats built at Tough's boatyard, Twickenham, where Johnnie Evans worked for many years, coming downstream to do battle.

In spite of being asked to reconsider her wish, Lady Bull retired from being President in February 1943, and Petty-Officer Herbert, having been proposed by Commander George Bull, R.N.V.R. and seconded by Frank Collis, was elected in her place. One of the least known bits of Club history was the sailing instruction given to R.A.F. fighter pilots following a request from R.A.F. Civil Defence Regiment Headquarters. Racing continued : Oxford University Yacht Club - winning a three-match race by three-quarters of a point, and there was also a joint race with Ranelagh and the West London Hospital race. Some Pool races were also held, with prizes of 7/-, 5/- and 3/-. Turnouts held up remarkably well, and Winifred Procter and Hobbie were out in almost every race. Michael Gilkes, still a medical student, made his first appearance. 'When I first walked into the Club, having been brought up on Jerome and Kenneth Grahame, I recognised it as a haven; the whole impression being of a place just made for 'messing about in boats.' Within a short space of time, Mike became a great force in the Club and not only on the water: he heroically extended the ladies changing room beyond the original 'loo.' Another new member who was to make his mark on the Club was Squadron-Leader J.A.

Charlesworth, who brought his 18 ft rater, *Oxbird*, to compete in the Handicap class.

Club races continued to attract up to ten or more out of twenty boats listed with handicaps, the first four in each race as usual having them adjusted. This happy scenario continued until on the night of 28th July 1944, a V1 flying bomb or 'doodlebug' as they came to be known, fell between Clark's Lead Mills and the Town Hall, blowing away most of the top story of the Club and destroying many nearby buildings, including Julius Sax, the electrical engineers adjoining the Club's west wall. The destruction of their premises left the dinghies on the Club's upstream pontoon vulnerable to vandalism and litter so it was moved in front of Clark's wharf, which resulted in immediate protests from the landlord. The V1 offensive began just after the invasion. The doodlebugs were hopelessly inaccurate but a powerful terror weapon. One launching site was obviously on a line north of the Club towards Ravenscourt Park Underground station. I was home on leave for a short time after the invasion in June 1944, and remember leaning out of the second floor window of our house with my mother and seeing them fall quite frequently.

The damage to all the buildings near Clark's was considerable. The minutes are a completely inaccurate record of what occurred, let alone a basis for a history. I gather from Elsie Bloor that what actually happened was that on the morning after the 'doodlebug' had landed, Francis and Winifred Procter rushed down to the Club and found Borough Council officials had already condemned the building and practically ordered it to be demolished. They were persuaded to change their minds. However this meant that the building had to be shored up and immediate repairs undertaken. These were carried out by the somewhat maligned Mr. Mason, (the ex-Commodore who had always 'just had my tea' when asked if he would have a drink) and other members. After that a firm had to be employed to provide the professional touch to their efforts.

Another heavy job was removing the billiards table for storage. The National Provincial Bank Rowing Club had kindly offered to let members use their premises for changing and also for the storage of sails and clothing. Forty bottles of gin having been sold to Club members for £2 a bottle, the balance of the bar stock was moved to the National Provincial Bank, but the bar was to be kept open and Club officers were to take it in turns to serve drinks. The steward and stewardess had of course been in bed at the time of the 'incident' - this was the word, regardless of its understatement used for all air raid reports - but although considerably shaken were unhurt. However their living quarters were uninhabitable so not surprisingly they decided to seek work elsewhere. A.P.H. presented the steward with 10 guineas to 'mark the Club's appreciation of his great efforts during this critical period.'

Although the future appeared a dismal one, steps were taken to make the Club more attractive from the outside, which it never had been. Winifred, Elsie and other ladies were asked to brighten up the garden and if possible clothe the dreary front of the Club with a climbing plant if possible. 'Winifred was a great gardener,' according to Elsie, 'and got us all working hard.' To cover the unsightly front of the Club Winifred chose a Russian vine, polygonum, whose rampant growth was thought in time to be holding up the building. One had to fight one's way through the foliage to get into the Club.

The Committee had not forgotten that 1944 was the 50th anniversary and it was decided that rationing or no rationing there should be a grand supper. This was organised almost entirely by the much derided ladies sub-committee for 21st October. It was held in the rooms of the West End Amateur Rowing Association and the price was 5/-, which included a cocktail, supper and beer. It was a great success. A guest list was included in the minutes and I see I was there with my parents, although I can't remember the occasion. I must have been on leave again - although not like the last time because my ship was in dry-dock after running aground off Arromanches on D-Day. The Commodore, Commander Sir George Bull, R.N.V.R., was in the chair; other Club officers and their wives included Morty Stephenson, Frank Collis, Jos Collins, Lt Bob Salt, R.N.V.R., and F.E. Procter (and his daughter Winifred). Guests included Jack Holt, Beecher Moore, Major-General Heneage Ogilvie, President of the United Hospitals, and Lady Ogilvie, W.W. Phelps, the great oar from Putney. Among members there were: Lt-Col Tom Fielding, O.B.E., Dr. Michael Gilkes, Dr. Magnus Pyke, the famous dietician who had been a member for many years and who later became a TV- star, and his wife, Vladimir Polunin, a much respected teacher at the Slade School of Art, who lived on Chiswick Mall, and many others. Then there were the Flag Officers of Ranelagh, Twickenham, Oxford University Yacht Club, Tamesis, and the R.O.R.C were asked and also the secretary of the Y.R.A. and the yachting correspondents of *The Daily Telegraph* and *The Times*.

    1945 marked the end of the war in Europe and there were no more restrictions on small craft sailing . Mike Gilkes recalls, as a young doctor, how the pre-war members returned and found that 'in spite of the sorry state of the building the almost unique atmosphere in the bar and general friendliness in the Club had somehow survived.' This was partly because after some unfortunate attempts at finding a steward, one Tom Ball was appointed. Tom over many years was a rarity - proving himself to be an honest man who put up with the dismal conditions of his living quarters - there was still no bathroom - but always provided a cheerful welcome at all times to members.

Arthur Tarrant remembers Tom with great affection. 'In those days things were rather more formal than they are now, and Tom was only ever addressed as 'Steward.' Equally he would never address a member by his Christian name, but always by his formal title, and always correctly remembering who was 'Mr.' or 'Dr.' or whatever it might be.

When you consider the appalling conditions under which this man had to live and work, you realised how well he carried on. I believe Tom had been a steward with P. and O. in pre-aviation days - when ships were ships and did not have stabilisers - and it showed. He was always attired in a clean white jacket and you only had to watch him putting sugar in a cup of tea to see him brace himself against the roll of the ship. He was always conscious of his station - he had a fund of anecdotes about his travels in the Far East, but would only recount these late in the evening when there were no senior members about.' In a completely different way, Dr. Sydney Browning, no sailor but bacteriologist at Moorfields, made a great contribution by paying out of his own pocket the subscriptions for two members elected by the United Hospitals, thus providing racing possibilities for a nucleus of active if impecunious young medical students.

In true British style and in spite of the Club still recovering from the doodlebug - the balcony and ladder were very rickety - the Club challenged Ranelagh to an inter-club race and they brought among other boats Jack Holt's prototype for the famous Merlin, *Kate*. There was also a memorable visit by a team from the R.O.R.C. to take on the United Hospitals, which included Alan Paul, the 'Apostle,' and Tom Thorneycroft of pre-war International Fourteen fame. Race results for 1945 are not clear as the Record Book was left open to the elements after the 'doodle-bug' had landed so it was damaged by damp. However the Kelmscott Cup and West London Hospital Cup certainly took place, as the Mayor was recorded as having given away the prizes.

The autumn will be remembered for a sailing exploit typical of medical students and unique in the annals of the Club. Two United Hospital members took one of their dinghies - they made better cruising boats than racers - down to Sea Reach to go wild-fowling. According to Gilkes: 'They shot one shell duck (which was found rotting in a cupboard in the digs we shared two months later) but claimed this was the first pleasure craft to go down to Sea Reach after the end of hostilities.'

The year brought a new title for the demobilised Petty-Officer A.P. Herbert as Sir Winston Churchill made him a Knight, but he will continue to be referred to in this book as A.P.H., which is what he would have wanted. Sir George Bull sent a telegram of congratulations on behalf of the Club and gallantly soldiered on as Commodore for another year. 1945 up to the mid-'50's were crucial years for many reasons. There was the rebuilding and pontoon and rotting piles problems and there were a number of new members who played an important part in the Club's future leading up to and after the move to Linden House: Philip Whitlow (1945); 'Storm' Roberts (1945); F.J. Snary (1946); Don Storrar (1948); Philip Withers-Green (1949); Simeon Bull (1950); Peter Strauss, Peter Calder and Arthur Tarrant (1951); Peter Curry (1955); and Hugh Davies, who was to become a notable Secretary, (1956). Tom Fielding had of course become a member in 1941.

For the Commodore, George Bull, 1946 was a busy and eventful year. Although the Club building was now reasonably secure, the pontoons and the campshedding on which they rested were in a dreadful state. Another damaged area was the causeway in between the moorings: in 1941 the tug Hero had got out of control and broken up the surface over a large area; but the Club managed to get compensation when the repairs were eventually done. Meanwhile A.P.H., who on occasions moored the *Water Gipsy* alongside Clark's wharf was asked by F.E. Procter, the Secretary, to invite Mr. Clark, the Club's landlord, to lunch and try to persuade him to let the Club use his wharf as accommodation for dinghies. Somehow Mr. 'Bessemer' Clark's reply has survived all these years and runs to two pages. He wrote in the friendliest way, but was obviously a frustrated and worried man. A meeting would be a waste of time 'inasmuch as what is going to happen is terribly obscure.... my company's works were damaged many months ago but no licence has been received to carry out repairs.... This is further complicated by the local Council.' This was true as he knew that the Council wished to purchase his land. 'I understand if they do this they intend to make a sort of fun-fair or in other words create a riverside embankment and an open space for the inhabitants, their children and dogs. I should have thought that bearing in mind that 95 per cent of my company's products are used for building houses, that the Government would have done everything possible to get the works into production again.'

Progress on renewing the campshedding and improving the state of the pontoons proceeded slowly, if only because of shortage of materials. Charlesworth had acquired free from the Government four 'sweeping skids.' These were towed up to a firm in Brentford and in time converted into a pontoon 72 ft by 18 ft. One of the old pontoons was moored in front of the Club, another in front of West Lodge wharf (next door to See's) which belonged to Frank Collis, while the oldest was put in front of Clark's wharf. Initially Clark said it would have to be moved when his business resumed, but shortly after that he consented to the pontoon staying as I think he realised he had lost the battle with the Council.

Early in 1947, before the arrival of Charlesworth's new pontoon, which was to be moored in front of the Club, there was a most unfortunate episode which illustrates how serious the pontoon problem was. The first three months of 1947 will be remembered by all those still alive who endured it, but particularly by the new Labour Government because of the great freeze which affected the whole country and brought the railways and many industries to a halt. Supplies of coal could not be delivered to power stations, let alone to the poor suffering public. The freeze was also accompanied by storms, during one of which a north-easterly gale caused the pontoon in front of the club, on which *Ace* and two other Fourteens were lashed down, to break adrift. The pontoon drifted up river and hit the 'lower boom' of *The Stork* - the lower boom on naval ships is for mooring boats used for going ashore. Much damage was caused to the Fourteens and *Ace* lost her mast.

The pontoon was evidently towed back by the police, but perhaps not very efficiently. Just before the incident, Olaf Bradbury, who was still at St. George's qualifying to be a doctor, had slipped on the ice outside his house and broken three ribs. Ironically he was carrying a large anatomical tome under his arm and this did the damage. 'So there I was out of action, but in spite of the ribs managed to get *Ace* down to Jack Holt's at Putney where amongst other things he put a splendid splice in the mast.' At a Committee meeting on 11th February, Bradbury asked whether the Club was going to pay for the damage done to the Fourteens. Some months later it was decided to make an ex gratia payment of £25 to owners whose boats had been damaged. It was also thought 'that it would not be politic to complain of the police action, but on the contrary to write and thank them for their help on this and other occasions and send a cheque towards their benevolent fund.' At the A.G.M. on 8th March, Sir George stood down after being Commodore for 14 years and Bradbury took his place, he and A.P.H. both paying tribute to Sir George for the great services he had rendered to the Club.

On a happier note the Y.R.A. Dinghy Committee, under the chairmanship of Stewart Morris, had been considering designs for 'a small seaworthy class between 12 and 14 ft long for beginners which must be cheap.' Uffa Fox and other designers were approached. Uffa replied in typical style by saying that he had 'produced the design ages ago.' This was in 1938 when the Oxford and Cambridge Sailing Society said they wanted a boat for beginners. Uffa drew the original design of the Firefly and christened it the Sea Swallow 'but other things intervened,' Charles Currey told me in his laid back way, referring to the Second World War. 'When it was over and the Y.R.A.'s plans were known, I told Uffa that Sir Richard Fairey wished the names of his aircraft to live on, so Uffa sent the original drawings to him with Sea Swallow crossed out and Firefly substituted. Sir Richard never noticed, but thought how clever Uffa was to produce the perfect design so quickly.' On 1st March 1946, the Y.R.A. Council not only approved Uffa's design and the name Firefly but made Fairey Marine responsible for production. Uffa left it to Charles, who in time ran Fairey Marine, to fit them out.

'I remember being rung up by the company's lawyer when we were just about to go into production and told that a rival firm was threatening legal action on the grounds that they had patented diagonal planking and also hot moulding. He said: "I'll give you a day to produce a defence." I went to the public library and after some research found a perfect illustration of *The Ark* on top of Mount Ararat and showing diagonal planking. With regards to hot moulding there was a mid-19th century firm who produced bowler hats in a hot mould.' Collapse of opposition. The Y.R.A. also wanted a more advanced class of dinghy which would be fast but whose price must not exceed £125. The result was the Swordfish, followed later by the

Albacore. So the scene was set for the post-war dinghy boom.

Fairey's could only produce the Fireflies - the first ones cost £65 - and other dinghies because they had large quantities of one-sixteenth marine 3ply left over from building the famous Horsa gliders that carried paratroops on many gallant assaults such as to Arnhem and the vital bridge across the Caen canal on D-Day, 6th June 1944. The London Corinthian had already set up a sub-committee to consider the whole question of class dinghies for the future, but having a representative on the Y.R.A. it heard early reports of the Firefly. In June 1946, the Secretary asked Faireys to send a Firefly to Hammersmith so that the Club could inspect it. This seems a fairly arrogant and expensive request, but it did not worry Charles Currey. He's always known the value of publicity and complied, suggesting a demonstration on the river. The Club replied: 'While willing to assist in demonstrating the Firefly, the Club could not act in any way as agents.' Charles wasn't worried about that. He would get the Press there and no doubt tip off other river clubs. The next winter, 1947, the first two Fireflies to be brought to the Club were (212) and (213). It was the beginning of a new era.

In spite of concern about the Club's future and possibly years of negotiations, the spirit of the members was one of enthusiasm and a desire to race and sail as much as possible, whatever boat they owned. If they capsized they were assured not only of a friendly welcome from Tom Ball, but also of a double rum for helmsman and crew, except in summer. 1948 opened with a visit to Burnham to race for the tankard presented by the Club to the United Hospitals. In spite of the cold conditions this was described in the minutes as a great success, but there was no mention of who won. A visit a month later from Ranelagh produced twenty seven starters. Jack Holt won in a National Twelve, which he had probably built himself before the war. However most of the fleet were Merlins, which was the first post-war class in England and designed by Jack. The West London Hospital Race produced thirty one starters, a considerable feat as petrol was still rationed and made visits from other clubs difficult; nevertheless ten arrived from Twickenham, while two sailed down from Strand on the Green. The winter season races were won for the second time, as already mentioned, by Dr. Bradbury, sailing *Ace* with Steve Bassett, the first occasion being before the war. 'The Club gave me a replica for each and when I had to take up my practice as a doctor down in Hampshire I gave both back to the Club.' Sadly like many other things they have gone by the wayside.

Providing 'safety' on rough days for such large turnouts meant relying on the goodwill of members with motor cruisers. The Club still didn't have a proper rescue boat, and was footling about with an outboard motor on the back of the Club dinghy. It wasn't until 1950 that the Club managed to find an ex-Dutch lifeboat which proved a suitable rescue boat. It cost £50 and the engine, after it had been embedded, another £86. Until then mooring the Barnes mark, particularly on Open Meeting days, always proved a problem, but Commander Grant, of *The Stork*, given twenty four hours notice would always arrange for his lads to row up there. Grant had also offered the Club a dory as a Club dinghy, as *The Stork* was soon to be towed away and broken up. Frank Cole was taken on as Bosun to drive the rescue boat, but he was getting on in years and did not prove very reliable. In the end Joe Cronk, a friend of many of us, took over the job. He later built his own boat and sailed away with his wife to Spain, but is now back and is still a member.

In 1947 before he retired as Commodore, Sir George Bull announced that A.P.H. wanted to present a trophy. It was not until the following year that it was decided that the trophy would be for International Fourteens and Swordfish dinghies, the first of which had just arrived at the Club. On 21st June the first race for it took place. The Trophy was a small silver tray of the kind used for visiting cards - a practice which has long since gone out of fashion. A.P.H. had written a poem which was engraved on the tray and signed:

> Sail on my friend. Your ship is small
> But in your ship, you have it all,
> The wind, the water and the will
> To win - if not, to sail on still.
> Through life, my friend, may you prevail
> With noble lessons learned in sail.
> Good fortune blow you there and back,
> Forever on the starboard tack.
>   A.P. Herbert, 1948

The race was won by the Commodore, Olaf Bradbury, in his beloved *Ace*. Up till 1955 the Trophy was always won by different helmsmen - twice in a Swordfish - but after that Simeon Bull had a winning streak for three years. A.P.H. had said he would like to present it outright if it was won three times in succession by the same helmsman. The Sailing Committee said they would honour this, provided A.P.H. donated another trophy in its place.

However it wasn't until I was doing research for this book that I discovered that Simeon wasn't even in *Serapis* for his third win as for some reason he was unable to sail. Determined to win the tray, Simeon suborned Mike Cooke, a noted Firefly helmsman, to be a 'hired assassin' with James Bridge-Butler, his regular crew. They were given a stern injunction which they found rather daunting: 'it's essential that you win,' and so they did. *Serapis's* name went on the Trophy but A.P.H. said that Simeon had to win it the following year, which he succeeded in doing, although by that time he was sailing *Fleur de Lys*.

When presenting Simeon with the tray A.P.H. mentioned to the assembled members that the winner was his godson, and later on referred to him as 'my distinguished son-in law,' which produced much mirth. So since 1956 the tray has been on Simeon's sideboard.

Afterwards A.P.H. said to me: 'That's the last time I give a trophy under such terms, but you better get another one.' This wasn't difficult as I was working at Christie's then and bought the present one, which makes a nice drinks tray, for quite a reasonable price. A new poem then had to be written and this is reproduced at the front of the book. Prior to A.P.H.'s Trophy the Club's Fourteens challenged the R.O.R.C. to a race which was won by Miss E. Dunbar-Nasmith, one of the visitors who may have been a relation of the Admiral who had been in charge of the Port of London during the war.

On a sad note Jos Collins, one of the oldest members and Harbourmaster for many years died, and in due course the Jos Collins Memorial Trophy in the form of a silver bailer was produced. A subscription list had raised £20 but the silver had been obtained from melting down the Van Moppes cup for motor boats with the permission of the donor. It was decided that the Jos Collins Trophy would be raced for on the day before the Shackleton Trophy. One of Bradbury's last announcements, which brought joy to everyone, was that the men's lavatory had at last been put into a sanitary condition - without resorting to any vast expenditure. He stood down at the end of 1949 and was succeeded as Commodore by Frank Herbert, or Herbie as he was affectionately known by one and all.

I am sure you will agree that it is now time to turn back to the arrival of the first two Fireflies, (212) and (213), *Judy* and *Pennyroyal*, owned by H.J. Palmer and P.D. Bradbury. From now on I intend to leave the arrival of another class and its success at the Club and equally the reasons for its demise to those who are or were particularly associated with them. It's quite impossible for me to write with any authority on any boat save the Fourteen.

Furthermore, to give you the results in the main text for every race would make for very indigestible reading. Thanks to the energy of Paul Williamson there is Appendix A which provides a summary from 1904 of the turnouts, the classes sailing and the Race Officer's comments (if he made any) on the helmsmen's or women's skill, allowing for wartime and other gaps. Thanks to Paul Truitt records are kept once more. There will, however, be times when it is necessary for me to intervene because of some special event which involved all classes of boats or visits overseas, and to insert the views of members of other classes.

Chapter 7

Fireflies

by

Gavin Robertson, Michael Cook

and

Peter Hinton

The Club was quick to show an interest in adopting Fireflies. Some years before it had introduced a Cadet membership for which they would be perfect just as they were for so many young people in clubs, schools and universities all over the country. Between 1950 and the mid-60's the Firefly fleet not only grew but was undoubtedly the strongest class in the Club with a large number of first-rate helmsmen and women. 'Robbie' joined the Club in 1950 and I always feel he is an elder statesman in the class, not only still sailing, but passing on his knowledge to new members. Here is his authoritative account of how the Firefly class developed.

'The Firefly dinghy was similar in general concept to the pre-war clinker built National Twelve and had a length of 12 ft and a beam of 4ft 8ins, with a 45 lb metal centre board and standard sails of 90 sq ft. Originally the hull and spars cost about £80, but this soon increased to £112. Unfortunately, owing to the shortage of marine quality plywood, the decks of the first 250 or so were of aluminium which was not ideal for winter sailing. They also had metal buoyancy tanks which could prove a problem as Virginia Strauss (née Shadwell) found: 'I crewed for Peter in his Swordfish which is how I came to meet him. A little after that I bought a Firefly (195) *Furore*. On her first buoyancy test she sank. However Laurence Martin, who was a member then helped to sort them out.' Even when marine plywood became available there were delaminating problems with the decks and buoyant wooden topmasts had to be substituted for the original aluminium ones. One method of doing this was to remove the bolts at the hounds, tie the top mast to a lamp post and the mast to a car, engage gear and drive on.

The Firefly was about the smallest dinghy that could reasonably cope with the tidal conditions at Hammersmith which are responsible not only for the time when it is possible to sail, but for many of the Club's problems over the years. The Firefly provided excellent training in obtaining the maximum possible from a small sail area under adverse conditions. Her disadvantage was the narrow transom which resulted in the boat rolling when sailing downwind in gusty conditions.

Before the Firefly was accepted as a class, a number of the cup races was sailed on a handicap basis. Because of the time the competitors were sailing against the tide, the faster boats such as the International Fourteens and the Swordfish had an advantage over the Fireflies. This gave rise to controversy regarding the use of the official Y.R.A. tables as the effect of the tide was not appreciated by that august body. Another aspect of the Firefly fleet was that we spent a certain amount of time sailing at other clubs. Very often boats used to be trailed or sometimes sailed upriver to the Easter and Autumn regattas at Tamesis, and all over the country. Although normally the upper Thames is more sheltered than Hammersmith, now and again there were unusual hazards, such as capsized Thames Raters with masts extending half-way across the river, or the occasional National 18 ft dinghy plaining wildly down stream.'

One of the initial successes of Uffa Fox's design for the Firefly dinghy was that it was chosen as the single-hander in the 1948 Olympics. Mike Cook took part in the trials week at Torbay having been selected in the Area Trials at Upper Thames where at that time he was not even sailing a Firefly, but a Fourteen. A friend had offered him his Firefly, *Gina* (13), to take part in the trials.

During the Finals Week he competed against the likes of Bruce Banks, Martin Beale, (who crewed for Stewart Morris for many years) and Air Commodore Sir Arthur MacDonald, from Ranelagh Sailing Club, who'd won the Burton Trophy for 12 ft Nationals before the war in *Farandole*. Considering Mike was only 23 it says a great deal for the selectors that they recognised he was an outstanding helmsman.

I understand it blew hard most of the week, and on one day owing to mast compression one of Mike's shrouds snapped, but he gybed the boat quickly and managed to save the mast. On getting ashore he went to a music shop and bought some piano wire with which he was able to re-rig it. His overall place for the week was 13th out of twenty eight. Arthur MacDonald was the selectors' choice, which Mike thinks was a mistake, as he was then in his early 40's, and too old to take on the likes of Paul Elvstrom, who won the Gold when they met at the Olympics. Considering what Elvstrom has done since, Mike was competing in historic times.

It's always interesting to know how the most skilled helmsmen started. Robbie learned after the war when he was at Chelsea Polytechnic. 'I was interested in boats, having sailed models as a kid, but I didn't really know anything about sailing. With me at the 'Poly' were 'Dickie' Dixon, Peter Calder, Arthur Tarrant and Don Storrar and we all decided to put in a 'fiver' each to buy *Ariel*, a half-rater we'd heard about on the Welsh Harp. We couldn't come to any harm there, and we all gradually learned enough to feel confident. It was really because I heard that Dickie had joined the Club that I joined.'

Mike first went 'sailing' at a very early age in a canoe onto one side of which he fixed a lee-board, Thames barge style. When he went about he had to change it to the other side. From this he progressed during holidays at Bexhill on Sea to another canoe with a lugsail rig and a 'ship's dog' to boot - once again Thames barge style. A National Twelve at Wroxham on the Broads came next. It is this experience with different types of boats which makes good seamen. He then joined Upper Thames having bought a National Twelve, but became so good at it that he found himself crewing and very often helming a Fourteen as a 'hired assassin.'

After the war Mike ordered a Fourteen from Uffa Fox, which cost him £275 inclusive of Ratsey and Lapthorn sails. It's interesting that as from late 1946 Purchase Tax was not levied on boats or sails in recognition of the contribution made by many small boat owners during the Dunkirk evacuation. The honeymoon ended with the introduction of VAT. One of Mike's Fourteen successes in *Verve* (502) was winning the Ranelagh Trophy in 1951. 'The Trophy was a beautiful 12-in high scale model of a Fourteen in solid silver.' However he found himself too light, in those days, for his Fourteen in the windy weather he enjoyed, so in 1948 although he kept her he ordered a Firefly - 'it would also suit girl crews.' Her name *Vector* (627) was apparently chosen by some newspaper reporters. His first big race was the Ranelagh Sailing Club Diamond Jubilee meeting on King's Reach in which he came 3rd, in spite of having had to borrow some sails from Charles Currey.

1950 was the first year the Fireflies raced as a class and the first year of the Morton Stephenson Firefly Tankard Open meeting. There were fourteen entries and the winner was A. Vines, a member of the great Vines' dynasty. The following year there was the first Nina Wood Firefly Team Race in which three teams of three competed, while in 1952 the enthusiasm among the fleet was shown when a single-handed race was organised, as it was for the 1948 Olympics.

It was also the first year of the Wally See Cup. Because of the pontoon problem, a number of members kept their boats on the pontoons of the late Wally See - he died only last year - the third generation of a family of Thames watermen and shipwrights. 'Wally' was a wonderful character. His barge was half home and half workshop, and came in time to have a *Swallows and Amazons* atmosphere.

Wally's personality was such that he attracted around him a number of the younger Club members - Jane Bluff, Peter Hinton, Christopher Buckley and Robert Bull to name a few of them. Although a shy man in some ways, he decided to present a cup for a team race between those Fireflies on his pontoons and those on the Club's. The winner of his cup in 1953 was Jane Bluff, whose father had joined the Club in 1931 and who in 1938 presented the Trophy that bears his name but was allocated to the Enterprise fleet when they were adopted as a class.

Mike Cooke joined the Club in 1953 and won the 1953-54 Winter Firefly Points prize. 'I very quickly learned to enjoy the intimate post-race atmosphere of the old Club bar. This was frequently enlivened by Dickie Dixon's repartee among a number of others. I remember also Anthony Lousada apologising to me for 'his daughter, Sandra's attempts to turn the Club into a bear garden.' I assured him that Sandra's ebullience and joie de vivre were enjoyed by us all and he should certainly not restrain her.' The following October there was the first of what was to become an annual event; the four a side team race in Fireflies called appropriately the Norwich Frostbite. All but one boat capsized.

Year by year the Club was increasingly well represented at Firefly Week. This provided those taking part for the first time with new sailing experiences, such as learning to gybe in the wave troughs and sailing onto a beach with a fixed tiller. In 1956 Mike Cook achieved glory by winning the Sir Ralph Gore Championship. 'It was sailed at Benllech, Anglesey that year. There were about 100 entries and the West Kirby Yacht Club, which was organising the week, put us up in caravans. On the day of the Gore it was very rough. My crew, Judith Hamilton Adams, had to spend a week in hospital afterwards healing lacerated and bleeding fingers on both hands. We were 2nd in the Sir Richard Fairey Points Cup.

Amazingly Judith returned for more the following year when we were victorious again and won the Sir Richard Fairey Points Cup. This was held at Westcliff and the conditions were the same as the previous year - a south cone flying from Southend pier. Robbie, Mike Collyer, Jeremy Pudney, Don Storrar, John Jupe and others will remember the week well. Only Don and Lee achieved the distinction of a photograph in *The Times*. It showed Don in the water holding on to his semi-submerged transom, the caption reading: 'Mr. D. Storrar steadies his Firefly, *Ragamuffin*, while his wife bails out their boat.' Mike Collyer was fourth and Robbie, who had Peter Bloor, Elsie and Joe's son, crewing for him, was twenty third.

Returning to somewhat calmer waters Mike recalls one of 'the fun' races run by Ranelagh from Putney to London Bridge and (following beer and sandwiches) a race back. 'I was fortunate to secure Miranda Seal (for many years now, Kemlo) who had just joined the Club, as crew. We all launched from Putney's sloping embankment and Miranda could not be persuaded by me to wear sailing shoes, whereupon she suffered a quite deep slash from broken glass, but refused to withdraw, which of course was noble but unwise. However I have always carried in my windcheater a small screwdriver, a penknife, glucose tablets and a bottle of brandy. While jockeying for the start, I 'scraped out' the wound until flesh and blood were visible and then sloshed brandy on it until it sparkled and smelled good. I strongly recommend this provisioning, especially for big open sea races.'

Peter Hinton, another of the Club's Firefly stars, had a distinctly *Huckleberry Finn* initiation to sailing. 'My first boat was a Cadet, but it was no ordinary Cadet. I bought the hull from Wally See for £5; stepped a London Transport handrail as a mast and made it into a gaff-rigged boat with sheets as sails. The vicar of St. Nicholas's Church, Chiswick, allowed me to keep her in his garden as I was one of the choirboys. I suppose I was about 15 at the time. We launched her from the old ferry causeway at the end of Chiswick Mall. I'd never read any book on sailing; in fact I'd always been told not to go near the river, as it was 'dangerous.' However we sailed every weekend as far as we could go. When the tide was on the flood, we sometimes made Richmond and came home on the ebb; and if it was ebbing we went downstream, sometimes as far as The Tower and came back on the flood.

When we got back on Sundays we used to go down to Wally See's where there was always a great tea party, with sandwiches and cakes. One evening Wally told me he had a Firefly for sale, *Fuego*, and did I want her? It was Walter Saxelby's old boat. He was asking £80 for her. I told him I would love to buy her, but didn't have £80. Wally told me he would lend me the money, which in those days was quite a lot, and he did. So having got a Firefly I joined the Club in 1958, and kept *Fuego* on Wally's pontoon, and so met Chris Buckley, Robert Bull, Jane Bluff and used to race regularly for Wally's cup.

Miranda Seal joined just after me, and I remember one afternoon after the race she asked me to teach her to get her Firefly planing. It was very windy, but I said 'O.K., Miranda.' We jumped in and I said 'off you go, Miranda.' We were halfway across the river when we broached and went in. We got the boat up and I told her she was allowing the boat to take charge. 'When a gust hits you bear away.' So off we went again and this time she bore away. Everything went quiet and we were running downwind, but when I looked back Miranda was 50 yards astern, having fallen out of the boat. In spite of this immersion she soon became very good.'

Whoever was keeping the Club's Race Records noted even in 1958 that 'Peter Hinton, soon to be one of our best helmsmen, appeared in *Fuego*.' This was fairly remarkable considering how he had learned to sail not having had the same opportunities for competitive sailing as many of the Firefly owners who had come from universities, 'polys,' or public schools. Unlike many to whom I've spoken about sailing on Hammersmith and Chiswick reaches, Peter is very unassuming about his success. Paul Williamson in his Synopsis of Race Results (see Appendix A) describes him as one of the Club's 'outstanding helmsmen,' while Chris Buckley told me: 'He was and still is a 'natural,' whether in a Firefly as then or the Yeoman he's sailing now at Queen Mary's.'

Jeremy Pudney, who joined the Club in 1955, like the Vines brothers started sailing Fireflies at Greshams (as already mentioned) and appears in the Race Records as being 'prominent' in 1956. 'When I joined the Club it was to sail Fireflies. There was Peter Hinton, Gavin Robertson, Jeremy Vines, Mike Cook and Mark Collyer to name just a few. We all did the racing circuit as well as the Club races. Peter was a very cunning, shrewd sailor, but a good sportsman and very fair. We sailed a great deal together in team races and he was great fun to sail both with and against, because of his approach to the sport. He would never push his luck to the limit or if he did he'd be the first to admit it and give way with a giggle. This is not a common virtue today.' All Peter says is: 'Having started at 15 I learned as I went along.'

Within a year of buying *Fuego*, Peter was competing in the Plymouth National Championship with the best Firefly helmsmen in the country. 'The Firefly class was at its peak, with two hundred and twenty five entries, the biggest fleet ever. I sent my boat down to Plymouth as a 'parcel' on British rail as I didn't have a car. Peter Calder took my mast and sails. When it came to the start the line was over a mile long, but even so you couldn't see the distance mark. Nevertheless it was a wonderful week with parties at the Royal Western and other clubs every night. Apart from Peter Calder there was Tony Jenkins and Dickie and Sally Dixon, and others and we went as a group to all of them. On the Thursday I was 3rd at the first mark and finished 6th overall.' Not bad for a comparative beginner. 1959 was the year terylene sails were allowed, so to remain competitive everyone had to buy them. It was also the year Mike Cook became chairman of the National Firefly Association remaining in that exalted post until 1961. After the shambles of the start at Plymouth, at the championship the following year at Herne Bay there was a 'gate' start.

About this time there were always regular turnouts of about fourteen Fireflies for Club races. There was also a large amount of team racing. Ranelagh began the London Pirates, and because of the enthusiasm of the Firefly class the R.Y.A. took it over and sponsored a National Team Championship for around 300 clubs. The London Corinthian team consisted of Peter Hinton, Jeremy Pudney, Keith Goulborn and Mike Collyer. 'We reached the final,' Peter said, 'but just lost the championship. It was held at Frensham Ponds - just a little ditch - and Prince Philip gave away the prizes.' Then there were a lot of races against local clubs, like Rickmansworth, Tamesis, London University Castaways and the R.N.V.R. Trophy. The Fireflies were a very active fleet.

In 1965 Peter became Firefly class captain. I asked him what was his most memorable race on the Thames. 'I suppose it was the 1963 Frank Livingstone Trophy. All the 'hotshots' were there: David Bacon, Jeremy Pudney, Mike Cook, Jeremy Vines, Hugh Kemlo and Mike Collyer - Keith Goulborn - was still a bit too young. It was a very windy day. The Race Officer estimated Force 6-7 gusting to Force 10. Well out of the seventeen starters, only six finished and we won, my crew, Richard Hawkes, had his hands ripped to shreds. Just a question of survival.' I remember the day well as I was O.O.D. It was blowing Force 7 plus.

Firefly sailors tend not to be deterred by heavy weather and three examples show this to be so. In 1966 the National Championship at Felixstowe Ferry was attended by several boats from the Club. On the way out to the start for the first race of the week, Tony Robinson, Commodore in Centenary Year, remembers seeing a launch with a TV crew going out to get footage for the evening news programme. It was blowing Force 6-7 and after battling out of the Deben over the bar competitors found waves so high that when in a trough helmsmen couldn't see the mast of the boat in the next one. Tony was running up and down the waves to the start when he was lifted off the gunwale 'by a wave the size of a garden shed and deposited in the 'hoggin' still hanging onto the tiller extension.' With the rudder hard over the boat remained upright with his crew, Liz Cratchley (that was), facing for'ard oblivious of the fate of her helmsman, until she joined him in the water when the tiller extension broke. About fifteen out of a fleet of seventy reached the start, but only seven or eight finished. There was nothing on the TV News that evening: the whole camera crew was seasick.

Another occasion was a Firefly cup race one Sunday at the Club when it was blowing a 'hooley.' On the Saturday, the fleet had sustained considerable structural damage: two masts broken, shroud plates torn out and other dramatic tales of woe. I happened to be Race Officer and Tony Robinson was class captain. We jointly decided to cancel the race. The disgust and dissent from the top helmsmen - and in the winter we then had some of the best Firefly sailors in the country sailing at the Club - was searing.

During the '70's there was a race for the Doreen Cup, the first trophy ever to be presented to the Club and eventually earmarked for Fireflies when the class was adopted. Once more the wind was horrendous and only three boats ventured out. The course was 5, 4, 3, 1 (the numbers on the mark buoys for any readers who are not Club members). By the island one boat was upside down and one deliberately went ashore to empty out water. Tony Robinson had been driven ashore with a bent plate. Somehow he managed to straighten it sufficiently to get it up and down, launched his boat and set off for No 5 buoy. Apparently in those days in heavy weather the technique was to lower the main and run under jib alone. All went well until the gybe at No 4 when the wind caught the loosely furled main, wrenching it out of the boat and lifting it to masthead height where it flapped like a flag, but in a frenzied fashion with a boom on the outer edge waving wildly and threatening to brain the crew - Liz again. The boat blew into the trees on the Surrey shore and the main halyard and mainsail became entangled in a tree. A passer-by tried to help and was astonished to be told to keep clear as the boat, although half full of water and enmeshed in the bushes, was still racing. After the tree was climbed, the main halyard unshackled and everything sorted out there came the problem of getting off a lee shore. Tony went into the water and shoved off, whereupon the boat took off like a rocket and he was towed right across the river to the lee of Hammersmith Terrace hanging from the transom.

In comparatively calm waters he climbed back in and sailed back to the start line, only to find that the race box was empty and everybody back in the bar. Eventually the race officer, Paul Williamson, was persuaded that the course had been properly completed and the cup was awarded. In the circumstances it was perhaps appropriate that the cup had a hole in it and the usual libation had to be retained by a 'tingle' of some kind.

'The class finally succumbed in the mid-'70's,' Robbie says, 'to competition from the Enterprise class, a particular difficulty being that there was a nucleus of expert helmsmen who could manage to dodge the worst of the tide and sail away from newcomers to the class. When this band of experts broke up, many of them graduated to Enterprises or, like Jeremy Pudney, Keith Goulborn, Hugh Kemlo, Jeremy and John Vines, Chris Buckley and many others, to Fourteens; there was nobody to take their place. By 1980 the sole representative of the class was David Edwards (senior), who of course now sails an Enterprise.'

Fireflies are still raced enthusiastically at clubs where the tide does not play such a part and those where there isn't any. There is even now a glass fibre version, which with youngsters in mind is much cheaper than the 420, but £600 will buy a good secondhand Firefly and once bought she will be much cheaper to run and provide plenty of sport for beginners as well as for experienced helmsmen.

Chapter 8

Memories of the Old Club
by
Arthur Tarrant

A.P.H.

The President of the Club when I joined in 1951 was Sir Alan Herbert. The first time I met him was after a race, as I brought the Firefly that I then shared with Peter Calder up to the Club pontoon. It was tricky getting in because there was precious little room between other boats and a strong ebb tide was ripping out. Amongst the clatter of flapping sails a voice hailed me: "Give me your line, Sir" - I was astonished to see that it was A.P.H. Astonished too, as a 22 year-old member of perhaps six weeks' standing to be so addressed.

* * *

A memorable evening was that before the Coronation of our present Queen - 1st June 1953. London was crowded with hundreds of thousands of visitors, and in those days road traffic was nothing like so well organised as it is now, with the result that much of Central London had become one colossal traffic jam. I had been in the Charing Cross area that day, and my homeward journey by public transport was more than heavy going. I decided to stop off at the old Club for a jar or two.

There I found several other of the younger unattached members whose thinking had been similar. It was a glorious summer evening, and with our own private waterfront, the old Club was as pleasant a place to be as any at such a time. I had not been there long when the phone rang. It was A.P.H. He had decided to proceed to Westminster (where he was to attend the Coronation ceremony) by water - as he had done for the 1937 Coronation - in the *Water Gipsy*, and he needed a crew. Could anyone help? I volunteered and he told me to come round to Hammersmith Pier immediately where he would pick me up.

    A minute later I was on Hammersmith pier as the *Water Gipsy* swept alongside - with the ebb under her - and still apparently going full ahead. "Jump on m' boy," A.P.H. called, "they charge me ninepence if I tie up." Jump on I did, and perilously clambered along the 'catwalk,' which ran fore and aft each side to the minute deck - perch might be a better word for it - from which *Water Gipsy* was steered and stood beside A.P.H. Almost immediately we passed the old Club, and of course the members saluted the President with blasts on the Club hooter and by dipping the ensign. 'Dip our ensign,' ordered A.P.H. I looked for a halyard on the short staff from which A.P.H.'s red ensign flew. There was none - his ensign appeared to be nailed to a broomstick in a socket on the deck. "Take the wheel m'boy," ordered A.P.H., thrusting me aside. I did so and watched amazed as A.P.H. pulled the broomstick out, and solemnly dipped the ensign three times.

    By the time he got it back in its socket, we were nearing Hammersmith bridge, and I carefully steered *Water Gipsy* exactly under the centre lights. A.P.H. asked if that was the first time I had taken a boat under a bridge. I told him it was the first time I had taken a power craft, but we often took our Fireflies under in jaunts to the Pool of London. Evidently he was satisfied, because he disappeared below, and for the first time in my life I found myself at the controls of a power craft. There were beside the wheel two throttle control levers and a push button, but nothing else. We were now in Ranelagh's water, and they were celebrating that evening with a race. Merlins, Merlin-Rockets and National Twelves were tacking to and fro across the river by the score. Now the only way you can stop a power boat in a hurry is by going astern. I banged on the hatch and shouted: "Sir Alan, Sir Alan."

"Yes?"

"Sir Alan, how do I make your engines go astern?"

"You come down here and change gear."

Somehow I managed to avoid all those racing, and we got through the bridges at Putney without incident. Then A.P.H. called up to ask if I'd like a drink. A few seconds later his hand was thrust through the hatch with a teacup full of clear liquid. It was neat gin. A.P.H. took over as we passed under Albert Bridge, where he rounded up to the pier and tied up for the night. He thanked me warmly, but insisted that I must have another cup of gin before I went.

My most precious memory of A.P.H. is that of the Morton Stephenson Trophy in 1956, which attracted forty Fireflies.There was a team race - the Nina Wood Trophy - on the Saturday and the Morton Stephenson race on the Sunday. On that occasion I was sailing *Nomad* with Peter Calder as crew. It was a no-wind day. We made a bad start, and with the rest of the fleet drifted up to the Barnes mark, and very slowly began to sail back to the Club at the rear of the fleet. Eventually the tide turned, with the result that almost the entire fleet bunched up to make a formidable sight - forty Fireflies abreast, gunwhale to gunwhale - across the whole river. We were some yards behind.

Then we got a puff. With the wind dead aft, *Nomad* surged forward. Miraculously there was one gap in the line - through which we shot before the puff died. Now a few yards ahead of the fleet, the tide swept us over the line to win. A.P.H.

presented the prize - there was only one because all the other boats were a dead heat - and reminded us that the day was Trafalgar Day, and this young man had not perhaps realised that he had done what Nelson had done at Trafalgar. I am sure that our win gave him as much pleasure as it did us.

The Flagpole

The old Club had an enormous flagpole, complete with gaff and yard-arm, from which the Red Ensign always flew. Before some great occasion it was deemed that it should be lowered and repainted, and I was endeavouring to finish the painting in time. Michael Gilkes, who was then Harbourmaster and had boundless energy and was particularly good at getting people to 'volunteer' for such jobs as I was doing, suddenly arrived. He said the flagpole must be raised immediately, and despite the fact that I was still busily plying my brush, he proceeded to get 'forces' to carry out the job.

Now the flagpole was supported by a tabernacle - a box round it perhaps four feet high, so that it could be lowered for painting and re-rigging There was no fourth side to the box and the pole was effectively on a hinge at its foot. In spite of the fact that it was covered in wet paint, a large crowd of 'volunteers' began pushing underneath to raise it, whilst another group got round the other side and pulled equally on the guy ropes.

Majestically the flagpole rose slowly from the horizontal, but everbody kept pushing and pulling like mad, with the result that the pole swept rapidly to the upright position - where it came into collision with the fixed side of the tabernacle. The foot shattered, and the pole swept over the vertical to plunge towards those who had been pulling a second before. By a miracle no-one was killed or injured, but Gavin Robertson had a narrow escape: the end of the yard-arm plunged into his pocket, leaving him wearing the upper half of his jacket. A photograph was taken afterwards of Michael Gilkes explaining to the Bosun: 'How I failed to kill some of the members' - or that was the caption it was given.

Votes for Women

In the days of the old Club, women could not enjoy full membership. Ladies could race if they owned boats, but they were Associate Members. Those without boats were Associate Members B; no lady could attend General Meetings, vote or hold office of any kind. Furthermore they could not nominate candidates for membership of the Club; if they wanted to propose a friend for membership they had to ask one of the male members to put the name forward. The situation was the same in fact as it was in the '20's, when it was suggested that women should have the same membership rights as men. To those of us who had been members of the University of London Sailing Club, where men and women were on equal terms, this seemed incredible, and led Don Storrar to take action.

What became quite a drama unfolded at the Annual General Meeting on 1st March 1952. It was a rather boring A.G.M., held in the Furnivall Sculling Club as there was no room at the old Club. Tom Fielding, the Commodore, and his committee wanted to clarify a number of Rules, which included Rule 5. This emphasized that 'Ladies are not eligible to be Full Members.' Before Tom Fielding could put the composite motion to the vote Don struck. He proposed an amendment, which was seconded by Francis Snary, that would have the effect of making women Full Members. It was late in the evening, and Tom Fielding put this rather tiresome amendment to the meeting. It was carried by a majority of twenty one to eighteen.

The Committee were flabbergasted - they were horrified - but that was nothing to their discomfiture when the next morning Priscilla Snary, Francis's wife and a lady member of long-standing, presented them with an application for Full Membership. This they could not take and some may even have considered resigning. Don Storrar was astonished at the storm he'd created. Mrs. Snary was told politely and correctly that her application would be considered at the next Management Meeting. A fortnight later a Special Meeting was held at which the whole matter was discussed. Tom Fielding made a very diplomatic speech in which he went out of his way to say that the Committee felt it was not 'the desirability or otherwise of Ladies being admitted to Full Membership, but it couldn't be done in the middle of the Club's financial year.' The Committee felt therefore that Don's amendment should be rescinded temporarily and a new notice of motion be drawn up and debated at the General Meeting in June. Don was quite agreeable to this, but Anthony Lousada suggested that before the June meeting the views of the Ladies should be sought through a questionnaire.

It would be unfair to say that the Management Committee had put out a three-line whip for the General Meeting on 13th June; perhaps it was only a two-line whip, but at that meeting there was a massive presence of the more elderly members who rarely attended general meetings. There were of course no women present. After everyone had equipped themselves with sufficient drinks to face the fearsome issue, the meeting started. Tom Fielding invited everyone to give his view but made a plea that however the vote went the issue would not become 'a hardy annual.' Pretty well everyone did give his view. At this distance of time some of the arguments look pretty ludicrous -

and frankly some of them looked ludicrous even then. Was it seriously suggested that women might become Flag Officers? Why, we might even have a lady Commodore!

Donald Storrar eventually proposed his amendment in a calm and diplomatic speech: 'The admission of lady members would be in accord with the ideas of today and it would be of value to the Club to hear ladies' ideas on management at General Meetings.' It was unfortunate for Don that the results of the questionnaire to lady members showed that only 25 per cent of those who replied were in favour of becoming Full Members and that more than half were against it. Anthony Lousada made much of this and said that his view was that 'if ladies attend General Meetings a different and more difficult atmosphere will be introduced.' David Edwards countered this by telling the meeting of a foreign sailing club where ladies enjoyed the same powers as men without there being any of the problems suggested by Lousada.

Francis Snary said: 'It was indefensible to afford equal facilities without giving equal rights. What may have been right thirty years ago was not right today.' Dr. Gilkes felt strongly that the fact that the Club did not move with the times was what made it such a pleasant Club. And so it went on. It was evident that everyone present had entrenched views one way or another and no one was likely to change as a result of discussion. When it came to the vote there was a majority of four against Don Storrar's motion. The Management Committee breathed visible sighs of relief and resumed their duties. Immediately after the meeting, Ted King-Morgan, the Rear-Commodore, remarked to me privately: 'Its got to come, Arthur; its got to come.' But it didn't come until 1961. Thirty-four years later we did have a lady Commodore - and a very successful one.

Frank Collis's Christmas Cup

One unforgettable member of the old Club was Frank Collis. He had retired in 1952 from being Treasurer after twenty seven years' service in various capacities on the Management Committee. He owned a substantial cruising boat, the *Seamark*, in which he made extensive trips downriver. Having become a member in 1910, he often bemoaned the lack of facilities following the 'doodlebug' damage to the club. For all that Frank was good fun and was always ready to socialise with members perhaps a third of his age.

It was the custom at that time after any race for the winner to fill up the cup he had won and pass it round for everyone to have a swig. A custom which is more honoured in the breach than the observance today. For this purpose Tom Ball had his own undisclosed mixture, which was as potent as it was delicious. We also had in the bar a collection of pewter tankards that had belonged to past members, many of whom were long dead.

It was after a rather unsatisfactory race just before Christmas 1954, - no wind, near-freezing temperature and a thin turn-out - that perhaps half a dozen of the younger members - including Bruce Fraser, Don Storrar, Simeon Bull's crew, David Shelley and me - were kicking their heels. It was about 5 p.m. and seemed far too early to go home, and far too early to start making an evening of it. Then old Frank came in. Instantly he judged our disconsolate mood. 'Here, it's Christmas,' he began. 'Let's have a cup. Steward reach me down old Jim's pot' - indicating one of the larger ones 'and fill it up.' Tom Ball did as he was bidden, filled it with his mix and it was passed round.

Jim's pot held quite a lot, and it went round several times. After we had all had several swigs, we felt better. Eventually Frank, left holding the empty tankard, recalled its owner: 'Terrible pity about old Jim,' he remarked,'he died of leprosy.'

Chapter 9

The Swordfish class

You may remember that the Y.R.A. dinghy committee had said that in addition to what ended up as the Firefly, there should be 'a more advanced class which would be fast. The cost was not to exceed £125.' Designs were submitted and Uffa Fox's were selected. Apart from his skill it is not all that surprising, as Mylne's designs did not arrive in time, and Wych and Coppock sent in a design for a sixteen footer. On 4th April 1946, the Council approved the National Fifteen at £100 plus purchase tax and its name - Swordfish. However according to Tom Fielding, Commodore for four years in the early '50's, the Swordfish was 'a relatively expensive boat,' which was partly responsible for its short life as compared with that of the later Albacore.

The first Swordfish arrived at the Club in 1948. It may have belonged to D.C.Maurice, who had become a member in 1946 and who is down as owning *Grey Goose* (72). There are only two Club Swordfish owners alive now - Tom Fielding and Peter Strauss - so it was quite difficult getting material for this chapter. The Swordfish was a hot-moulded dinghy with three skins of two and a half mm marine ply built to Uffa Fox's lines. She had bench seats which provided the buoyancy, a steel plate of 70 lbs and a mast weighing 20 lbs, which even Charles Currey agrees now was too big in section, so it was not surprising that it was a heavy boat, weighing well over 400 lbs. Peter Strauss, who joined the Club in 1951, had never done any sailing before but immediately started crewing for Hobbie, which he continued to do for three years. His friend Edward Edwards crewed for Winifred for the same length of time, until Dr. Glossop decided to sell his Swordfish, *Piscator* (25), and sail offshore, and Peter and Edward bought her.

Tom Fielding, Peter Strauss, Winifred Procter and Hobbie were the first to race regularly and in 1951 the Swordfishes were given a separate start with the LC/3, as opposed to being with the Handicap boats 'Winifred and Hobbie were amazingly keen sailors,' Peter recalls. 'The Swordfish was a stiff and stable boat to sail, but very wet in heavy weather. For me it was learning all the time. As the boat was so heavy, if you were sailing her hard she would tend to heel first and you would have to watch out for this because it took some time for the boat to accelerate. She was slow to pick up. The centre-board was hard work, of course, and at that time there was always an argument about whether you should lower it before gybing, or raise it. Quite quickly I learnt to do the latter.'

As well as turning out for Club races - eventually there were ten of them - the Swordfishes went almost as a team to the annual class championships. For Winifred Procter, who forsook her Fourteen *Dauntless* in 1951 for a Swordfish, and Hobbie who followed her example, getting to the championships required considerable motivation, because neither of them had cars. Peter Strauss continues: 'Today it's inconceivable, but Winifred and Hobbie used to take their boats to the championships via British Rail. A lorry would be hired to take both boats and masts and a gang of members would carry the boats, sails, masts and everything else from the Club to Mall Road, near The Rutland, which was the nearest the lorry could get to the Club. On arrival at the championship station, transport had to be obtained to take them to the host club.

Even for those of us towing trailers it was hard work getting the boat off. Tom Fielding provided the answer: a strong box was placed under the stern and two people bore down on it. This took most of the weight off the trailer, so that with another two people holding the bows the launching trolley could be substituted for the trailer.' We never got anywhere in the championships, but Winifred and Hobbie did fairly well, which for women was pretty good, as the competition was quite hot. Tom Fielding was also always well up. I remember the first one we went to was at Harwich, and Jack Knights was 1st one day. But they were all good fun. There were always between twenty five and thirty six boats. We went to Shoreham, Poole, the Medway, Aldeburgh, where there was always a good turnout, because it was their local class, and Brancaster Staithe.

It was in 1953, the year that the Y.R.A. 'by Royal Command' became the R.Y.A., that Gordon Bassett said he'd like to give a trophy for the Swordfish class, although he didn't actually sail very much himself. The Trophy was the Tilney Tankard, an Open meeting event. There were only eight entries, so there can't have been many visitors. A considerably larger event that year was The Round the Island Race -The Isle of Wight, not The Eyot. 'Tiny' Mitchell, Commodore of the Royal Corinthian at Burnham on Crouch and also of The Cowes Corinthian, thought a dinghy race for boats no longer than 18ft round the island would be a great event. So did over four hundred other sailors, including Peter Strauss and Edward Edwards in *Piscator*, Michael Gilkes in his Fourteen, myself in one of Uffa's West of England Redwings, which he thought was a wiser choice than *Dark Wind*, and a number of other Club members. Sleeping accommodation, if you could call it that, was provided in the basement of the town hall, schools and other large buildings. The start was at 6 a.m., and when we were roused an hour before to have a rushed breakfast I remember feeling ghastly. Peter had obviously slept better: 'Dr. Glossop fancied the race so we were going to go three-up. He made a wonderful start. The wind was unexpectedly in the east and we'd borrowed a large spinnaker. I remember looking back and seeing over two hundred boats behind us with all their spinnakers set. Quite unbelievable.'

Tiny Mitchell, who was of course one of the largest men I've ever seen, and his committee had thought there would be the usual prevailing westerly wind, so that it would be a beat down the Solent with the ebb tide to help us, and a run/reach eastwards after the Needles, by which time the tide would soon be on the turn. Instead the wind was in the east, as I have said, so that the whole fleet arrived at the Needles unexpectedly early, and were faced with plugging the tide round the south of the island. There had been no real inspection of the fleet, and some extraordinary boats had entered; of no recognisable class, some very like those in the Handicap class at the Club. Many could make no headway against the tide and started drifting westwards towards Anvil Point. There were a great many rescue boats, but they would not have been able to cope with the number of capsizes if the weather had turned nasty, particularly in well-known danger areas like St. Catherine's Point. Anyhow fortunately the weather remained good, although it took us a terribly long time to get round: I found myself falling asleep while sailing the boat. Peter Strauss said that they were relatively well up for them, but Michael Gilkes did very well coming 15th. The Management Committee congratulated everyone who took part. But the race has never been held again, quite rightly in my opinion.

The Swordfishes raced regularly in the winter series, normally with the Fourteens and I note that Peter Strauss and Edward Edwards come in for a mention one year. 'Of course there were no wet-suits in those days,' Peter told me, 'so we used to wear loads of jerseys. It was not even compulsory to wear life-jackets but we didn't capsize often, although there was the famous occasion when I lost my glasses when we went over. Fortunately we were close to the Surrey shore and at low tide I found them lying on the stony beach. In 1958 I joined the Medway sailing club where there was quite a big Swordfish fleet. I preferred sailing in the estuary there, because there was always much more breeze than on the river, without its being rough as it often was in the Championship races out to sea.' It was in 1958 that the Portsmouth Yardstick was introduced for handicapping much to the relief of O.O.D.s and Sailing Committees all over the country. It was also the year when there were twelve entries for the Tilney Tankard, the largest turnout ever for the Trophy, but there still couldn't have been many visitors.

Tom Fielding was still sailing his Swordfish, *Fantome*, until mid-summer of the following year, when he appeared in the first Enterprise to be seen at the Club, as you will read in the next chapter. Tom sold his Swordfish 'in a huff', following a spillage of Bemax which was a breakfast mood made among other things by Vitamins Ltd, the riverside factory between the Old Ship pub and Linden House. The raw material for Bemax, was delivered by barge in those days. 'The spillage caused masses of greasy substance to foul the river, so coating the hulls of craft and making them repulsive to pull out of the water.' So he went down to Holt's and bought one of his Enterprises. The Swordfish was a relatively expensive boat, and sales slowed down to a trickle when Fairey's produced the Albacore. This craft without the built-in buoyancy of the Swordfish sold for two-thirds of its progenitor.' By 1961 there was only one Swordfish at the Club and that soon disappeared.

The Albacore was Fairey's answer to the demand for a family racing dinghy. She had Uffa's lines and was basically the same as the Swordfish, with three skins of two and a half mm marine ply, but her freeboard was two inches higher. More important her wooden plate weighed only 12 lbs, compared with the Swordfish's 70 lb steel plate, and her mast of the same section as the Firefly, at 10 lbs, weighed half that of the Swordfish. As she relied for buoyancy on inflatable bags she was not only cheaper but much lighter.

Black Lion Stairs, which have been known as Bell Steps for many years, was the old Club's 'station' (sic) from which races were started before the Lower Mall premises became available in 1897. The sign on the Black Lion pub was painted by the author's mother.

Photograph by permission of Hammersmith and Fulham Archives

II

One of the founders of the Club with his boat at the original moorings off Black Lion Stairs which are in line with the main mast of the boat. To the right are the old water works. which were pulled down after the war. Up till then they were

The entrance to the old Club, Lower Mall, which was rented from Mr. F.A. Clark, the owner also of the Phoenix Lead Mills, the other side of the path, in 1897.

A contemporary photograph of the old Club from the river showing the crowded moorings, the Phoenix Lead Mills to the right and other buildings to the left.
Both photographs by courtesy of Hammersmith and Fulham Archives.

IV

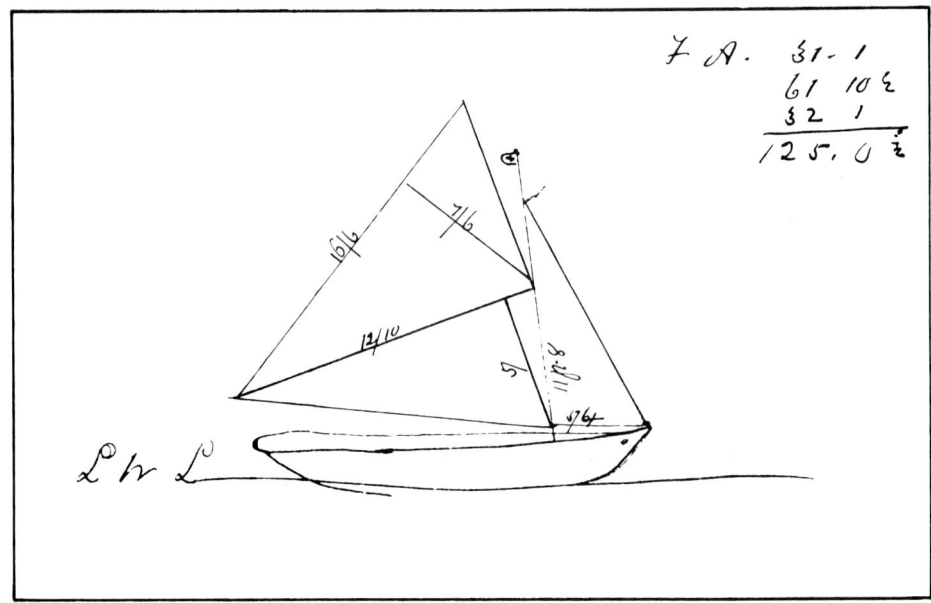

Every boat had to be measured in order to get a rating or handicap. This is the Dixon Kemp 19th century Point 3 formula and is for a Half Thames Rater, of which there were quite a number in the Club in its earliest years. It was based on sail area multiplied by waterline length divided by 6000.

LONDON CORINTHIAN SAILING CLUB.

No.

This is to Certify that we have this day measured the ____Rip____ ____Mr Halliday____, in accordance with the rules of the Club; and find its dimensions to be as hereunder stated.

Fore Area 31ft 1 in. Main Area 93ft 11½in = 125 ft⁰;
L.W.L. ____ ft. Sail at ·3.

____N Lewis____
____W E Burgess____ Official Measurers.

N.B.—ANY ALTERATIONS TO THE HULL OR BALLAST CANCELS THIS CERTIFICATE.

The waterline length has not been filled in - perhaps because Half Thames Raters were a special case. This formula was not satisfactory for such a mixture of boats, so by the '20's handicaps were worked out according to the performance of each boat.

v

A group of members with their ladies - 'welcome as guests ... not permitted in the bar' (circa 1913).

The Creek, the cradle of Hammersmith, just east of The Dove. (circa 1919-1924).
Both photographs by courtesy of Hammersmith and Fulham Archives.

The saloon of the old Club was decorated with flags, trophy shields and for twenty years was lit by gas mantles. Through the half-glass doors at the far end was the hard and the river wall. It was this proximity with the river and the glow of the gas mantles that made it a perfect snuggery. Male members could have their pink gins or whatever was their fancy and discuss sailing and life, albeit without their wives and women generally; or they could play draughts or cribbage. Some women, who were allowed to be members because they sailed, found passing through the saloon quite intimidating because it was a jealously guarded male sanctuary. Even in 1936 ladies were not allowed in the bar and the steward served them in the billiards room on the first floor. After sailing the bar was always packed with men, but nobody minded the crush as the atmosphere was exactly what a sailing Club should have.

VII

The great flood of January, 1928. The scene after the river wall near Digby Mansions, Lower Mall, collapsed from the pressure of water which had poured over. Some of the river walls of the houses in Hammersmith Terrace disintegrated in the same way.

Photograph by courtesy of Hammersmith and Fulham Archives.

A.P.H.'s canal barge *The Ark* towing boats back from Greenwich after one of the races before the war. Frank Bluff, who presented the trophy for Fireflies in 1938, is standing in the forepeak.

A Club race in 1939 showing the variety of boats (all reefed). On the left is *Dart*, the third of the Club's one-design made by Jack Holt and owned by Ted King-Morgan, a future Commodore.

IX

The 1938 Shackleton was a breezy day. Four Uffa Fox designed boats in the lead; all visitors. The eventual winner was *Spider* (389) E. Bruce Wolfe

A little trouble at the gybe mark in the same Shackleton

x

Doodlebug devastation. The Phoenix Lead Mills (centre) and Julius Sax (right) with the triangular roofing next door to the old Club. Today the Great West Road runs where the furthest people are standing.
Photograph by courtesy of Hammersmith and Fulham Archives.

The battered old Club during the mid-'50's. No money for a lick of paint. The billiards room was to the left of the starter's box. Spars and sails were kept in the sloping roofed shed to the right of the hard. No sign of the lead works.

XI

Tea on the hard wall. The crane was used originally by the Lead Mills to unload the barges which came alongside where the pontoons are. Wally See's barge in the background.

Late '50's. The growth in the Firefly fleet made the wharf essential accommodation for the boats. Everybody helped getting them down to the pontoons before a race and back up again after it. Background left: Houses have been demolished showing the beginning of the Council's open space plan.

One of the Swordfish Open Meetings for the Tilney Tankard in the '50's.
The class petered out towards 1961.

The start of the 1960 Royal Thames Yacht Club Trophy race for Fireflies.
Some Firefly Open Meetings had 47 entries.

XIII

Wally See in his barge presenting Jane Bluff with his cup as winner of the 1953 team race between Fireflies on his pontoon and the Club's.

Cheerful faces saying 'Goodbye' to the old Club in 1962. On the left Sir George Bull. Commodore from 1933-46 and later President of the Club. Behind him is Miss Winifred Procter, while in the middle are Miranda and Una-Jane in their 'teens.

A.P.H. presenting the Shackleton Cup in 1962 to Stewart Morris who had won in *Gossip*, a Souter-built Procter V.

A good breeze for the 29 entries for the 1967 Shackleton Trophy. This was the golden period for Fourteens. In 1970 the Club had a fleet of 31, the largest in the country.

XV

The start of a Club Enterprise race. The Enterprises raced as a class from 1960 and achieved remarkably good turnouts for 15 years. There is still a fleet of over 40, many of which are raced regularly.

A good turnout for one of the O.K. Open meetings. The O.K.s raced as a class from 1964 and achieved medium-sized turnouts, but by 1982 had virtually gone because of the arrival of the Laser.

Gil Winfield in a typically relaxed position in the rescue launch which he drove for many years in every type of weather. apart from being Rear Commodore (Bosun). A much-loved member.

The 1962 Tideway Race. Part of the City of London Festival. Some of the hundreds of boats which took part drawn up on the beach below The Tower. prior to racing back to Putney.

Photograph by courtesy of The Evening Standard.

XVII

Jack Holt presenting Enterprise 15,000, the Golden Enterprise, to Commodore Simeon Bull in 1970 as a result of the Club having enrolled the greatest number of new members to the Class Association.

Stephen Aris, Rear Commodore Sailing, and Chris Kidd, deputy class captain, with the four Enterprises kindly donated by the Sports Council in 1993.

Tony Robinson, Commodore. 1979-1981, as well as this year, setting a good example in the days of wooden pontoons.

Other members of the working party: (extreme left) Gil Winfield; Johnnie Evans, the expert, in overalls and behind him Woodie, another stalwart, who took over the rescue boat from Gil. Centre in yellow seaboots (and shorts) Chris Williams; Sue Midleton; Vicky Bradburn and Liz Robinson (then Cratchley). *Both photographs by Paul Williamson.*

'King' Kemlo, a worthy winner in his Laser *Tin-Tin* of the R.T.Y.C. pursuit race on 13th March 1994, when it was gusting Force 7. Martin Dixon had led all the way in an Enterprise but just before the finish ended up in the trees.

Photograph by Bruce Fraser.

The 'Golden Oldies' lunch organised by Chris and Sally Buckley the following Sunday for everyone who had been a member for 25 years or more.

Photograph by Glen Campbell.

Hammersmith reach's infamous sou'westerly about to send Peter Mack in *Distress* swimming in spite of his crew being on a trapeze in the mid-'70's. Charing Cross Hospital and Hammersmith Bridge are in the background.

Similar conditions in 1982. Jeremy Sibthorpe in *Rampant* appears to be completely in control. I presume he had a crew.
Both photographs by Bruce Fraser.

Chapter 10

The Enterprise Class
by
Bill Simpson

As early as 1959, the Sailing Committee was concerned by the decline of the Swordfish fleet, which was confirmed by the bad turnout for the Swordfish Open Meeting the following month. The adoption of a new class, suitable for young and old, yet fast enough to cope with the tide, was needed. The G.P. Fourteen or Enterprise were thought to be worth trying. Jack Holt, the designer of both, agreed to lend the Club an Enterprise and the Sailing Secretary, J.C. Jupe, undertook to find a G.P. Fourteen so that members could compare them during a weekend at the end of May. The Enterprise was regarded as most suitable, not surprisingly as many other clubs had already adopted them.

The Enterprise was inaugurated by *The News Chronicle* in 1956 and the dinghy was recognised as a national class soon afterwards. The first members of the Club to invest in one were Tom Fielding and Elsie and Joe Bloor, who had found their Fourteen a bit too much for them in heavy weather. Later in 1959 they went afloat in *Westerly* (2842) and *Easterly* (3680) respectively. Bill White was soon to follow their example. *Easterly* was triumphantly transported from Jack Holt's stand at that year's Boat Show by a squad of volunteers from the Club.

The use of marine ply in the construction of small boats had been demonstrated by the appearance of the *Yachting World* G.P. Fourteen and the Cadet, which Jack Holt told me had a huge success behind the Iron Curtain, particularly Poland. Both boats had a 'hard chine' flat bottom form. However the 'half' or 'double chine' design of the Enterprise allowed for a boat with a round bilge characteristic constructed from sheet ply and still within the scope of the D.I.Y. enthusiast. Jack Holt was the first man to design boats capable of being made from kits and they were a huge success. An owners' association for each class was incorporated with all his boats. Jack intended with the Enterprise to attract the family cum cruising people as well as the racing enthusiast by including in the specifications a smaller cruising sail, provision for rowlocks and easy mounting for an outboard. There were also spinnakers in the original design, but these were ruled out by the class association. No doubt they wished to maintain the simple one-design racing appeal.

The launch of the Enterprise was spectacular. On the night of 7th January 1956, Enterprises 1 and 2 crossed the Channel from Dover to Calais. In one boat were Bruce Banks, the Olympic helmsman, four times winner of the P.O.W. and an occasional visitor to the Club for The Shackleton and his wife Rosemary; the other was helmed by Bobby Pegna and crewed by Mrs. Flavia Nunes, retired now but a much respected headmistress for many years. Still a member of Itchenor, Flavia's skill at the helm of her X-boat is well-known. The new dinghies performed well. The only trouble the crews experienced was fog on the French side. Jack, who had been in the accompanying launch, was warmly congratulated on his design. Later that year *The News Chronicle* sponsored a race from France to England for six Enterprises to be sailed by leading helmsmen from other classes. One of them was Beecher Moore, Jack's partner. All this was good PR stuff and helped to establish the image of the Enterprise as a good seaboat - shades of Uffa Fox's great sail to Le Havre in 1928.

In this respect one has a vivid memory of a 'Blue Jib' event organised by the Sussex Yacht Club at Shoreham in the

1960's. Twenty-six Enterprises drifted a mile or so offshore in a near calm before the start. Suddenly a freak 'hurricane' burst out of a sky turned to copper, instantly capsizing twenty five dinghies, many under bare poles. In the mounting seas and blinding rain the Shoreham lifeboat together with club rescue boats collected all the crews and got them ashore, leaving their boats to the elements - no argument. Conversation in the changing rooms was of new boats and insurance claims. But as quickly as it had come the wind died. Motor cruisers from the club put to sea and recovered all the dinghies; many little the worse for wear. The exception was a boat crewed by Shirley and Ray Rouse who had joined the Club in 1965 and bought an 'old Enterprise' before taking up Fourteens. Ray and Shirley had managed to stay upright and scuttled back to the river under jib. It must be admitted that any class of dinghy would have suffered the same fate in those conditions. There is the example of the Fourteens at Whitstable in the 1961 P.O.W. when the race had to be abandoned because of Force 6 winds and huge waves kicked up by the comparatively shallow water.

Again in the first Evening Standard Tideway Races in 1962 some Enterprises had difficulties in the fresh breeze. Perhaps the sail area although much appreciated on the river when punching the tide in a light summer wind is on the generous side. The first Tideway Race was organised by Ranelagh Sailing Club with the help of the London Corinthian as part of the City of London Festival. At least a third of the three hundred-odd boats were Enterprises with a sprinkling of Club dinghies from other classes. In the last race in 1966 a Club Enterprise, *Custy*, came second overall, just missing the Golden Triton Trophy, the top prize. [Author's note: Bill shouldn't have been so modest. *Custy* was helmed by him and Elaine and they received a great hamper of food as a prize].

At the time of the Tideway Races - they continued for a

number of years - there were about thirty five Enterprises in the Club undercrofts and over 10,000 boats registered in the class. By 1970 the score was 15,000 and to mark the occasion a competition was organised in which the prize was to go to the club enrolling the greatest number of new members to the Class Association. Jack Holt provided a prize: a new G.R.P. Enterprise with a gel coat speckled with gold and the number 15,000. After a considerable amount of press-ganging - at Tuesday nights at the Club by Clive Norris in particular - the *Golden Enterprise* was ceremoniously handed over to our then Commodore, Simeon Bull, at Putney by Jack. The introduction of the G.R.P. version towards the end of the 1960's did not find many takers in the Club, although David Edwards has been sailing his glass boat regularly since about the mid-'70's. How extraordinary it is that a hull shape designed with sheet ply in mind should now be produced in plastic and continue to grow in popularity against the competition from those classes designed for plastic production such as the Lark and the 420. Our continuing to sail this class should be good for growth in our Club, particularly after the the Sports Council's generous donation of £17,000 last year, which provided for four more Enterprises plus a new rescue boat. With these and the encouragement of more members to use their own boats we can look forward to a higher turnout.

Paul Williamson's tireless research has produced an account of performance and strength of turnouts for as long as records have been kept. During the dinghy boom years a fleet of fifteen or more Enterprises in a Club race was not unusual. Regular home water sailors also trailed to many Open Meetings. The Royal Corinthian Crouch Rat Trophy at Burnham, where Hugh Kemlo did so well, was a favourite. Other host clubs were: Waldringfield, Felixstowe Ferry, Hayling Island, the Broads, Twickenham and Laleham. An example of motivation by the Class captains was demonstrated in the mid-60's when Simon Fraser led ten Enterprises to the Open at Wraysbury Lake.

As with other classes, many members of other clubs visited in the summer became winter members of the Club. Among the Enterprise class, Peter Gimpel and Jerry Wade would bring a gang from the Royal Corinthian at Burnham while Doug Bishop and others came from the Sussex Yacht Club. Then there were Peter Brewer and Philip Rayner, our one-time Commodore, who at that time was sailing at Laleham Sailing Club. This all made for good competition and a high turnout in winter sailing. To capsize in the reservoirs in mid-winter was a murderously freezing experience before the advent of all weather clothing, while on our reach of the Thames unsolicited swimming was tolerable even when it was snowing. The automatic hot rums and black current in the bar were traditional.

In the '80's top helmsmen attended and took line honours at many Open Meetings and championships, leaving little time to sail at Hammersmith other than at Open Meetings. Prominent among these were Alan and Dave Beaney, Steve Grant and Dave Manson, always high in the National Championships. Alan and Steve were up in the top ten in the World Championship in Thailand in 1989 and Dave Manson was doing well in the 'Worlds' in Bombay in 1991. Bear in mind that the Enterprise had had International status since 1972. Mention must be made of the crazy 24-hour race organised by the West Lancashire Yacht Club when up to a hundred dinghies (a mix of Enterprises and G.P.14s) raced around the marine lake at Southport for twenty four hours; crew changes at the discretion of the club teams. Here, London Corinthian successes were 6th overall (1st Enterprise) in 1985 and 1st overall in 1986. Again with Alan Beaney, Steve Grant and Clive Norris in the team. In the same year Steve Grant and Alan Beaney won the Thames Valley

Spring Championship, and Steve Grant went on to win the East Coast and South-West Area Championship. Long before this, in 1966, Hugh Kemlo had won the Thames Valley Bowl and Thames Valley Trophy.

In the broader aspect of yacht racing we will remember Phil Crebbin racing an Enterprise at our Open Meetings. He became National Champion in 1974 and an America's Cup helmsman in recent years. Many other top helmsmen started by sailing in Enterprises: Harold Cudmore, Lawrie Smith, Brian Willis and Jack Knights, yachtsman and journalist whom older members will remember as he was a member of the Club for some time. In 1961 Jack was National Enterprise champion.

It is a Club tradition that each year there are Flag Officers' races when the latter provide the prizes. Rear Commodore (Sailing) has been responsible for the Enterprise race and this seems to have produced some odd prizes. Signed copies of books written by the presenter were very acceptable. 'Yards of Ale' and salad serving spoons were O.K. But in one year Mike Collyer had a lavatory pan to spare when building his new house at Bourne End. This he duly presented to the winner of his race. Cries of 'Fill it up' were ignored. We were glad to have come second that year and receive a hip flask of more modest capacity.

Crews: The Enterprise is an admirable boat for husband and wife crews of which we have many. The average weight is satisfactory and space so generous making it possible for the cramped limbs of the 'wrinklies' to cope and go on sailing as the years go by. It was a tough lady who could cope with a Fourteen, as they developed through large genoas and yards of foresheet (not good when short tacking on the river); then one trapeze, then two trapezes. One year at Grafham Water, with the wind gusting to Force 5 plus, the lady crew was too scared to come in at the windward mark - disaster. I must admit though there is quite often a lot of shouting and in-boat criticism with husband and wife, probably born of familiarity. Such behaviour is less likely between helmsmen and sought after lady crews. Examples abound, but I'm sure they will forgive us if we refer to those intrepid offshore sailors, Bruce and Ann Fraser, whose altercations in Bruce's Fourteen *Rhythm* could not have been more audible if wired to a public address system. For our part, the only time in our lives that impatient criticism moving on to stony silence has been when sailing. When people have been dinghy sailing together for many years, the advantages of synchronised reflex movement and actions are some compensation for the growing arthritic handicap.

At the old Club when crossing the start line in light winds care was needed to sail well clear of Hammersmith pier and berthed craft projecting well out into the river. I remember being unable to make it on one occasion, and being trapped against a large transom by the force of the tide. Our watchful Harbourmaster, Peter Roberts, and the Pier Master were at hand to haul the wife crew to safety and shove the dinghy and hapless helmsman out into the stream to carry on single-handed. Fortunately the rescue boat had laid all the buoys and was available to tow me back to the pontoon. I went to find the wife who was none the worse for her experience particularly after being given a number of gins by Peter and the Pier Master in his hut. Also at the old Club we witnessed what must be a record when Tony Jenkins capsized three times before the start; each time returning to the pontoon to collect another ill-advised lady crew - all the time never losing the yachting cap he was wearing.

In all classes of dinghies, finding and keeping crews is a problem and so often Enterprise sailors would fail to turn out because of crew problems. On one occasion an off-duty policeman was passing the Club and Johnny Underwood persuaded him to crew him in his Enterprise race. Later the officer was heard to remark that he felt sure his wife would not believe his reasons for being late for lunch. Another of Johnny's stories, again with an inexperienced crew, was when with nil wind at the Barnes mark he drifted under the railway bridge and lost his topmast to a passing train. A regular sailor for nearly thirty years, Johnny was always prepared to take out and teach new crews. It was while sailing his Enterprise that Johnny suffered a fatal heart attack; a traumatic experience for Katie Jupe, his young girl crew, and a sad loss to the Club.

Johnny had a well-earned reputation for 'ouching and pumping' as a means of propulsion. But this was peanuts compared to the roll tack now so well-developed by the quick helmsman of today and much aided by their crew ability. One recalls an Enterprise Open Meeting at the Club, when a committee boat start against the tide was arranged in very light wind conditions. Despite I.Y.R.U. Rule 54 the leading boat had virtually roll-tacked to complete a round of the course to meet the bulk of the fleet still trying to cross the start line against the wind and tide

The Commodore has so often been left holding the baby. I expect past Commodores will have told of their experiences when entertaining visiting Mayors of Hammersmith, teams of sailors from France and Holland during Jumelage years and officers from other clubs. From 1955 when the Royal Thames Yacht Club awarded a trophy to be sailed in Fireflies, officers of the club would turn up for the race each year and many a good session was held in the bar. In 1971, our Commodore, Simeon Bull, entertained the Royal Thames Commodore to lunch, after which the trophy race was due to start. There was some embarrassment when only four Fireflies turned out, while our visitor was armed with prizes for the first six boats home - ('you really must do better, Simeon!'). The following year, not wanting to repeat the debacle, the Club obtained permission to switch the Trophy to an all classes pursuit race.

Sadly we do not see the contingent of Royal Thames officers attending the race these days. No doubt the Serpentine Cup team racing better reflects their interest in Thameside dinghy racing. Despite the decline in turnout, attributed by some to competition from board-sailing, the growth of interest in off-shore racing and the appeal of the tideless conditions at Queen Mary and other reservoirs, it has been demonstrated recently that a good lead from the Sailing Committee and the class captain can produce a hefty turnout of Enterprises for prominent events in the sailing programme. Three other developments should help achieve this aim: the new 'Sports Council' Enterprises to be sailed by Club members who do not own a boat; Paul Truitt's organisation whereby well-used Enterprises can be borrowed for a race and Robbie's evening teach-ins for new members which are of such great value to our Enterprises and the Club itself.

A Few Words More About the 1962 Tideway Race

I hope Bill will not mind me chipping in on his excellent article on Enterprises, but I was delving into some of Sally Buckley's files which she kept on all sailing matters with commendable discipline and came on one relating to the first Tideway race. It even contained a list of the results and on studying those of the Firefly class I saw that Patrick Goodison was first, sailing his dinghy *Fortune*. By an amazing coincidence Patrick, an advertising man, has been my next door neighbour for forty years or more. I rang him up to congratulate him. 'Yes,' he said, 'I was first. Actually the whole idea was mine!' Patrick is no longer a member of the Club, but he was at the time, having joined in 1959. I feel the original inspiration for the Tideway Races should be recorded and I must admit it would give me a chance to describe what it was like from the Fourteen's point of view.

Over a drink Patrick told me he was approached by another advertising man involved with the City of London Festival and co-opted onto the Lady Mayoress's Committee which was planning all the events. Lady Hoare, the chairman asked Patrick if he had any special ideas and he said: 'Yes. I've always wanted to see the river crowded with a mass of boats; a larger version of the London Corinthian Sailing Club race down to Greenwich. Why not hold a race from Putney to The Tower and back?' "What a splendid idea. Can you get it done?"'Lady Hoare asked. "I know who to approach, if you give me a little time," Patrick replied. It didn't take long. Barry Bewick, general manager at the the time of *The Evening Standard*, agreed that his newspaper would sponsor it. Barry also personally spent days looking for a suitable prize for the overall winner and eventually found the Golden Triton. John Stokes, Commodore of Ranelagh, was wildly enthusiastic to help as a 'launch-pad.' It was then that our Club was drawn into helping with the administration.

Saturday 21st July was a lovely sunny day and there was a tremendous atmosphere of excitement on Putney Embankment. There were a total of three hundred and thirty two entries - Solos - G.P. Fourteens - Fireflies - National Twelves - Enterprises - International Fourteens and Merlin Rockets. The Fourteens started first. I was being crewed in *Little Billee* by James-Bridge-Butler and we had a nice easy run down. Ranelagh had timed the start to perfection because we had little trouble getting under any bridges. Fortunately there was a large number of rescue boats about, although they weren't really needed till the sail back. However on the bend of Battersea Reach, just past where Fulham Power Station used to be, James and I were horrified to see Wally and Joan Maddison, from Tamesis and old friends of the whole Fourteen class, moving straight for the swimhead of a dumb lighter moored to a buoy. The wind must have dropped away so that they didn't have steerage way and an eddy took them in. Their mast broke with a crack, and within seconds the boat had disappeared under the barge. Wally and Joan going underneath as well. To our relief they popped up the other end just after their somewhat mangled Fourteen had appeared. A rescue boat picked them up and took them and their dinghy to Cadogan Pier in a state of shock, but otherwise all right.

Sailing through London, past the Houses of Parliament, The Savoy, St. Paul's Cathedral and the many spires of other Wren churches, Somerset House, Billingsgate Fish Market, as it used to be with its wonderful golden fish weather vane, where Chris Newnes, my normal crew once worked, was always a marvellous experience. On that day it was even better to see a mass of boats behind us and then a nice sandy beach beneath Traitor's Gate for us to pull up our boat. Simeon Bull, Tony Newman and I went off to one of the many pubs in Wapping, but not before watching the arrival of the other classes. The mass of boats was an unforgettable sight.

The start of the return race was very different. The wind had got up; it probably wasn't much more than Force 4, but in the narrow Upper Pool, where there were still warehouses and actually cargo ships, the wind seemed to be much stronger, funnelling down through Blackfriars, Southwark and London bridges. There were only seven Fourteens, so the start wasn't too difficult, but as we tacked through London Bridge, watching all the time the top of our mast nearing the curve of the arch, we felt for the first time a sudden and unpleasant buffet of wind off the arch we were approaching which required an immediate crash tack and this was repeated through the next two bridges. Curiously it wasn't until we got through Blackfriars that we came to grief. Either I tacked too quickly, or there was an extra strong gust and over we went. Fortunately the wind was strong enough for us to get the self-bailers to work and plane across the river which by now was wider and empty the boat.

After that it was all plain sailing for us, but in Chelsea Reach, by which time it was a fetch, Tony Newman and Eve France, who were ahead of us in *Boanerges*, suddenly went in. We passed on and bore away into Battersea Reach and began to put on speed. Suddenly there were four loud blasts from ahead, and saw that one of the colliers that used to supply coal to the London power stations - they were nicknamed 'flatirons' because of their long low shape - had decided that there was enough water for them to get away from Fulham power station wharves. The flatirons were large ships built specifically for this trade. To get under London's bridges when empty needed accurate timing - 'threading the needle' - the skippers called it and they needed to be going quite fast to have proper steerage way. Looking astern I saw the Thames was littered with upturned Enterprises. *The Evening Standard* rescue boats did a great job as they quickly cleared a gap for the 'flatiron' to pass through.

We got to Putney without mishap and Tony Newman came in shortly afterwards. He obviously hadn't enjoyed it as much as I'd done. "God what a purgatorial race," he said. I don't think he even signed off as his name doesn't feature in the results list. Meanwhile Patrick Goodison and his wife Edwina 'were having a wonderful sail.' "Everything was going fine until Edwina's bra strap broke." "Bra strap?" I queried. "Oh yes, she thought it was bikini weather. The only trouble was from then on I had to hold her bra straps in one hand, and the sheet and tiller in the other."

Retirements totalled a hundred and fifteen, which said something for the conditions on the return trip, leaving a hundred and seventy three boats which completed the course. I didn't bother to stay for the prize-giving, but the following day at the Club I was handed a small pewter mug for coming 3rd in the Fourteens while Simeon Bull was 4th. Ranelagh Fourteens were 1st and 2nd. Bill Simpson was 4th in the Enterprises in that first Tideway, which in view of the conditions was no mean effort. It was a great day and full marks for Patrick Goodison for initiating it.

Chapter 11

The Hard Beat to Linden House
and
The Move

For Olaf Bradbury, Frank Herbert, Tom Fielding, Storm Roberts, Ted King-Morgan and PhilipWithers-Green, successively Commodores between 1947 and 1962, this period after the war involved months and months of exhausting negotiations with Hammersmith Borough Council, which must have tried the patience and diplomacy of all of them, and also of their officers. Temporary repairs had been carried out and the Club had received £230 from the War Damage Commission. However the Commodore and his officers were faced with the problem of rebuilding the Club on its original site or recognising as the years rolled by the inevitable alternative, forecast by Mr. Clark, the Club's landlord, in his letter to A.P.H.

Mr. Clark, you may remember, was exasperated because he was unable to get a licence to rebuild his premises, and blamed Hammersmith Borough Council and in particular its plans for building a promenade from Hammersmith Bridge and transforming the blitzed area into gardens for the public. Mr. Clark even mentioned a 'funfair' in his letter to A.P.H., which was of course pure euphemism, but he can be forgiven as he thought building materials which his factory could produce if rebuilt were a greater priority. 'Open spaces' have for years been accepted as being socially desirable, but in those immediate post-war years some felt such policies, however well-meaning, had a *Brave New World* ring about them.

Socialist Britain did not approve of riverside alleyways.

The river should be open to the public and sanitised. If the riverside lost a lot of its character that was the price of progress. The Council's plan originally provided for a bowling green, tennis club, rowing club and a sailing club, as well as a large promenade for the general public to take the air between Hammersmith Bridge and Chiswick church. It was inevitable that the latter would prove to be the course following the bombing and immediate opportunities for replanning, even if not unnaturally most of the plan proved too grandiose.

It is all water under the bridge now so probably is of little interest to most members. However this book is meant to be a history, so some record should be made of this period, if only because of the interminable negotiations and 'Catch 22' situations which, because of the lack of finance, the Club's officers found themselves embroiled in. If anything we face worse problems at Linden House now.

The desire of the members and indeed the committee was not only to rebuild but to improve the Club. Since the war there had been an influx of members and in 1948 the Club was accommodating forty one boats when there was only room for twenty six. The departure of the United Hospitals did not help the pontoon space problem - it was not to be 'Goodbye,' because the Club proposed a trophy to be raced for every year at Burnham. There were complaints at General Meetings that it was impossible for owners to work round the hulls of their boats. The reply to that was that a balance had to be struck between providing the best possible facilities on the one hand, and maintaining the Club's income and active racing membership on the other. This can't have cut much ice with Douglas Maurice, a newish member with a new Firefly who had no pontoon berth. It was decided therefore that there should be 'a more stringent scrutiny of applicants' credentials.'

The pontoons provided a seemingly insuperable problem;

they continued to be in a leaky if not sinking condition and the late and much-liked Wally See, apart from accommodating about ten dinghies on his pontoons, was kept busy repairing the Club's as best he could. Over the next six years many substitutes to new steel pontoons, which was what were really needed but which the Club couldn't afford, were tried: bridging pontoons and a cut-down barge, which buckled owing to overlapping the Club's campshedding, were just two. All in all the Harbourmaster had a thankless task in spite of the help of members replanking pontoons, when wood could be obtained.

The pontoon problem was never really solved until after 1952, thanks to the efforts of Ted King-Morgan, then Vice-Commodore, Storm Roberts and his engineering colleagues at work, Mike Gilkes, Simeon Bull, and a gang of volunteers. This particular pontoon was christened the 'Sandys' pontoon because Mr. Sandys, the driver of the rescue boat, designed it. It was made with alloy angles and oil drums supported the planks on which the boats rested. This seems to have been the only successful one, until the Club were forced to have one made professionally at considerable cost on moving to Linden House.

The Club's architect said that it was unlikely that the War Damage Commission would pay the Club the £2,000 which was the estimated cost of rebuilding including such improvements as inside accommodation for some boats. The Club had a balance of only £159 so if it was to borrow the money it would have to be at a low rate of interest which would mean it would have to have a 99-year lease. Clark said this was out of the question and would only grant a 21-year lease. The cost of this would be too heavy for the Club. Pleas for help went to the Borough Council and L.C.C. but to no avail. For at least the first four years after the war building materials were in short supply, so it followed that licences were as well. That is unless you were Uffa Fox, who when he wanted more wood, told the authorities it was for an export order for dinghies and he got them immediately.

The breakthrough came early in 1950 when Clark asked the Club if it would like to buy the freehold for £2,600. He had obviously decided that he might as well get as much from the Club as he could as the Council were obviously going to proceed with their plan. Provided that the freehold included the wharf, the idea was welcomed by the members in spite of the cost and the fear that the Council would either evict the Club or rebuild it according to their wishes. The surveyors warned the Club that they had to recognise that the redevelopment plan would eventually go ahead, at which time the Club's property would be compulsorily purchased at a price mutually agreed between valuers or through arbitration. There was a risk therefore that compensation might not equal the Club's expenditure. In spite of this warning the members were all in favour and sanctioned a loan from Westminster Bank - the Club's balance at that time was £24.

It became clear gradually that the Council intended to acquire the freehold, either compulsorily or by negotiation. Sure enough on 1st September an application for a Compulsory Purchase Order was served on the Club. Sir George Bull drafted a well-reasoned letter of objection. The Council's letter appears to have been more of a threat, because it was still prepared to purchase the freehold through the Club for £2,600, rebuild the Club and give it a 21-year lease at a rent of £200 a year, with safeguards against dispossession. Before the Club committed itself, Philip Whitlow, the Secretary, pointed out that assignment of the Club's rights to the Council could not be considered unless a satisfactory agreement about the future of the Club had previously been reached, and that it might therefore be necessary for the Club to complete the purchase.

He then very generously offered to provide the money on a short-term basis and this offer was gratefully accepted.

Early in October, the Town Clerk, Horace Slim, confirmed that in spite of the Compulsory Purchase Order the Council was prepared to agree to the Club remaining on its present site 'subject to a strip of land some 20 ft wide on the southern and eastern boundaries of the Club property being surrendered so as to enable the promenade which has been started, to continue round the riverside of the Club premises.' Under the circumstances Herbie Herbert, had no alternative but to agree. Knowing how arguments can erupt these days at General Meetings over quite minor things, it is amazing that there was no outcry about the Club having a public footpath in front of the hard. A few weeks later the Council withdrew their application for a Compulsory Purchase Order, after hearing Sir George's representation on behalf of the Club.

However the Council continued to try to acquire Clark's wharf by negotiation and in 1952 the Borough Surveyor, Mr. M. Scrase, produced the most grandiose plans for a new three-storey clubhouse, 'like the bridge of the *Queen Mary*' with covered accommodation for fifty boats, and was 'anxious to proceed directly he got a licence.' A year later the Commodore reported that he had had a long unofficial talk with Mr. Scrase concerning the walk in front of the hard. Mr. Scrase had worked out plans to build a cantilevered path over the eastern end of Clark's wharf so that it would pass behind the Club. This was good news.

1953 had started badly for the Club because as if it didn't have enough problems regarding its site, at the end of January at about 3 a.m. on a Saturday morning there was 'the great flood,' brought about by three natural forces coinciding: a storm surge in the North Sea flooding up the Thames; a spring tide and excessive floodwater from upriver. Fortunately it was not quite as 'great' as the flood in 1928 and no one was drowned. I remember the night well as I had come out to spend the weekend with my parents. We were woken by police launch loudhailers telling everybody to get up. Typically the police were a bit late as even in the darkness I could see that the ebb had already set in . However it was a near thing. When I went down to the bottom of the garden the level of the river was only one inch from the top of the wall.

My father and I put on seaboots. On the way to the Club we sloshed through quite a lot of water in Upper Mall which had seeped in through the tideboards of Linden House, Latymer School and St. Paul's School. Things were much worse at the Club. The water had seeped through the tideboards, the hard was awash, and some water did get into the bar, but only to a small extent. The Steward had been woken by the police boats' loudhailers and came out into the bar and got his feet wet, but his quarters weren't flooded. The real problem was the pontoon which had drifted on to Clark's wharf. With the tide ebbing the danger was obvious. If we couldn't shift the pontoon it would eventually slide off of its own accord and the boats, if they hadn't been lashed down, would go first.

Fortunately my father and I weren't alone; there were Sir George Bull, Gordon Bassett, B. Rogers, my friends, Jane and Martin Bluff and no doubt others. With an almighty heave we managed to push the pontoon off the wharf, and put some beams between it and the wharf to stop it drifting on again. Dealing with the boats was rather like corralling a herd of wilful ponies. However directly the tide dropped all was well, although as always there was a vast amount of flotsam and unpleasantness left behind there and also on the hard. The next day was Sunday, and a call for volunteers went out to clean up the Club. There was going to be another high tide in the afternoon and members watched anxiously, but the storm in the North Sea had died down. Tom Fielding, who was still Commodore, thanked us at the next meeting for our night's efforts.

To return to the Club's rebuilding problems, it was finally in 1954 that Mr. Scrase, Borough Surveyor, put his final plan to members and it was approved. Amazingly the 'three-storey bridge of the *Queen Mary*' had not been watered down, but there would only be accommodation for fourteen boats inside the Club; there would, however, be undercover accommodation on Clark's wharf for forty boats. The promenade would pass to the north of the Club, and the Council would provide launching brows and pontoons for the boats on Clark's wharf. The rent for the new clubhouse would be £200 a year and rates would be £100, while the rent for Clark's wharf would be £120 and the rates £70. Considering the estimate for rebuilding was £7,000, the Council appeared to be doing the Club proud. Mr. Scrase hoped to start work the following year. The only problem was where was the Club going to go while the new premises were being rebuilt? However this never had to be worked out. In 1955 there was an economic crisis and local authorities could only borrow for essential projects. The Club was not one of them.

A year went by and no progress was made in spite of desultory negotiations. However early in 1957 Linden House, the sports and social club of Joseph Lyons, Ltd before the war, was mentioned verbally by the Borough Council for the first time as a possible new Club headquarters. There would be accommodation for boats underneath a block of flats which was to be built adjoining Linden House and the right of access to the existing pontoon moored to the piles. In spite of the Commodore's warning that the Club might be forced to move, the general feeling of members was that they would prefer to stay at the old Club.

Storm Roberts, privately, was more realistic than the

members and maintained a calm and objective attitude through a frustrating year of inaction by the Council until 11th December 1957, when the Town Clerk wrote to the Commodore as follows: 'It would be to the advantage of the Club and the Council if the Club was to move to Linden House which has now been purchased by the Council. The building would be in a good state of repair; there would be undercover accommodation for boats; in addition to access by the existing pontoon, the Club could have additional ramps if they desired. Subject to the Club agreeing, the rent would be what had originally been agreed.' The Commodore's view was that *prima facie* it appeared to be a generous offer by the Borough Council. Nevertheless when put to members at a special meeting they felt they would like to know what would be the reaction of the Council if they were to decide to remain on their present site and demand the rebuilding in accordance with the terms of the lease.

Carey Randall was now Town Clerk and his reply was unusually quick and blunt. On 7th February 1958, he wrote: 'The Club would get no facilities if it stayed on its present site, no piles and no use of Clark's wharf, but there was an assurance that the Borough Council would be helpful over Linden House.' Undaunted Storm Roberts wrote a diplomatic reply before a meeting with him and other officials a week later: 'I realise what a busy man you are and how many more important affairs you have to deal with, but I must point out that I wrote to you on 19th March last suggesting an early meeting, and in fact seven weeks will have gone by without our moving an inch forward.'

This achieved nothing. There was an agonising four-month wait for the Council to give their revised proposals. Finally on 9th May, Carey Randall wrote offering the Club a seven-year lease of Linden House and promise of renewal. The subsidised rent would be £250 a year and the estimated rates would be £260 a year. If the Club agreed, he would submit a lease. A five-page memorandum giving full details of the present lease and the terms the Council were offering for Linden House and what facilities the Club would get there was sent to every member. The Management Committee emphasised that apart from undercover accommodation for boats, proper changing rooms and showers, there should be at least two extra hours' sailing time from the Linden House premises which would provide a greater choice of racing courses. At an historic meeting on 23rd June the committee asked members to empower them to negotiate, 'subject to satisfactory arrangements for security of tenure,' a lease for Linden House on the Council's terms. After a remarkably short debate A.P.H. proposed the resolution, which was seconded by Simeon Bull, and carried unanimously. The Town Clerk was notified of this.

There were of course many loose ends: the length of the lease; the rent and rates; the unwillingness of the Council to pay for more piles and a new pontoon, and the total number of boats which could be accommodated underneath the flats. The prospect of a 'seven-year' lease had not unnaturally aroused criticism. However the latter was not a question of the Council being 'cagey.' The Council could not authorise a 21-year lease; only the Ministry of Housing and Town Planning was able to do so. As the Council was leasing Linden House at an uneconomic rent this might raise problems. However by the middle of August the Town Clerk wrote saying that the Ministry official responsible thought a 21-year lease would be possible. This in due course proved to be the case.

Negotiations continued and were so time-consuming let alone exhausting for the Commodore, then Ted King Morgan, that it was decided to form a sub-committee to deal solely with Linden House problems. It was essential to have a lawyer on the sub-committee so Sir George Bull was ideal; the remaining members would be the Commodore and 'Elder Statesmen' - Tom Fielding, Storm Roberts and Philip Whitlow. All agreed to serve. To many members, the Club did not appear to be getting anywhere, and suspicions grew that the Council was not sincere in its wish to bring the move to a satisfactory conclusion. At a General Meeting at the Furnivall Sculling Club in June, which was being chaired by Chris Buckley, Vice-Commodore, as Ted King-Morgan was ill, Frank Collis, probably the oldest member present, implied that the move was a great mistake and that the Club should remain where it was. Chris Buckley, then aged 27, told him in no uncertain terms that this was not a helpful suggestion. The members at a special meeting had voted unanimously to accept the Council's offer in May 1958 and there was no going back.

Finally in December the Club received what could be called an ultimatum. The Town Clerk offered a 21-year lease at £250 a year exclusive of rates; the Council to pay for all external repairs and the Club to pay rates as determined by the District Valuer and internal repairs and redecoration. The Club could exercise its right to stay where it was, but it would soon have to lose the wall. The Club should regard the letter as preliminary notice of the Council's intention to terminate the licence which was the Club's present authority for using the wall. The Council set a time limit of two months in which to enable the Club to decide to stay or move. Members although still reluctant realised that they had to bow to the inevitable and agree to the Council's terms. The lease was signed by the Trustees - Sir George Bull. A.P.H., Tom Fielding and Philip Whitlow.

Long before this there was a meeting which had nothing to do with a new Club house, which will no doubt be a relief to the reader. On 23rd June 1961, there was a Special General

Meeting to vote on making ladies Full Members and what was more, pay the same subscription. The Commodore and other officers had emphasised in December when the subject had been discussed at length that they had not been under pressure in raising the matter. It simply was time that it should be given an airing. Readers may be shocked to learn that another reason for at last taking this step was that with Linden House in view more people would be needed to serve on committees and women could do that as well as men and 'apart from those considerations surely the time had come when it was the right thing to do?' All the usual arguments, for and against, came up but in spite of the controversy the motion was carried, with only four voting against. Parity with men's subscriptions would be raised at the first General Meeting in Linden House.

Early in 1962 there was light at the end of the tunnel for Philip Withers-Green, Commodore, regarding the move. Sub-committees had been formed to deal with the interior of Linden House, the organising of social matters and to advise on pontoons and piles. The tentative date for taking over Linden House was 1st May, however the flats over the undercroft were not yet finished. Until they were, the rent would be £20 a year. When completed the rent would be £250 a year, with a 'break' clause in the 21-year lease after five years' tenancy, in case Linden House proved uneconomic to the Club. The Council would be responsible for the exterior and would bear the cost of the design and erection of the starting box - it eventually won a Civic Trust award, but in some ways has always seemed to me be impractical, certainly for one O.O.D.

Prior to this they would provide a small hut for the same purpose. Access would now be by Oil Mill Lane, not Upper Mall. The one stumbling block was the refusal, or inability, of the Council to provide funds for sinking the extra piles needed if the Club was to have three pontoons. With some reluctance

Tom Ball, the faithful steward, was given three months' notice and a leaving fund, which in the end totalled £150, was opened on his behalf. Linden House would definitely need a steward with a wife to provide meals and the service members would expect. Members were glad to be told that Tom had found another job, with accommodation quite quickly.

Linden House had been built in the mid-18th century and was a noble Georgian building until in the 19th century wings were added at each end and later still a hideous bow window. These were removed before the war. When originally built Linden House was part of a large estate which included Grafton House to the west and Beavor Lodge to the north. To the east was Seagreens, which belonged to Mr. Louis Weltje, after whom the road is called; he was Clerk of the Kitchen to the Prince Regent, and is believed to have lived in Linden House at some time. When Mr. William Bull was invited to dinner by the London Sailing Club in 1887, the tenant was a Mr. Arter, but he had let the premises to a girls' school. The 1915 L.C.C. Survey of London describes Linden House as as 'an excellent example of mid-18th century style worthy of better neighbours than the present oil-mills which disfigure the riverside and which Hammersmith could well afford to lose.' There had been oil-mills, or firms such as Vitamins Ltd, for at least sixty five years before the Club took over Linden House - there are references in local histories to the 'stinking oil mills.' It is true that the narrow path between The Black Lion pub and Upper Mall was somewhat smelly, but, with the beam-engine operated water works beyond Vitamin's premises, the whole area had a Dickensian character.

In the '20's Linden House, as I have said, was bought by Lyons and became their social and sports club with a special emphasis on rowing. The skiffs and eights were kept in a boathouse where the undercrofts and flats are today. This also had a four-man practice rowing tank in which David Widdowson, when at St Paul's School opposite, spent many hours rowing 'miles and miles.' Another great interest in those days was rifle shooting and there was a range in the basement. During the war it was an A.R.P. headquarters, but when the war over, the building became very dilapidated, until the Council seized on it as the future home of the vexatious London Corinthian Sailing Club. Having edged the Club out of its cosy premises, the Council's next target in order to complete their riverside promenade was Vitamins Ltd, but this was to take them another ten years to acquire.

P.C. Dickie Dixon, as Rear-Commodore (House) was the driving force directing the different teams responsible for all the work that there was to be done to make Linden House habitable. Dickie had joined the Club in 1948, the same year as Don Storrar and they shared a Fourteen for a time before buying Fireflies. This was fortunate because Don Storrar was House Steward and both wives knew each other and the four made a powerful team. Dickie, apart from giving instructions, did a lot of practical carpentry ranging from the washbords in the changing room to the shelves behind the bar. He was also responsible for organising the copper top to the bar.

Don Storrar's description of what it was like working with the Council officials and getting the interior of the Club ready is interesting: 'In the early 1960's I was House Steward. I remember the very good rapport we had with the officers of the Borough Council. They adapted their plans to our needs and painted the inside of the premises to our colour scheme, but when that was done it was up to us. It wasn't easy to begin with because there was no detailed plan. Unlike the old Club there was too much space. What was the best way of allocating rooms? Where would be the best place for the clubroom and bar? Some wanted the bar separate from the clubroom; some wanted bar, clubroom and kitchen on the ground floor with accommodation for visiting yachtsmen on the first floor; some wanted a small snug bar in the basement. Eventually after hours of reasonably amicable discussion an outline plan was agreed.

After that it was the members' working parties, weekend after weekend, that fitted out Linden House. One of the first things we did was was to build a proper carpenter's bench. It still stands in the basement. Members did most of the joinery and plumbing in the kitchen, for which a catering-size cooking stove had been acquired for nothing and a refrigerator for a song, thanks to Hugh Davies. Plates, cutlery and kitchen utensils were donated by members. To give an example of the huge number of little but essential things, there was a list of twenty two jobs to be done in the changing rooms and workshop area of the basement. Lee Storrar and Sally Dixon (as she then was) made the very large curtains for the clubroom, having selected, bought and transported the material.They also chose the paint colours for the whole building. The Borough Surveyor was so taken with the orange colour in the changing rooms that he later specified it for the fancy metalwork on Hammersmith Bridge. We built the bar to a design drawn up by the design department of the B.B.C., thanks to the keen interest of Richard Levin, head of the department. Brian McCann did most of the joinery, while Bill White installed the plumbing.Watneys donated £100 towards a bar; a hundred chairs came from a school in Ealing for £20 - while armchairs and tables were made by members. In this way we equipped the Club's new home.'

It was obviously a gigantic effort. During all this time materials had to be bought to keep the working parties going; the brewers' deliveries had to be received and the money taken by the bar had to be accounted for (as the Club did not yet have a steward). Before the commissioning of Linden House there was a bar service of sorts in the dining room and simple catering. This was run by members some of whom, for the security of the clubhouse took turns to sleep (not always alone) in what became the steward's flat. Alan Cawthorne (the father of Simon or 'Killer' the professional skipper) was responsible for laying out the garden. So far as the move was concerned in order to to allow members to move their boats, the Sandys' pontoon and another were brought up and placed against the wall of Atlanta wharf (which was still Vitamins's property and cut off from the public path by an eight-foot wooden slatted fence but was directly in front of the Club. These pontoons were soon to be joined by a brand new one which would be able to take the weight of the ramp and which had been paid for by a Sports Council Grant.

Linden House was formally taken over by the Club on 28th April 1962. Members were told that the old Club would be closed as from 9th June and a temporary bar would operate in Linden House as from that time. Sailing, however, would continue from the old premises until mid-July by which time the new pontoon and ramp should be installed at Linden House. Boat owners were advised that they should then bring their boats up to Atlanta wharf and use the two other pontoons for rigging boats. They could then start racing. Before this there was a farewell party at the old Club and from the photographs, regardless of alcohol, everyone appears to have been in good spirits and looking forward to the move. Two weeks later the Commodore had a letter from the Town Clerk saying that he had a heard a rumour that the members were going to burn down the old Club. He replied in suitably forceful terms that it was completely untrue and was amazed that the Town Clerk could take such a suggestion seriously.

At the first General Meeting to be held at Linden House on 29th June, Philip Withers-Green told members how pleased he was to preside over it and gave a brief resume of the damage done by the 'doodlebug' and the problems of repairs and then the whole question of rebuilding, which in the end had proved impossible. Successive committees had experienced many promises and disappointments but this first meeting was the realization of success. He expressed his thanks to all those who had worked so hard, in particular to P.C.Dixon, Rear Commodore, who seemed to be always on the job with two or three consistent henchmen, Brian McCann, Geoff Freestone and Bill White. Also Don Storrar, the House Steward and his team. Then there was the pontoon committee - Chris Buckley, Vice-Commodore, Peter Roberts, Tom Hill and Geoff Freestone.

'The Club would have to expand considerably - a few non sailing local residents would not be detrimental, but sailing members were essential. It would be wrong to be too rigid; the ultimate election must rest with the Management Committee. However members should be careful to propose and second only people whom they felt would be desirable members.' The Commodore finally said that he wished to present a trophy to be called the Linden House Trophy to commemorate the opening of the Club's new premises.

The Committee decided that this would be competed for on 11th November, the day after a house-warming party. Invitations would be sent to the Mayor, the Town Clerk and other officials connected with the move and their wives; the Commodore of the Royal Thames Yacht Club, Castaways, Laleham, Minima, Ranelagh, Thames, Twickenham, Whitstable, Strand on the Green and Upper Thames Sailing Clubs; the Furnivall Sculling Club and Kensington and National Provincial Bank Rowing Clubs; Stewart Morris, Captain Lovell of the P.L.A.; the chairman of Vitamins; the Chief -Inspector of Hammersmith Police and Barnes River Police; and the Editors of *Yachts and Yachting* and the *West London Observer*.

It must have been a good party because a hundred and forty four bottles of champagne were consumed in a short time. The Commodore, his Officers and all those who had helped with the move certainly deserved to celebrate. However the Management Committee and its successors would find that there was a lot to be learned about running a club which expected greatly increased social activity, as Don Storrar, who was later Commodore for two years, pointed out to me. Whether this has ever been done is doubtful bearing in mind the Club's present situation. A nice gesture by the Mayor, Miss Edith Woods, at the party was her wish to donate a cup to be sailed for as the Sailing Committee decided, which put to rest the tension there had been at times between the Council and the Club during the Hard Beat to Linden House.

Chapter 12

The O.K. Class
by
James Bridge-Butler

As early as 1963 the subject was raised at the June General Meeting of another racing class 'to replace the depleted Firefly class.' Mr. G. Freestone was bold enough to make the suggestion and got a flea in his ear from the Firefly class captain. 'The Firefly class is not moribund, although a little dormant at present.' Nevertheless by August the subject was being discussed by the Management Committee. There were twenty five Fireflies in the undercrofts, yet it was quite an event if six raced and most hadn't been out for months. This sad development may have been the result of the popularity of the Enterprises, which being faster, had their starts before the Fireflies. It doesn't explain, though, why Fireflies should be just left in the undercrofts, anymore than why the same happens to the Enterprises today.

At the A.G.M. early in 1964, Dr. Paul Smart, a noted Fourteen sailor, advocated the introduction of a single-handed class and by March the Sailing Committee recommended that the O.K. should be adopted as a fourth racing class, racing to begin as soon as there were sufficient boats. The International O.K. was designed by Knud Olsen in Denmark, hence the title, which is a reversal of the designer's initials. The class developed in Denmark, the O.K. conveniently using the same mainsail as a pirate dinghy of which there were many in that country, but rapidly spread to France, Norway, Sweden, Denmark, Germany, Great Britain, and later Australia and New Zealand.

The first boats were extremely difficult to sail due to the lack of restraint on the boom, but Paul Elvstrom sailed one and immediately overcame the difficulty by using a wedge as for a Finn of the same period. Even so the boat always gave the impression that it was about to take charge of you unless you used a firm hand. The flexible rig, with an unstayed mast, could be tuned to the weight of the helmsman quite easily and as the wooden masts on the earlier boats were very flexible there were many capsizes, especially down wind. Some helmsmen, like Robo, who bought one in due course, regarded the masts as 'telegraph poles' and to tune them planed a bit off the front to make them bend. If, of course they planed off too much, they had to stick it back on again. O.K.s gradually became more sophisticated and acquired kicking straps but still if the boat was not properly set up it was very difficult to control.

The first O.K. appeared at the Club in 1963 and was bought by John Ogle, normally a Fourteen helmsman; he had apparently decided to buy the O.K. to amuse himself when he couldn't get a crew. It was thought that other Fourteen helmsmen might like to buy them and thus produce a small class when no crews were handy. The exact reverse took place; the Fourteen crews began to buy O.K.s and get away from the undue demands of their Masters.

At first, as they were given the same rating, the O.K.s raced with the Enterprises. The first O.K. race to have a separate start was on 7th November 1964, with Eddie Kirkwood-Lowe, Martin Wheatley and myself. The class proved quite popular and numerous boats appeared usually with rather odd names - *Yok, Pussy Galore* and such-like. A number of the more well-known and active members of the Club also bought boats, such as Paul Williamson and Chris Buckley with a boat called *T-in-C*.

A week after our first separate start, six members of the Club set off together for their first Open Meeting which was held on a tiny lake in the Midlands. Tony Warren, who owned *Pussy Galore*, suggested that we stay overnight at the Rising Sun near Silverstone, with which he was familiar from his motor racing days. We had the usual boozy evening and set off the following morning very much the worse for wear. The journey which we thought was going to take half an hour took an hour and a half and we arrived at the club just as everybody was launching.

After some frantic rigging we all got off. It was a bitterly cold day; none of us had had time to read the racing instructions and the tiny lake appeared to have many shallows and islands and what appeared to be thirty marks scattered over it. Robin Dent didn't have time to change and sailed to the start dressed in a grey lounge suit. He then promptly went aground in one of the shallows, jumped over the side to push off and found himself up to his chest in water. Nevertheless he continued to sail and we had great difficulty in thawing him out afterwards.

The start was hilarious as the wind went round through 180 degrees and I arrived second at the first mark in front of about sixty boats The leader then promptly retired and I found myself leading the fleet with no idea of where the next mark was, let alone the rest of the course. I shouted to the second boat to overtake me and asked the helmsman to let me know when we were approaching the last round. This second helmsman was Robin Kemp, who was also at his first Open Meeting. Robin led round the tortuous course for what seemed to be about fifteen laps. He called out to me - I was only about two feet behind him - when he thought we were going into the last lap and as he called so the gun went for the end of the race. On the way home on the M1 I was proceeding at over 70 m.p.h. when I was passed by my boat in the outside lane. She eventually parked herself on the hard standing and I stopped behind her, causing some amusement to other O.K. helmsmen on their way home.

John Martin and I presented trophies to the class and the first Open Meeting at the Club was in October 1965, with class racing for the Martin Trophy on the Saturday and the Bridge-Butler Trophy on the Sunday. There were about twenty entries including various well-known helmsmen from other clubs such as Robin Kemp and John Dawson-Edwards from Oxford. However, it was Chris Buckley who won both races. At a later Open Meeting, Robin Kemp won in his boat *Hoof Hearted*. Our dear President, A.P.H., found this a bit of a mouthful and in announcing the winning boat seemed to run the two words together, causing great hilarity, and raised eyebrows from A.P.H., who didn't realise what caused the laughter.

At an Open at Shoreham, Martin Hunter capsized at the gybe mark in a very strong wind and while the boat was upside down with him inside in the cockpit, he was more than surprised to see the bow of John Dawson-Edward's boat come right through the side to join him. Martin's boat was a rather peculiar one, painted black, white and orange and built out of alignment by a home builder so that the transom was twisted in relation to the stem. Nevertheless Martin seemed to make it go quickly enough; that is when it did not have a large hole in the side.

Members of the O.K. class from all over the country were familiar with the London Corinthian because I was class chairman and the A.G.M. had therefore been held at the Club since 1965. The class often had helmsmen from other classes in the Club who would borrow a boat when they could not get a crew for their own. Whenever Peter Hinton borrowed a boat, usually Chris Buckley's, he won, although Paul Williamson always did well. All in all the class flourished and in 1970 there were forty three entries for our O.K. Open Meetings; both won by the great Herb Sweetman. With 'comedians' like Simon Bullimore and Robo in the class, the party on the Saturday evening was always catastrophic. The best racing tended to be in the winter, as the class rather like the Fourteens, dispersed to Open Meetings during the summer.

The first Lasers appeared at the Club in 1973 and these spelt the downfall of the O.K. class. O.K.s needed fairly regular maintenance as the loadings on their fittings, especially mast mountings with no rigging to support them, was quite high. The Lasers offered single-handed sailing with virtually no maintenance at all. In 1974-75 there were only very light winds for the O.K. Open Meetings at the Club and this did tend to discourage visitors who were not familiar with attempting to sail in such conditions over a tide.

The class struggled on but in 1976 there was the first Laser Open Meeting. In the O.K. Open Meeting the same year there were only ten and thirteen starters and in 1977 they were back sailing with the Handicap fleet. O.K. Open meetings were still being held in 1981, but the following year the winds were very light again which finally put paid to Hammersmith as a place to race so far as visitors were concerned.

By 1983 the class had virtually disappeared from the Club, which was a pity because the International O.K. offered very exciting sailing, especially in heavy weather; the boats could be tuned by the helmsman and they were very satisfying to sail to windward as a proper hooked position could be achieved in the cockpit. Unfortunately dinghy sailing was now entering the age of plastic standard boats, such as the Laser, on which it was virtually impossible to alter anything (and with a sitting out position which I always regarded as hideously uncomfortable).

Perhaps the O.K.s were too much of a good thing for the more modern inhabitants of a London riverside club who did not want to work on their boats or agonise about the particular finish or placing of fittings. Maybe they were just too difficult for the later generation to race! Whilst they were sailed at the Club they provided great amusement and splendid close racing often on the edge of disaster, with a cast of characters the like of which will probably not be seen again.

Chapter 13
The Laser Class
Miranda Kemlo Talking To
Nick Paine, Paul Williamson, Hugh Kemlo,
Robin Johnson and Una-Jane Hodgson

The Canadian, Bruce Kirby, well-known also for his Fourteens, designed the Laser. It was launched at the New York Boat Show in 1971 and was an immediate success. David Widdowson, who was Vice-Comodore at the time having joined the Club in 1965, and Katie Clemson were the first members to buy a Laser. David bought his in 1972 from Gerry Kitching, the West Wittering shipwright, for £225 all-up and named her *Meltemi*. Katie's boat was *Down Under*.

'The initial reaction from members to my many capsizes and somewhat dramatic sailing at that time was similar to my attempts to get the Thorpe Water Scorpion fleet accepted when their own club waters were buried beneath the M 25.' Considering their success in America and other countries including the U.K., the Laser took some time to catch on at the Club. There is a minute of the 10th October meeting in 1972 that 'Lasers were to be welcomed in order to keep abreast of the times.'

David and Katie were joined the following year by Bob Fisher, Paul Hillman, Simon Cawthorne, Hugh Kemlo and members of the Fourteen fleet. It must have been the very simplicity of the Laser, compared with the technological 'dream in time to be realised by the state of the art Fourteen' that tempted some Fourteen sailors to treat them more as a toy than a serious boat. Bob Fisher, the yachting journalist and later for some years Rear-Commodore Sailing, was not particularly amused when Tom Trevelyan and Robo borrowed his Laser to test it out in a Force 6 when normal sailing had been cancelled. Both had returned from Lowestoft, where the Royal Norfolk had also cancelled sailing, having first naturally over-indulged themselves in sampling the local beer. They were still 'over the top' when they returned to the Club. Refusing to be done out of a sail they decided to take Bob's Laser out - not two-up - in spite of the fact it was still blowing a near gale. The result was that Bob's brand new sail was completely blown out, and Tom had to replace it.

The new single-handed boat was resisted at first by the O.K. class, only one or two defecting to them. The advantages of a one design production line boat, where hull shape, weight, mast bend, sails and fittings can all be rigidly controlled to fine tolerances, gradually became apparent. Nevertheless compared with other clubs in the U.K., let alone the rest of the world, the Lasers took a surprisingly long time to gain real favour at the London Corinthian, which the Management Committee found disappointing. However in 1974 there were enough Lasers to have four starts to themselves, with Bob Fisher leading the fleet. The following year the Lasers were accepted as a class with John Hallett as class captain, and in 1976 there was the first Laser Open Meeting which attracted twenty entries. It was about this time that the turnouts of the Fireflies and O.K.s diminished to such an extent that they sailed with the Lasers in the Handicap class.

The Laser has gone from strength to strength and is up to sail number 151,285 world-wide at the time of writing and has been chosen, much to the fury of Fourteen sailors, for the 1996 Olympics. Laser owners speak of the boat as a thoroughly good design - exciting, fast, quite difficult to learn at first, but without any incurable vices. Most of our serious Laser sailors have sailed a variety of boats before buying one and for some a Laser is just one of the many boats they own. I spoke to some of the various owners in the Club

Nick Paine bought his first Laser in 1976, when he was 42, having graduated from a home-made oak framed Cadet to a captain's 'gig,' while in the Royal Navy; then 12 ft and 18 ft Nationals and a Merlin Rocket. 'I came to Lasers mainly because of the difficulty of getting a crew. I thought at first that sailing a Laser would be quite dull as it had only one sail, but actually I've never enjoyed sailing so much. It's absolutely marvellous. The prime reason is that in a Merlin you always thought it was your boat which was making you go so slowly, whereas in the Laser it can only be you and there is no excuse.

There were some difficulties at first. For example the mainsheet always catches round your transom when you gybe, and it's very difficult to get the kicker on and off, and you can quite easily roll in to weather on a broad reach unless you watch what you're doing. There's no doubt it takes a little while to learn to sail a Laser competently, and it takes much longer to arrive at sailing it fast, especially if you are over 40.' Nick obviously learned quite quickly because he won the Laser World Master's Championship (the Master's is for over 45 year-olds) in 1980 and 1981 and was placed on four other occasions.

I asked him if there were any special difficulties downwind. 'Well, bear away is the answer to nearly everything. You must not let them heel; you really must sail a Laser flat. It is disastrous if you are on a reach and you luff up; the boat gets out of control. The only thing to do is to yank the helm hard and bear away - that is if you've got room. For example in the Grand Masters (for over 55s) in Aarhus, Denmark, in '89 it blew so hard during the first race that only a third of the fleet got back under sail. The only thing I could do on the reach was to make it a run, and the thing was then to come back upwind with perhaps only half the sail drawing, because I found that if you try to broad reach in a gale you just get blown in; the boom being quite long can so easily catch on a wave, even with the kicker right off. I find that other than submarining, which is a problem, a run is quite stable provided you steer, as with other boats, to keep the foot of the mast under the flag.

My most memorable moment in Lasers was when I came first in the 1980 World Masters. That was the first Championship I had ever been to and it was held at the Ile de Bendor, opposite Bandoles, in the South of France. There must have been about a hundred boats. On the first day I made an awful start; so I tacked away out to sea to get clear. The wind dropped to light and the sea breeze came in, and I was first round the weather mark, not having worked it out at all. So I won the first race and everyone thought I was some whizz kid. I was dead lucky. I think I managed to win two other races that week.

Then two days before the end of the series a mistral blew up which produced enormous seas and a Force 6 wind. It was a real struggle. I don't think I've ever sailed in such big seas; I was amazed that off the French Riviera in summer the Mediterranean could get so rough. I got round the weather mark and bore away on to the reach. Unfortunately I couldn't see the leeward mark and I think I went too low and lost a place or two. One of them must have been to Paul Millsom, one of the Australians. Unknown to me at the time he had broken something on the mainsheet so had no cleat and no centreblock and therefore hardly any purchase. He was holding the mainsheet down by sheer muscle power yet somehow he managed to do quite well. Anyway he was ahead of me which was very impressive in the circumstances. He was really tough. I just scraped round about seventh or eighth. What was particularly nice was the conveniently situated bistro where we all met for dinner in the evenings and in spite of our competitiveness relaxed together. We all enjoyed our time on the Ile de Bendor so much that they held the championship there the following year. It was much more of a struggle, but I still managed to win.

My most disappointing moment in my Laser career? Well there was this chap Friedhelm Lixenfeld - I think he was the City Engineer in Hamburg - and he won the Grand Masters for the first time in 1988. I first joined the Grand Masters in '89 at Aarhus, Denmark, as I said earlier. At the time I was lying second to Friedhelm; that was I think race three or four. We were reaching along and I had just got past him when in that moment of elation I let the sheet go and rolled in to windward. It took me so long to roll the boat right over and come back up again that of course I had blown it. However I came in fourth. Lixenfeld won the Grand Masters not only in 1989 but the following year as well - three times in all. The next year the championship was in New Zealand, and not surprisingly, having won it three times, he decided it was too far to go.'

Nick joined the Club in 1982. 'I found it very valuable sailing on the London Corinthian reach for seven or eight years because sailing Olympic courses on the open sea can make you very unconscious of tides, whereas at Hammersmith you are supremely aware of the tide, or if you aren't you won't do very well. There is a great deal of satisfaction in getting it right and you can do well even if you are not inordinately fit because it is all a matter of cunning, guile and luck, and judging when to cross the river and so on.

One very good trick was to watch what Hugh Kemlo did. I like sailing in tight company and in very close proximity to the shore. I find that jolly, quite cosy really. I have to admit that I have become quite irritated in a northerly, because the wind is so cut up that you constantly get put aback; but it is pleasant in a south westerly when you beat up river and then run back; then life is easy. The most difficult part is in an easterly when you've got to beat against the tide.

The other thing I like about Hammersmith is the relative informality of the racing, the tremendously good spirit and pleasant company and very few people exploiting the rules and being too sharp and that sort of thing. It is gentlemanly but people do know what they are doing. You can go to many clubs and find that people have no idea of the rules.'

Robin Johnson taught himself sailing as a child using model yachts on the Round Pond in Kensington Gardens. He bought his first Laser in 1980 having previously sailed almost every sort of boat from an eight-berth cruising catamaran to Hornets, Fireballs Simeon Bull's old Fourteen *Fleur de Lys* to a Flying Dutchman. Robin was in the F.D. Olympic Training Squad in 1978 with Rodney Pattison.

'I was attracted to the Laser because of its simplicity and the fact that there would be no problems about replacing gear or getting repairs done. Having sailed such a variety of boats, I found no great difficulty in sailing my Laser. The main thing, I think for the beginner, is tying all those knots and then when you undo them remembering how to rig her properly again. Sometimes it is quite difficult to remember which bit of rope does what and also some of the adjustments are quite hard to reach once you are out on the water - especially the kicker. Another problem for beginners is knowing how many purchases to have on the kicker, the clew outhaul and the Cunningham, as these can vary between 13-1 and 2-1. I have my kicker at 6-1 which gives me the purchase I want.

Of course launching at Hammersmith when it's wind against tide can prove difficult; those conditions will also need a lot of short-tacking when racing. Then there are the gusts of wind coming in between the trees and buildings and the real windshifts, and you must decide what course to steer when the wind is light and you are running back against the tide. You can never tell exactly what will happen at London Corinthian; you may get four hundred yards ahead on one lap and lose it on the next one.

Some of my worst moments on the river, or funniest which ever way you like to look at it, have been in windy weather when the race has just started and one has capsized just beforehand, so drifting upstream one is already over the line. Then there was a particularly embarrassing race when Nick Paine and I got our mainsails tangled - my boom was between his main and boom - when going round the mark. We finished 1st and 2nd but decided to retire, much to the delight of Una-Jane who was behind us and ended up the winner. Then in *Fleur de Lys*, with Vivien Cherry as crew, capsizing and finding a fish swimming in the bottom of the boat when we managed to right her. Sailing aside, our stretch of water must be one of the best places in London to enjoy the sunset, and some of my most memorable sails have been in the evening with that wonderful orange glow lighting up the sky and colouring the water.'

Paul Williamson was brought up in the depths of Hampshire reading Arthur Ransome books and longing to sail, but unable to do so as there was nowhere suitable nearby.' I made do building life size boats which could be 'sailed' on the lawn out of greengrocers' boxes, with broomsticks lashed together for spars and sheets for sails.When I moved to Strand on the Green in 1946 it was a marvellous opportunity to learn to sail. I did it by borrowing boats locally. No buoyancy either in the boat or on oneself but nobody seemed to mind, and I remember sailing great big 14 ft clinker built boats with bamboo spars, and thinking how clever I was to allow the water to run along the top of the gunwhale without its coming over the edge. I had not learnt then that from every point of view it was better to keep the boat upright.

The first boat I actually bought was a Heron and I used

to sail her single-handed even down to Hammersmith for Strand on the Green's annual visit to the London Corinthian. That was when I first saw the Corinthians in action and I remember the Fireflies, with coloured cotton sails in those days, and thinking how marvellous they all looked and longing to come down here again. I joined the Club in 1957 but prior to that I was acting in Birmingham for some years, and it was not until 1959 that I was able to start sailing seriously at the Club with my very old Firefly, *Whistler* (159), which had a suit of beautiful mulberry-coloured sails. It was just about this time that everyone was turning to terylene and one had to follow suit in order to compete. By 1961 coloured sails were a thing of the past.

I bought my Laser in 1978 and called it *Roxanne* after the heroine in one of my shows, Cyrano de Bergerac. The reason I like the Laser apart from it being one design is that I find it easier to sail and very responsive compared particularly to an Enterprise which I think is not a well-designed boat although marvellous of its kind and I enjoyed mine thoroughly, but they do get out of control very easily going into a death roll from which it is impossible to recover. The O.K. was excellent, but the problem was that one had to spend an awful lot of time shaving bits off the mast from one place and sticking them on somewhere else to modify the bend of the mast. It was a relief to think when I bought the Laser that I would have more time to spend on my acting career rather than on constantly titivating the boat.

I find when sailing the Laser that it is much easier to control in heavy weather than an Enterprise; on a run for example when a gust hits you, if you get aft quickly you can dampen out the death roll by very strong movement of the tiller and mainsheet and by keeping the boat completely upright.

I have been very happy sailing at the Club and I think one

of the reasons is the very good atmosphere there. The rules are observed but they are applied in a friendly and courteous manner. When people do get too keen and there is a shouting match out on the water things tend to get resolved in the bar over a pint or two. There are protests occasionally, but I think that this probably has to happen in order to maintain standards. One of the major improvements to the racing scene since the days when I started sailing is the change in the rules which allows you to do a 360 or 720 as appropriate rather than retire the minute you make some minor error of judgement such as touching a leeward boat or a mark, however slight the contact. That was sometimes very disappointing.'

Hugh Kemlo started sailing with his father when he was three and learned dinghy racing while crewing for Paul Williamson at Strand on the Green. Hugh joined the Club in 1959 with his Firefly *Bamboozle*. He met me there when I turned up with a brand new Firefly and absolutely no idea of how to sail her. He bought his first Laser in 1978, probably called *Tin-Tin*. He buys a new one every four or five years, calling them either *Captain Haddock* or *Tin-Tin* alternately.

'I enjoy Laser sailing because it is a superb design - very simple, a true one design, light, easily-handled and very exciting to sail in a blow. The only negative aspects, for me, are that sailing a Laser does not involve the teamwork and camaraderie of a two person boat like, say a Fourteen, which I particularly enjoy. That is why I seldom do any serious Laser Open Meetings, as it is a bit lonely driving all those miles on one's own. That having been said the Laser is a near perfect one design boat; there are no rig adjustments that are either needed or permitted; whereas with a Fourteen, tuning and rig adjustments were a time consuming if enjoyable obsession. The Fourteen also needed plenty of care and varnishing, so I do find that the Laser feels a little bit sterile by comparison. It is more like owning a car - a machine from which you expect and receive a certain amount of performance for a few years and then finding it is time to trade her in for another. This of course, suits me with my career demanding more and more of my time.

I always enjoy sailing at the Club as the constantly changing conditions mean that no race is like another. One can never relax as one is constantly thinking about the tide; where it is strongest; where the eddies are and unless the wind is straight down the river you have to hunt for it. These local conditions train excellent sailors with skills in all departments other than fast reaching. River sailors always do well wherever tides or fluky conditions are a factor.

The main snag with our water is that you never get any decent fast reaches, and it is on this point of sailing that the Laser comes into her own. The problem for our stretch of the river is that when the wind is either in the north or south it gets cut up by the buildings on the one hand or trees on the other. The best conditions for the Laser are when there is a strong south-westerly with planing conditions. When the wind is in the north-east and there is all that short-tacking to be done, I prefer the Enterprise which is particularly effective in those conditions. Of course it doesn't always work out this way, as I might have booked up my crew before I know what the wind is going to do.'

I next talked to Una-Jane who took up Lasers at a much younger age than Nick, Robin, Paul and Hugh. 'I first learned to sail with Peter Hinton, crewing for him in a Firefly. He was and still is an excellent instructor; patient as well as being an expert sailor, so I gained confidence quickly. I bought my own Firefly at the age of sixteen and sailed her with Diana Clarke at the Club for two years, taking turns at helming and crewing.

The Lasers were just beginning to arouse interest at this time. After Diana left home (and me) I had no permanent crew and thought that the answer was to get a single-handed boat. Although I regretted losing the opportunity of pottering about mending and varnishing a wooden hull, I was enthusiastic about the very short time needed to prepare a Laser to sail because I was nearly always behind schedule, so often arrived at the Club at the last moment just before the Blue Peter. I managed to slip the mast into its stepping and launch the boat into the river without centre plate, rudder or boom in position and usually sorted it out in the next few minutes!

To begin with I found learning to sail a Laser frustrating. I had two specific difficulties. I found the boat slid sideways a lot more than I was used to in the Firefly, and I was not accustomed to the need to keep the boat absolutely flat on the water. I puzzled about why this should be and blamed my lack of weight for the second problem. The best days were those with light flukey winds, for instance north-westerlies, when I was able to plane on the gusts sooner than anyone else.

I was still learning the importance of playing the windshifts on our stretch of the river and the solution to both problems gradually emerged. Lasers are very sensitive to oversteering; they need to be controlled through the tilt of the hull as well as the rudder. The need to control the angle of heel led me to adopt the correct steering position on the beat; sitting right at the front of the cockpit, leaning forwards as well as out on the toestraps. In strong winds I found it was essential to keep the boat flat in the puffs by getting my weight out instantly and simultaneously letting out the sheet according to how quickly the boat was starting to heel. It's also essential to sail her fairly free while on the wind. I found myself steadily improving. I was no longer being lapped; then I was a tail-ender and next challenging Hugh Kemlo and Robin Johnson - I even beat Hugh once for the Dark Wind Trophy, I think, fairly recently.

I have been to Open Meetings at Hayling Island Sailing Club and at Derwent Reservoir. The H.I.S.C. sets courses in Chichester Harbour, with its many sandbanks. It was blowing hard and I missed the start, capsizing twice before crossing the line. I persevered though and only gave up when I had gone twice round the circuit and been lapped by the leading man. I saw the leading lady at the prize-giving; she was a big girl and probably weighed about 12 stone. No wonder she kept quite a few of the men behind her.

The R.Y.A. Ladies Championship is held in the autumn in Lasers, 470's and Toppers. It is an Open Meeting; and at the end of the two day series there was a video and discussion of the highlights and tactics, led by Jim Saltonstall, the R.Y.A. coach. I didn't disgrace myself, coming fifth or sixth in a fleet of ten, but the same heavy lady won.'

In spite of the obvious enthusiasm of those I spoke to and others such as Philip Rayner, class captain and Rear Commodore Sailing in 1980, the late Andy Hewett, Justin Scott, Simon Beeby and Mark Dowling, the Lasers never really caught on at the Club as much they did elsewhere. Open Meetings attracted up to sixteen boats sometimes, but as with the O.K.s they were often unlucky in having very little wind; that and the tide might well be the reason for so few visitors and equally the small turnouts today.

Chapter 14
Linden House, 1962 - 1994
and
the Battle over the Lease

Since 1962 many of those who have passed the Club on their weekend stroll, particularly during winter months up to 1982 when turnouts were bigger, must have stopped and watched with interest members sailing even if they shivered inwardly at the idea of capsizing. They no doubt turned to admire the mid-18th splendour of Linden House and thought how lucky and rich the members must be to have such a clubhouse; probably one of the finest sailing clubs architecturally in the land.

After allowing for losing for perfectly valid reasons the Fireflies, the O.K.s and in time the Fourteens during those years, the members enjoyed splendid sailing, even if in summer quite naturally there was almost an exodus to Open Meetings at other clubs. However passers-by would have been wrong in their impression of our clubhouse. We have all had many happy hours there and I hope we will continue to do so, but for those responsible for the Club it has been an uphill struggle from the start; I have no wish to labour the point, but anyone who thinks otherwise should read the thirty years of Management Committee minutes. It makes depressing reading.

The Commodores during these years were: Philip Withers-Green, 1960-63; Christopher Buckley, 1964-67; Simeon Bull, 1968-71; Bill Simpson, 1972; Bob Salt, 1973-74; Sir Anthony Lousada, 1975-76; Don Storrar, 1977-78; Tony Robinson, 1979-81; Philip Rayner, 1982-85; Sally Dixon (now Buckley) 1986-88; Francis Brown, 1989-90; Simon Beeby 1991-93; and Tony Robinson, 1993-1994. They and their officers and many others brought in to help on an ad hoc basis deserve great credit and the fact that the Club has survived at all is due to their unstinted effort. Members may be relieved to read that this chapter does include some sailing matters and is not purely about the much greater domestic and financial problems of Linden House compared with those encountered at the old Club. There are also some members who are no longer with us but must not be forgotten.

In 1961 the Borough Council asked the Club if it would join in a goodwill 'Jumelage' visit to Zaandam, outside Amsterdam, which would feature sailing as well as a number of different sports. All the visitors - and there was a third group from Boulogne-Billancourt, a suburb south-west of Paris with access to the Seine - would be housed and entertained by Dutch families. Sally with her usual thoroughness has kept all the details including a press-cutting or two from Hammersmith papers of the results. Chris Buckley was responsible for organising the Club's team of eight and he and Mike Cook won their races when they got there. Everyone - the Hammersmith contingent was fully representative of the Borough apart from the Club - appears to have had a good time.

Following this there was a return visit to Hammersmith in 1963 when the Club was responsible for finding beds for the Dutch and French sailors. I haven't been able to find out who did this, but someone succeeded in coping with the problem and there were two days racing in Fireflies and Enterprises. After the racing everyone naturally repaired to the changing rooms. I gather that John Salt and other male Club members were somewhat awestruck to see a highly nubile Dutch girl emerging stark naked from the shower, and towelling herself down completely unconscious of the silence that descended on the normally noisy changing room scene. Changing rooms in Holland were evidently unisex.

The next Jumelage visit was to Boulogne-Billancourt in 1966. The Club team was Mike Cook, Tony Newman, Lee Storrar, Hugh and Miranda Kemlo and Simeon and Annick Bull. They won convincingly, in spite of a noisy collision stem to stem between a Dutch boat and Tony Newman's. After the sailing was over Mike Cook was prevailed upon to give a speech of thanks - in French. He wrote it out in English and had someone translate it. When he got to his feet he found it was virtually illegible - probably Annick's writing - so there were many stumblings and pauses till in desperation he said: 'C'est tous. Merci, mille fois voiliers Francais et Hollandais.' and sat down. Whereupon there were roars of laughter and the French Commodore in excellent English complimented him on the speech he had made with such 'esprit.'

The fourth, and last Jumelage visit, was to Hammersmith again in 1969. Simeon was Commodore and when I mentioned the subject his face went white. Having a French wife and having made frequent cruises to France, Simeon knew that young French sailors were 'très sportif.' It is a fact that French sailors, of all ages, pride themselves on sailing into harbour. I've seen six small keel boats plane into Concarneau from the Isles de Glenans sailing school without causing any apparent damage to anyone. 'If you go down below you just find a lot of smelly sleeping bags,' said Simeon.

With that in mind, Simeon thought an easy way out of the accommodation problem would be to billet the young ones on the Club, although part of the aim of the visit was to further mutual understanding by the British inviting the French to stay in their own houses. When I taxed him on these arrangements he said it was one of the worst problems in all his time as Commodore. 'I knew the 'jeunesse' were used to hardship and thought they would be quite comfortable on the Club floor.' His one concession was hiring two metal coathanger racks.

Unfortunately among the young were some middle-aged French sailors. These were found homes, but one man, the Commodore of the French club, objected to the quality of his host's home and demanded to be re-housed. I asked Simeon if it was true that he had to wake his parents late at night, probably only Lady Bull took any action, and ask them to provide the French Commodore with a bed. "Quite probably. There are some things in one's life one tries to blot out of one's memory and the 1969 Jumelage was one of mine."

In 1962, the year the Club took over Linden House, Gil Winfield became a member. Gil was American by birth and lived next door to The Dove, with his wife Elizabeth, son - 'young Gil' and daughter Una-Jane. He became one of the most popular members on account of his charm, sense of humour, laid back manner and willingness to help young members and the Club. He owned a lovely Thames sailing barge yacht, *The Seagull*, on which he used to take many members on fairly boozy trips to Pinmill and elsewhere. *The Seagull* was also 'committee' boat sometimes on races down to The Tower, and on one occasion was in attendance at P.O.W. week at Lowestoft. More important he took over the rescue boat chore from Peter Roberts, whom I have already mentioned, and drove it every weekend for about ten years and also served as Harbourmaster for the same time.

Although I capsized many times, Gil never bothered to come to my aid, as I think he knew I preferred to right my boat by myself; this was no reflection on Gil's boathandling ability but some drivers and indeed the river police were not as seamanlike as he was. Thus I never experienced the almost Bateman cartoon-like experience of being asked, as were those crews who appeared to be in real difficulties and hung spluttering and shivering to the gunwale of the rescue boat: 'Do you have water with your whisky?' Whenever Gil went out in the rescue boat he took with him a square grey metal case which contained six metal beakers, a bottle of Islay Mist malt whisky and a small metal bottle of water.

Gil's wife Elizabeth was also wonderful and each year made a quite amazing Christmas cake illustrating a different theme or book, which together with Gil's rum punch went down very well at the annual party after carol singing along the riverside organised by Mrs. Christopher Clarke.

In January 1963, there was the series of team races against the Norwich Frostbite Sailing Club; this event began in 1954 and still of course takes place even if not in Fireflies. At that time the Club fleet consisted of forty three Enterprises, twenty seven Fourteens and twenty one Fireflies. In the autumn of that year, the Royal Thames Yacht Club celebrated the reopening of its splendid new clubhouse in Knightsbridge by holding a regatta on The Serpentine for Fourteens, Merlin Rockets, 12 ft Nationals, Enterprises and Fireflies sailed by teams from Ranelagh, Tamesis as well as our own Club. There were two boats per class per team. The Club's team were: Tony Newman, Dr. Paul Smart, John and Jeremy Vines, Mike Cook, Jeremy Pudney, Chris Buckley and Peter Hinton. I don't think the police had been informed, so there was quite a lot of official aggravation about the park being invaded by boats on trailers - trailers being strictly forbidden. Diplomacy prevailed, the races were sailed and then everyone repaired to the R.T.Y.C. where there was excellent hospitality, for competitors and spectators who needed thawing out. The Club won this contest for the first time in 1969 and the regatta is sailed for each year, but not with Fourteens.

1969 was the year in which Jeremy Pudney came 2nd in the Burnham Icicle to which a few stalwarts went each year. The Fireflies had done well in the R.N.V.R. Trophy and come 2nd in the Bosham Belle. Then there was the 24-hour West

Lancs race at Southport, the London Pirates Trophy, the visits to Seaview Yacht Club and no doubt many other races apart from all those on class 'circuits.' As far as I know, these races continue to be sailed to this day.

The domestic and financial problems which faced the Club in 1962 were virtually a question of: 'Plus ça change, plus c'est la même chose.' They can be summarised quite quickly. Rising expenditure and poor financial husbandry; dishonest stewards; a virtually static membership and the usual arrears in subscriptions and mooring fees; loss-making social events; the high cost of maintaining pontoons, piles, ramps, the rescue boat and delapidations. The last item can be dealt with quickly.

Although the Borough Council had supposedly renovated Linden House, the roof leaked into the steward's flat from the start and there were many other faults which needed attention. The Council took full reponsibility, but the problems had not been anticipated and caused more work for the Commodore and his officers. I do not think the repairs to the roof were ever carried out properly as the leaks have recurred several times over the last thirty years, according to the minutes, and must be partly responsible for the dry-rot and wet-rot which was discovered last autumn.

The really serious problem was financial. Even in 1964 fears were expressed about the Club's position. Expenditure had risen alarmingly since 1963; rent, rates, insurance, heating and lighting had gone up by £800. Income was down: membership was down; and social events had been poorly supported, which prompted Chris Buckley, the Commodore, to say: 'If members want social functions they must support them.' There would be a loss in 1965 and subscriptions would have to go up to bring in at least £1,000 extra. The Club had so far only been liable to half the agreed rent, but in 1966 the full amount would be payable.

The Club could not have foreseen that the Wages Council Standing Orders, 1963, would increase the steward's pay to an amount far beyond what the Club could afford if overtime was to be included. Club hours would have to be changed which could have a knock-on effect on membership. It was a Catch 22 situation. In an attempt to make the Club more attractive and bring in members a bar billiards table and a 'fruit machine' were hired, and a deep freeze bought for the kitchen. Such items, however, justifiable, were expensive. Aggravating the expenditure was the drop in bar profits.

The succession of unsatisfactory stewards might have had its funny side had it not meant such serious financial loss and waste of the Treasurer's and in the end a whole sub-committee's time. For some months the members took over the bar and the profit soared to 24·5 per cent, almost twice what it had been with the last steward. Barbara King-Morgan, Ted's widow, came up from Devon and for some weeks ran the bar full-time, staying in the Club till the next steward arrived. He turned out to be an ex-River Policeman; a year or so later there was a Dutchman - ex-Holland-America Line - with an English wife. If they weren't dishonest, they were 'tipplers' or gave short measures. The last reprobate, before I leave the subject, was a Jekyll and Hyde character. The immediate impression he gave was of being a pleasant man and one who had strength of character. He and his wife had been taken on in June 1969. By 1971, in spite of being considered by many members to be a very good steward, the writing was on the wall to the Treasurer, Nicholas Christoson. In July he resigned as his repeated complaints to the Management Committee regarding his suspicions about the steward fell on deaf ears. His assistant, Miss Barbara Robinson, succeeded him, thereby becoming the first lady officer to serve on the Management Committee, a position which was confirmed at the 1972 elections. Barbara reported that the Club was running at a loss of approximately £1,200 a year. In the last 12 months £247 had been lost on social occasions. The Commodore, like Chris Buckley before him, went on record as saying that he felt members were just not interested in social activities. Furthermore, Barbara continued, the membership situation was as bad as ever. Fifty-four members had resigned and fifty five had joined. The Club could just survive until October when the subscriptions for 1972 were due. Coming to the catastrophic drop in bar profits, Barbara reported that the steward was refusing to give her detailed bar transactions and even the till rolls. Under the circumstances she asked: "Who is running the Club, the Committee or the steward; he has delusions of grandeur?"

Simeon Bull, Commodore at the time, set up a special sub-committee to investigate the whole bar situation, and recommend how the finances of the Club should be run in the future. Dudley Vaughan was chairman. Other members were Gerry Speidel, Barbara Robinson and Chris Buckley. The financial sub-committee reported that bar profits should be at least 30 per cent - when the steward had been on holiday and the bar was being run by the members they were 36·6 per cent - whereas on investigation they amounted to only sixteen - 18 per cent. Their recommendation was that the steward should be dismissed. However such was his popularity that James Bridge-Butler organised a petition to persuade the Management Committee to think again, and even Gil Winfield stressed the humanitarian aspect '.... wife and children.' The Commodore replied that he did not think the steward's financial situation 'was all that bad' because his children were educated in Scotland.

The steward accepted the Club's demand for his resignation which was to be as from 22nd October, but he did not finally leave until early in the New Year. What is more before the Management Committee's meeting on 9th November, a bugging device on a wire lead which led up to the steward's flat was found behind a radiator and had to be neutralised. I wonder how long it had been there. The final piece of villainy was discovered in August 1972; the steward had forged references from the Club in order to get a similar position elsewhere.

Directly the steward was relieved of his duties, David Widdowson, who was Vice-Commodore for four years, organised a House-Committee of Mrs. Lavender Clarke, Mrs. Stephanie Nicholls, Miss Caroline Brace, Mrs. Rita Vaughan, Simeon's wife, Annick, and Frank Jones, who would be responsible for catering; while Johnnie Evans, Gerry Speidel, Bill Buckley and Alex Edwards would take it in turns to look after the bar. Obviously measures would now have to be taken for the Management Committee to control and approve all expenditure and a means had to be found to increase income, one being the immediate sale of the *Golden Enterprise* to Cambridge University for £275.

The Management Committee had come in for a bit of criticism from the Finance Sub-Committee, and Simeon, who was in his last year as Commodore, realised that the adminstrative nettle had to be grasped. At the A.G.M. in January 1972, he emphasised how the Club had grown into a large financial unit, calling for a continuing system of paper work. It was essential that each Officer, on his appointment, should be provided with full instructions in writing from his predecessor regarding the nature of his duties and how they should be carried out.

By April 1972, Christopher Clarke, assistant Secretary, and later Secretary, had found a new steward through the Ex-Officers' Association - he also had the tedious task of redrafting the Club rules. Alistair and Nan Wicks arrived in April and quickly became very popular although it was their first time in such a job. They lasted until 1978 when Alistair died of a heart attack. Jim and Avril Earle followed them for a few years and left of their own accord early in 1983. 'Bonzo' and Kate took over the catering for three months and not only produced good food, but also enhanced the general atmosphere in the bar. Then in April, John and Anne Billington were engaged as steward and cook and were a great success, increasing bar profits and income from room hire considerably; they stayed until 1989.

Bill Simpson, who took over as Commodore in 1972 had proposed the previous year at a Club meeting that a portrait should be painted of A.P.H. and suggested that Ruskin Spear, who lived locally, was the obvious artist to approach. This received unanimous agreement and Bill and Tom Fielding saw Ruskin who agreed to do it for £500. Ruskin would have to paint it from a photograph, as A.P.H. had had a stroke from which he died in November 1971. Early the following year Ruskin told the Commodore that the National Portrait Gallery had heard of the commission, and had asked for 'first refusal.' The Management Committee decided that they would not stand in Ruskin's way, particularly as he said he'd do 'a copy.' Bill Simpson and Tom Fielding told him, according to the minutes, that the Club would like A.P.H. to be wearing if possible a reefer and the Club tie.

However it was only when it came to write this chapter that I discovered from the N.P.G. that in the original portrait A.P.H. was wearing everyday clothes including a green tweed jacket - which obviously was not very suitable for the Club. I'm ashamed to say that none of the Herbert family have ever been to the N.P.G. to see the original; in my case because I thought it would obviously be similar to the one that has hung on the staircase for so long. Ruskin must have got a photograph of A.P.H. in his petty-officer's uniform from my mother, but she never said anything to me about it. Regardless of all that, I and everyone who knew him think the portrait is an excellent likeness of him, and it was a considerable achievement of Ruskin's to 'dress him up' correctly with the right First-World War medal ribbons and petty-officer's crossed anchors and two 'good conduct' stripes. Ruskin finished the 'copy' in January 1974. VAT had by that time raised its ugly head, and Ruskin reduced the cost of the painting to allow for that, which was nice of him.

The financial scenario of 1964-65 continues to the present day. Inflation, higher rates, the arrival of VAT; the problem of social functions, falling membership - it was five hundred and twenty in 1965 and dropped to an all-time low of two hundred and twenty five in 1985; the loss of the Fireflies, O.K.s and all but two Fourteens - the others having gone to Queen Mary's in the winter and elsewhere in the summer - must have been a contrubutory factor; falling bar profits and the cost, let alone work of keeping the pontoons afloat and eventually buying new ones; and also the rescue launch. All these factors resulted in subscriptions and entrance fees having to go up ten times in twenty years.

For years there was concern about the safety and reliability of the blue rescue boat which had been bought second hand in 1952 and came with us from the old Club. Peter Roberts had even made the long trip down river and through the Swale to help out in the 1961 P.O.W. week at Whitstable; this meant nothing to him after his experience driving Air Sea Rescue craft during the war. On the Thursday, the day of the P.O.W. race itself there were gusts of more than 35 knots and only seven boats out of fifty survived before the race was stopped. First in was Mrs. Robert 'Mouse' Birkett, followed by amongst others Simeon Bull crewed by David Shelley and myself, crewed as usual by Chris Newnes, for years now known as 'Knuckles.'

About the time Simeon Bull became Commodore in 1968,

a Pool of London Race was about to start when Peter Roberts, the rescue boat driver who had taken her to Whitstable, yelled out to Johnnie Evans in his O.K., *Paper Tiger*, that the launch was taking water. Someone managed to caulk a hole which was found with some rope and the passengers were sent up for'ard for the day. Peter Roberts on his return asked Johnnie to look at the boat, knowing he was a boatbuilder. 'Only one look told me that the boat was on her way out. David Widdowson, Rear-Commodore Bosun, later in the bar asked me if I could help him find a diesel G.R.P. launch cheap. At the time I was working for 'Water Craft' at East Molesey, making ships' lifeboats.

'We were shown a boat under a tree and covered in leaves which had obviously been there for some time. When we'd cleared away the leaves I saw she was a class 'C' lifeboat which had been made for a Water Board but didn't suit their purpose. It was fitted with a Lister 'L.O.2' engine. 'Just what we want said David.' Mr. Abrahams of Water Craft said the price was £650. David gave 'Abe,' as apparently everyone called him, a deposit and he and Johnnie motored back to the Club, very pleased with their purchase.The balance was paid, but a few days later 'Abe' rang Johnnie in a state of some anxiety. He'd given him the wrong price. It didn't even cover the cost of the engine. However philosophically he said it was his mistake and he'd at least got rid of 'the boat under the tree.' The Club may have got the boat cheap - it is the same one that is moored downstream of the pontoons - but a vast amount of money over the years has been spent on it: a new engine has been bought and lifted in and many new rebuilt propellers, a new shaft and bearings fitted. Johnnie's postscript to me is rather sweet: 'David Widdowson got A.P.H.'s permission to call the new rescue launch *Water Gipsy* after his war-time M.T.B.!'

The matter of safety was obviously occupying Simeon

Bull's mind. When I saw him he said: 'There were always two schools of thought - one said we've never had a bad accident yet so we needn't bother - and the other who said statistically we've never had a bad accident yet so we should bother. I took this point - getting closer every day. Rescue boats always seemed to break down; there should be some form of backup.' Simeon had the brilliant idea of asking the Royal Lifesaving Society if they would like to use the Club as a winter HQ to practice on. So for many years they helped with their dory to provide rescue services.

The pontoons and piles problem was the most unsatisfactory feature of taking over Linden House. Christopher Buckley was chairman of the sub-committee set up to deal with it. Other members were Geoff Freestone, Peter Roberts but undoubtedly the most qualified was Tom Hill Tom was a professional Civil and Structural Engineer, employed in those days by the old L.C.C.; he only left County Hall when Maggie Thatcher weilded her axe.

At the time of the move the pontoon sub-committee's plans for the accommodation of dinghies was for the Sandys pontoon and another pontoon to be brought up from the old Club and placed alongside Atlanta Wharf. A new wooden pontoon, which was to be made by Richmond Slipways and paid for by a Sports Council Grant, would be placed where the Lyons pontoon had been till it sank and take the main launching ramp. The contract for the pontoon was organised by Johnnie Evans, who was Rear-Commodore Bosun at the time. Thanks to his Tough Bros training he knew who would produce what was needed at a reasonable price.

The next problem was the Sandys pontoon. This was twenty years old and showed signs of sinking. The 40 gallon oil drums, which originally had been found by Storm Roberts, and the aluminium framework which kept them in were beginning to corrode. Quotes were obtained for a steel pontoon, but the Club did not have the money. Substitute oil drums were found to be very expensive, Thanks, however, to Johnnie Evans's father, thirty six plastic 'Kosher' barrels, originally used for importing Israeli wine, were bought for £59.40. I presume there was a working party to help Johnnie substitute the barrels, but there is no mention of one. However 'Woodie,' was probably there, as apart from becoming Rear-Commodore (Bosun) and driving the rescue boat when Gil retired, he like Johnnie and a few others were the hard core who kept the pontoons afloat. The upstream pontoon was the next to need attention. At Gil's suggestion polyurethene foam was pumped into it.

The ramps - in time there would have to be two - were a real problem. Tom Hill was appalled to find that the Lyons launching ramp at low or even half-tide must have been at an acute angle; eight strong men could carry a rowing 'eight' up or down, but it would be hazardous for dinghies on trolleys. This is where the Club was lucky to have a professional engineer at hand. There is not space to go into details, save to say that although the Club could not afford the two steel pontoons and robust ramps which Tom would have liked the ramp problem was solved and two of them were paid for to a large extent by the Central Council for Physical Recreation.

Three pontoons were essential, because in the late '60's until the late '70's there were often forty-boat turnouts, whether for an Open Meeting or for a three or four class Club race. This obviously meant a second opening in the river wall, which the Council had anticipated, but only the L.C.C. Public Health Department could authorise it. It was fortunate that Tom worked in the L.C.C. and knew the 'right people.' Initially the officials were worried by the risk of flooding and tideboards not being replaced, but thanks to Tom being a colleague they approved the Club's application quite quickly. The L.C.C.

provided the criteria for the design, and Tom produced working drawings and specifications. These were approved by the L.C.C. and Tom put the job out to tender on behalf of the Club and it was completed in 1968. Prior to this, Captain Dear, of the P.L.A., had condemned the piles - another legacy of the Council's - so four new wooden piles were driven in by Tough Bros at considerable expense.

The time and money spent on keeping the pontoons afloat did not stop until 1988 by which time the Club had two steel pontoons. To get the first of these was the decision of Don Storrar, Commodore in 1977, who organised an appeal fund, which raised approximately half the £3,845 needed. To help the appeal Sir Duncan Oppenheim, who joined the Club in 1950 and used to sail Fourteens offered screen prints of the 1977 Shackleton for £35; one-time chairman of British American Tobacco he painted in his spare time.

At the A.G.M. in 1973 Bob Salt became Commodore. Sir George Bull got up and said that he had list of officers in 1933 - forty years ago - when Bob was Vice-Commodore: 'It is a very happy thought that he has now been elected Commodore.' Having at last attained what he referred to as the 'hot seat,' I doubt if Bob really enjoyed his two years as Commodore, because of the problems the Club was suffering from, and the completely different spirit or almost lack of it in Linden House compared with the old Club. In his opening speech he said: 'The Club is facing a difficult year with rising prices and the effects of VAT. More than anything I would like to see a new spirit of enthusiasm and freedom from apathy in the Club; volunteers are needed for all manner of jobs around the place and it is quite wrong to expect the Steward to do everything.'

A year later referring to Simeon Bull's 'valuable analysis about the Club's needs in the matter of administration, the response by members had been disappointing.' Then in his valedictory speech as Commodore he spoke of apathy and complacency. 'Volunteers for working parties fail to materialise. We can't afford a paid bosun to clear out the mess in the undercrofts so members should do a little more to prevent the utter mess we can usually find there. The clubhouse is second to none and there is scope to putting it to greater use, and by not leaving all the donkey work to just a faithful few.'

In 1979, when the Club needed to carry out its responsibility for maintaining the inside of the Club and decoration generally, Tony Robinson, Commodore at the time, said he would organise working parties on a 'squad basis for two non-sailing weekends in the autumn to decorate the Clubhouse and clean out the undercrofts.' This meant that instead of merely announcing a date for a working party and hoping someone would turn up, definite commitments were required in advance and lists of names were prepared and posted on the notice board. It worked.

At the next Management Committee meeting, Philip McDanell, who was Vice-Commodore for four years, said he was attacking the decoration of the Club with the assistance of a sub-committee and by a mixture of working parties and contractors. He told me he had difficulties in getting working parties, so organised a visit to Young's Brewery in Wandsworth purely for the volunteers: 'It was a wonderful brewery with great beam engines and all very interesting. Eventually we reached the sampling room and everyone was given a half-pint mug which was a bit of a disappointment. But then we saw all the barrels of different ales. After half an hour our delightful guides said: 'Well gentlemen we think that's it.' Everyone looked very crestfallen, as they'd hardly had two pints.

Just then Mr. John Young came in. I'd taken the precaution of asking Stewart Morris to come along. 'Stewart,' Young said, 'I havn't seen you for thirty years.' Somehow I'd learned that

Young and Stewart had been fellow fighter-direction officers on an aircraft carrier during the war (Stewart got his OBE, not for winning a gold medal in Swallows in the 1948 Olympics, but for his manual on Fighter-Direction Procedure which was adopted by the R.N. after the war). The lovely ladies who had been escorting us looked very glum, as they realised that this was the beginning of a big session as indeed it was.'

It was only one example of Philip's initiative in getting things done, but it shouldn't, in my opinion, really have been necessary to organise such an operation to get volunteers. Phillip's efforts were remembered at the next A.G.M. when someone applauded them with the words: 'At least no one can accuse Philip of not being unable to organise a piss-up in a brewery.' There obviously were other occasions when people responded readily - during the redecoration in Sally's time as Commodore is a case in point; but there are too many mentions in the minutes, by different Club officers of all ages of volunteers not turning up when they said they would, for the point not to be made.

Another problem were social functions. It is true that many of them to begin with made a loss which must have been aggravating to Commodores generally, even if the bar profits had shown a considerable increase. However there had to be social functions if only for PR purposes, because otherwise members, certainly new members, would have thought the Club was absolutely dead. Obviously they had to be budgeted, promoted properly well ahead - making sure that the date didn't clash with some important Open Meeting on the circuits - and they didn't always have to have a marquee. If kept simple there was little danger of a financial disaster and there might well be a profit, but the members would certainly have had a lot of fun.

The most ambitious example I can remember was in the

late '60's, when John Salt and a team had the imaginative and nostalgic idea of transforming the men's changing room into a replica of the old Club's saloon. Two girls painted a mural of the saloon from photos, and the actual mahogany bar was produced from somewhere and French-polished. 'We found some of the original curve-backed chairs, little old tables, glasses and other mementoes. The shields made by Jack Holt and others for different trophies were hung up together with flags and contemporary cartoons. There was one of 'Dicky' Dixon standing in front of the Honours Board and saying: 'Perhaps I'll be Commodore one day;' another showed two girls chatting together with the caption: 'Of course once he's married me, I'll tell him I hate sailing.' The discotheque was in the changing room recess and in the darkest corner there was room for members to discuss other things than knots. In order to change its appearance even the clothes hooks were unscrewed and removed for the night. It was very successful but could never be repeated.

Philip McDanell told me how after joining the Club in 1971 he bought a Laser. After an Open Meeting I said: "When's the party?" He was told there wasn't one as they only lost money. I thought this ridiculous so I, Jonathan Hughes and 'Bonzo' put on a party. We charged 75p a head. 'Bonzo' cooked the chille con carne and I provided the music with my Hi-Fi equipment. We made a profit of £5.50 and handed it in to the Management Committee the next day.' Some parties made larger profits, such as those which featured Boulle, run by Dudley Vaughan or Gil Winfield. Then there was the Cowboy/Western all-night party. Three hundred people enjoyed a seven piece band; a steel band on the forecourt and a basement disco throughout the night. Gil Winfield ran the upstairs casino with 'slugs' of whisky at 25p a time and there was a constant barbecue. The suitably attired members, from Cavalry to

Redskin, enjoyed it immensely.

Simeon Bull, when Commodore, was aware of the need for the Club to be used and asked me to carry out a market research project to try to find out what members expected of the Club. The result was: 'A New Course To Steer.' I received over a hundred questionnaires back indicating what people wanted. I'm not certain whether it achieved anything, but I'd asked apart from catering and discos, did members want occasional films, lectures, and even 'bridge' evenings, which Johnnie Underwood did run for a time? What is relevant are the highly successful series of lectures given by Jonathan Clark over a series of years. As most people know Jonathan is highly qualified to give such lectures being an R.Y.A. coach and having won or been placed in a large number of different dinghy National Meetings.

Tuesday Club nights are not what they were. I am not being critical. There are lots of reasons. However I think it's worth recalling that for most of the '70's the Club every Tuesday evening was the centre of dinghy sailing for the country. This may sound an exaggeration but Philip McDannell and John Salt used virtually the same words. 'On Tuesday nights you could meet the top dinghy helmsmen and even top Admiral's Cup crews. They'd all be mixing in the bar, which was far more fun than going to the posher clubs in town. Bob Fisher, who was Rear-Commodore Sailing for several years, was influential, not only as a journalist and sailor, but in the earlier years with the Hornet fleet who originally met in a pub in Covent Garden. As a result Hornets raced for a time at the Club. Bob and Robo attracted a lot of people to the Club and increased the socialising between other clubs. The atmosphere - and the drinking - was great because everyone knew each other or got to know each other.'

In 1961 at the historic meeting which granted women

members full status with men, it was agreed that their entrance subscription would remain the same, until the Club had actually taken up residence. However it wasn't until December 1977, that the matter came up for discussion by the Management Committee. Tony Robinson, Rear-Commodore Sailing, said it was proposed to abolish the difference at the next A.G.M., but first he was going to look into the law on sex discrimination. The following month, he confirmed that male members were being discriminated against, an unusual misdemeanour, and entrance subscriptions were raised in line with those of men. Whether this was popular with women I don't know; perhaps not, but it meant that after eighty years women members had complete equality of rights and responsibilities.

In January 1982, Philip Rayner left the comparatively easy post of Rear-Commodore Sailing to become Commodore. He is a brave man because he must have known that most of his time would be spent negotiating the new lease with the Council from a not very strong position. However he received invaluable help from a sub-committee consisting of Hugh Kemlo, Peter Calder, Len Hawkes, John Salt and Philip McDanell. There is no point, let alone space, in doing anything more than summarising the lengthy negotiations which finally ended in a four-day Court action.

On 11th September the Council informed the Club that they were terminating the tenancy, but would not oppose an application for a new one. Philip Rayner replied that the Club wanted to stay in Linden House and asked for terms of a new lease. Early in 1983 the Borough Finance Department valued the Club rental at £9,000 a year and the Council proposed a 10-year lease for this sum. This was quite impossible from the Club's financial situation. Paul Collard had been engaged as the Club's solicitor. At an E.G.M. in December Mr. Collard reported that the Club had the right to the lease of the whole building and that it was improper and illegal of the Council to introduce a new tenant without a new lease being agreed by the Club. This was a reference to an application by the Council for a 'change of user' and notices had been fixed to the railings giving local residents twenty one days to object. The proposal was that a suitable tenant would be found for the downstairs rooms of the Club, which would mean of course that the Club would lose valuable revenue, without which it couldn't survive. Mr. Collard advised also that Linden House should be surveyed regarding its value and a reasonable rent.

Early the following year the Club on Mr. Collard's advice suggested a rental of £1,750 for seven years and engaged Counsel. The matter would probably go to Court, but the Club must be resolute. Philip McDanell warned that this sum for the next five years would use up all the Club's reserves and might therefore threaten sailing. Michael Beaman, the Club's surveyor endorsed the legal view. There were few, if any, comparables - especially a market value for a sailing club on a river. He advised the Club to look for a rent it could afford. In Court 'the ability to pay could have a significant factor in determining rent.' Neverthless it was not altogether surprising that the Council demanded a much better offer by 2nd August to avoid a Court action, so the Club suggested £3,000 a year.

In November 1984, the sub-committee had its first meeting with Counsel, who thought the Club had a good case. The Council had asked for a rent review. There was no progress in 1985. Paul Collard in September told the sub-committee that he did not think the Council had sufficient evidence yet to go to Court. The Council were rumoured to be thinking of asking for an even higher rent. Meanwhile Michael Beaman on the Club's behalf was collecting evidence. However early in January 1986, the Council asked the Club if it was ready to exchange evidence. Paul Collard replied "No." Philip Rayner stepped down, and Sally Dixon (as then) succeeded him as the Club's first lady Commodore and took up the cudgel in what had become the battle over the lease. The Club had raised its £3,000 offer to include 50 per cent of the net letting profits. The Council replied £5,000 plus 40 per cent of the gross income with a £1,000 minimum. The Council said it would not negotiate below this. The Management Committee voted to 'decline their offer.' Thus the Council would have to take the matter to Court.

It was a very anxious time for Sally because it was rumoured that the Council was thinking of a rent around £16,000. However Paul Collard in February said he was fairly optimistic, as was Michael Beaman who completed his report in April 'from which it would seem the Club had a strong case.' Amazingly nothing happened until August when Paul Collard wrote to the Council and said he had had no communication from them for eight months and wanted an exchange. Silence. The following January (1987) Paul Collard went on the attack and told the Council that as he had heard nothing from them, he would take out the appropriate application to the Court. To Court it went on 27th June and the case lasted until the 30th June. Sally and Philip Rayner were the Club's witnesses. When he had heard all the evidence, the Judge said in view of the complexity of the case he needed time to consider it. He would give his views therefore in mid-September.

In spite of the optimism of Paul Collard and Michael Beaman, Sally, her officers and the sub-committee were full of anxiety and the long wait until September was agonising. 'I was having sleepless nights and biting my nails with worry,' Sally told me. Hugh Kemlo asked Sally what she proposed to do if the judge's decision made the Club's future at Linden House impossible. 'I think we should go out with a splash rather than a whimper and have a great party in Cowes on members' offshore boats.' At the same time Sally went as far as making an approach to Ranelagh who said the Club members would be very welcome. The weeks passed all too slowly but eventually early in September Sally and Philip with the expert witnesses were summoned to the West London County Court.

The Judge's decision was that there should be a 14-year lease with two reviews at five and ten years. The Club was not to be charged for the maintenance of the exterior, which the Council valuer had sought during the case. The rent was to be £3,500, with an interim rent of £2,500. Costs, which were likely to be about £28,000, were granted in the Club's favour at the highest scale. The Club had won. 'We were over the moon with joy and relief,' Sally said, 'We opened a bottle or two of champagne back at the Club to celebrate. We also decided to have that party in Cowes in October, and the following year we said let's do it again. That's how the Offshore Rally started.'

Paul Collard told Sally in May 1988, that the Council had agreed to pay £23,000 of our costs, and the Club would only have to pay 15 per cent of the total fees plus VAT. The reason why the Club won so convincingly was due to the Judge being overwhelmingly impressed with the evidence of the Club's expert witnesses, Paul Collard and Michael Beaman. The Council's valuer in his evidence concerning other sailing and rowing clubs did not compare like with like - in particularly the Club's tidal disadvantage compared with clubs above Teddington. Also his arguments re a proposed rent were based purely on the square footage rather than 'the ability to pay,' which as Michael Beaman had prophesied early on would be very relevant.

Returning to the sailing scene, the Management Committee in October 1988, were considering 'can we really support next year's racing programme' because turnouts were so poor. Happily, however, there are grounds for optimism. Today the membership has risen to over three hundred and fifty. Paul Truitt's initiative in 1989 regarding Club Enterprises for members without boats and Simon Beeby's idea for 'beginners' nights which now have been formalised into 'Robbie's' regular instruction must have helped considerably and must be backed by other experienced helmsmen. This policy is just what is needed to encourage new members.

At the same time there has been an increasing interest in keelboats. A number of members have their own small cruisers. When therefore the Manhattan Yacht Club in 1988 invited the Club to send a team to race J.24s in New York Harbour there was no difficulty getting one together; and another one the following year, and yet again in 1990 when Monaco suggested a J.24 regatta. The Club's Offshore Rally has become more and more popular as indeed has offshore cruising, let alone racing, which will be dealt with in the final chapter. All this offshore sailing has brought members closer together. Finally the evening navigation classes, which were started in 1989, and more recently Bill Matcham's R.Y.A. approved diesel engine classes are welcome positive steps which have already brought new members to a Club paradoxically ruled by the tide. So I am glad to be able to end this chapter on a happy note.

Chapter 15

Ocean-Going Corinthians

One of the features of the last ten years or more is the growth of interest in offshore racing and cruising. It may not be too much consolation to successive Commodores wringing their hands over low turnouts on the river, but there's no doubt that our Club has a larger number of well-known ocean racers than have many sea-based clubs which is remarkable and something we should be proud about. There has been the occasional account of ocean races in the news letter, but there is seldom enough space there to tell what it is really like to race across the Atlantic the hard way, let alone to Australia.

Peter Hopps has supplied me with a list of the Club's ocean-going Corinthians who have competed in races. Apart from Peter himself, of course, they are Vivien Cherry, AnneFraser, Laurel Holland, James Chrismas, Mike Dunham, Jonathan Callow, Paul Rouse, Tony Short and Tony Blofeld. If there are others, I apologise. I'm going to take Peter's list of races and voyages in the chronological order.

The 1979 Parmelia Race

This was a race from Plymouth to Perth to commemorate the 150th anniversary of the founding of Western Australia. It was called The Parmelia Race after the barque which took the first settlers there in 1829. Mike Dunham, who joined the Club in 1975 was in the Merchant Navy before turning to the law and is a Master Mariner. In 1976 he went to the Boat Show with Jonathan Callow, who'd joined the Club a year after him and who had been a friend since their teens. Although now only in their early thirties, both had considerable experience of offshore racing and long-distance cruising. They saw some publicity about the race and entered there and then. Their non-existent boat was the first entry for the race, which ultimately had fifty seven entries from twelve countries and became the largest inter-ocean race ever staged. Mike was going to design the boat, while Jono as co-owner would look after the financing.

The boat was built by Len Last, a well-known boat builder, and a friend of Mike and Jono. All three decided that the boat was to be a fast easily driven two-masted schooner. Her overall length would be 55ft and her beam 9ft 6ins, very skinny by modern day standards. Talking to Peter Hopps, I remarked how narrow-gutted she was, and Peter quipped: "Well she had to get down Len Last's country lane didn't she?" Last's workshop was up a country lane ten miles outside Exeter. The actual design of the yacht was only settled after several models had been constructed and tested in Mike's bath at his home in Ealing.

The design was based on the highly successful *Sundancer*, which Last built, and which has sailed round the world four times. She was to have a steel frame on which three diagonal layers of mahogany would be cold-moulded. An unusual feature was the long hollow dagger board containing over 4 tons of lead which together with her 4ft keel would give her a draught of 10ft 6ins and a displacement of 12·5 tons. Her sail plan would be comparatively simple and designed to keep the centre of effort low. It would keep the yacht driving in stronger winds, and because no individual sail was too large, a crew of seven plus Mike, the skipper, would be able to handle the rig with ease. This was a much smaller crew than is normal for a boat of this size, making for less weight in people and provisions. Mike and Jono mortgaged most of their worldly goods to start the great work.

By early 1979 the hull was ready for painting and transporting to water. What they needed now was a sponsor to pay for fitting her out, buying the sails and provisioning her for the long voyage. Jono eventually found one in The Selection Trust Group, which then had world-wide mining interests. John du Cane, the company's chairman, had already read about the race and thought sponsorship of a yacht might be good for the Company's image in Western Australia. After meeting Mike and Jono he readily agreed. Not surprisingly it was decided to call the yacht *Seltrust Endeavour*, but she was going to sail under the Club's burgee.

In addition to the usual working up trials, *Seltrust Endeavour* more than 'qualified' for the 12,500 mile voyage to Perth by taking part in the disastrous 1979 Fastnet. During the beat across the Irish Sea to the rock they were under storm jib only. There were gusts of over 60 knots and waves heights sometimes 30-40 ft high. The late Bob Harris, a member of Selection Trust, was one of the crew and wrote a brilliant log of both the Fastnet and the Parmelia races: 'At 0400 when the storm was at its worst we were halfway across the Irish Sea. The waves now reached their maximum.... An unforgettable sight in the moonlight were the long ridges of water stretching away to the north-west and south east, coloured silver. It was, as Mike Dunham said, like standing on the North Downs and looking out across the Weald of Kent.' The yacht weathered the storm and performed well. Peter Hopps was in an Oyster 37 which although much smaller got round without any real trouble apart from extreme discomfort.

The Parmelia race started on 2nd September. There was one girl in *Seltrust Endeavour*'s crew; Terri Paul-Edwards, a qualified nurse whose services were going to be needed, over and above her work on deck; another was Paul Rouse, a member of the Club. What follows are extracts from Bob Harris's log when the yacht was in the South Atlantic and the Roaring Forties.

September 18th: Position: Lat. 28 degrees 24 mins N; Long. 13 degrees 30 mins W. 1,458 n.m. out from Plymouth. The waves built up during the night and we had a hectic run. The helmsman could not be on for more than half an hour at a time because of the concentration required steering the boat.... The wind freshened to about twenty five knots and when we caught a wave we did anything up to 15 knots. Most of the time we were doing between 10-12 knots. Christian came on deck and noticed that a little strand of the steering cable, which operates the quadrant on top of the rudder, was fraying where it went over the starboard shieve wheel. Mike and I looked at it.... and discussed what one could do if it broke. However we were fairly complacent that this would not happen - but even as we were talking about letting go the sheets and getting the sails down, the wire parted. We immediately had to put into effect all we had discussed. This could have been a very fraught operation, but the entire crew was on deck immediately and the whole thing was over in three minutes. The boat behaved very well during this time: she was still surfing when the wire broke, but ran on straight and didn't curl away either to port or starboard while we were dropping the sails.

We had the emergency tiller bolted on quickly.... It now fell to Mike to repair the broken cable with the wind still blowing twenty five knots. While he was removing the compass to get inside the steering pedestal and after that the various wires from the quadrant itself, I had to steer, using the tiller and lifting it to clear his hands.... which was rather tiring. Steering by tiller is extremely heavy as we found on the

Fastnet.... particularly when travelling at over 10 knots. After three hours' work Mike had rigged a new line and life returned to more or less normal again. We were not to know that the steering wires were to part several times before we reached Perth.

October 25th: Position: Lat: 32 degrees 38 mins S. Long: 08 degrees 06mins E. Total distance run 6,897 n.m. We had a real spot of excitement during the night. I woke to the sound of the flapping of sails. It sounded as if one of the sheet cars had come off its track. I lay there listening but the noise didn't go down. I then heard someone say the forestay had gone. I jumped out of bed, grabbed my harness from the loo and went on deck. I was still in my blue longjohns and red thermal socks. There was a chaotic scene on deck. The forestay had indeed broken and was flying out to starboard carried by the No 2 genoa, which was still hanked on. The wind carried the whole sail up to nearly masthead height, rattling and cracking in the darkness. The deck was bathed in light from the deck lamps which also lit up Mike, Paul and Sandy who were struggling to pull in the runaway No 2 by its starboard sheet. The foremast shook alarmingly while the forestay was thrashing around and I remember thinking that it was not going to stand much of that treatment before the whole thing came down. Paul, Sandy and I pulled the sail in while Mike slackened the halyard. I stuffed the sail, which had huge tears in it, down through the companionway.

We then took the end of the forestay - the deck fitting which held it had in fact broken, not the wire rope - and tied this to the sampson post. We also tied all the spare halyards to the same post and tightened them. The foremast steadied up although we were not able to get these jury support ropes nearly as tight as the forestay used to be.... The whole operation didn't take more than half an hour, although there was tremendous activity on deck during the course of it. While all this was going on, Harry was steering. The sea was reasonably rough, although it wasn't breaking over the boat, which was fortunate considering my state of undress. The wind was blowing about 30 knots and Harry had quite a time keeping the boat steady while the rest of us were cavorting about....

November 19th. Position: Lat 44 degrees 23 mins S; Long 79 degrees 48 mins E. Distance run from Cape Town where there had been a stopover 2,979 n.m. A day to remember! All through yesterday afternoon and the night we made good time speeding along under the superstar spinnaker with 12 knots on the meter, giving probably 15 knots actual. During the night as the wind rose we took down the spinnaker and the mainsail and drove along under the No 2 and the staysail.

The wind rose and we were often dealing with 50 or 60 knot blasts. The seas were huge now with 40 foot high waves that followed us forming great valleys and troughs behind us.... Steering was difficult and we had to keep two people on deck and sometimes three. When dawn came my watch was on deck and Mike came up and suggested that we reduce sail from the No 2 to No 3. We went for'ard to take down the No 2 and got frozen doing so. We managed to pull it down after a great struggle in the high winds and breaking seas and put it down the hatch. We then went back and sat in the galley to get our hands warm before going for'ard to put the No 3 up. We were now going under staysail alone.

Phil, who was steering, had already had several experiences of waves breaking over the stern and washing him about.... This time he was sitting in the rear cockpit steering when a largish wave came by which caused the steering wires to break. He turned round leaving the useless wheel and struggled with his cold fingers to release the rope and catch to secure the emergency tiller to the pushpit. Having watched him struggle for a few moments from the companionway, I threw Sandy, who was sitting beside him, a knife so he could cut the securing rope. It was quite a hectic moment, as while the steering was being changed over the boat was out of control on the huge waves. After this Mike and I went for'ard to put up the No 3, which made steering easier.

Mike and I had just gone below to get warm when there was a terrific crash on deck as a wave came over and we looked out to see if everyone was all right. By now it was quite light.... a large wave had come aboard and thrown Phil across the steering cockpit and then as the boat righted herself, the tiller came back and Sandy, who was also thrown into the steering cockpit.... landed on Phil just as the tiller caught the latter under the ribs. Poor Philip was completely incapacitated and we took him below, waking up Terri to start her nursing experience. We laid him on the galley floor.... water was sloshing all over the place.... Sandy took over the tiller and we took down the staysail in an attempt to slow down and reduce the violent motion, while the remainder got Philip into Terri's bunk, where he would be less likely to be thrown about. It seemed that Philip might have broken a couple of ribs as he was having great difficulty in breathing and in considerable pain so Terri gave him some of her special pills to reduce this.

After many attempts Mike finally got through to H.M.A.S. *Moresby* who we knew was going to be on station 1,000 miles from the Australian coast. We received good medical advice from the surgeon on board and the captain said they'd try to take Philip off by helicopter on the 21st - in two days time. Mike said later that he thought the winds during the night were stronger than they had been in the Fastnet. Not long afterwards there was another terrific bang on deck while Paul was steering. We looked out but saw no Paul. Mike and Jono dashed up on deck and found him hanging over the rail by his lifeline. An enormous wave had come in and swept him clean out of the cockpit, over the boom which was lashed to the deck, over the rail and into the sea. Mike and Jono hauled him aboard and brought him down below, perfectly all right, but soaked through and a bit shocked.

November 21st. Position. Lat. 43 degrees 18 mins S. Long. 89 degrees 33 mins E.... We then started a long talk with *Moresby* which by now had devoted herself to finding us but was experiencing great difficulty. We gave her our position, but by the time she had got there we were 10 miles further on, and we had difficulty giving her new positions because it was not sextant weather. *Moresby* finally put up her helicopter which found us after being told of the cloud formations and where the rain squalls were coming from. The helicopter came and hovered about 10 yards astern of us and then lowered their first man on board. A hair-raising exploit, because he swung to and fro narrowly missing the mast and backstays, and the winch man had to raise and lower him as the swell, running at 15 feet or so, moved us up and down. He finally came between the backstays and collapsed in a heap on top of the lazarette. The wire was sent up again and this time the surgeon came down in much the same way, except a line from the boat was attached to his feet so that we could guide him down in a more accurate fashion.

We got Philip on deck with some difficulty and lashed him onto the stretcher, all togged out in waterproof clothes. a helmet and lifejacket. Philip was shot out over the side of the boat on his sling, lying horizontal, and the helicopter, though rising fast, didn't fail to dunk him in the water on the way. As he splashed into the waves our hearts leapt into our mouths, but then he was dragged out clear again high into the air. We heard shortly that they had all arrived safely on the *Moresby* and that Philip was in good shape, although it turned out later that he had four broken ribs. Once all this excitement was over we set sail to the north-east on our original course having probably spent some six hours or more loitering in this portion of the ocean.

Seltrust Endeavour crossed the finishing line in Freemantle Harbour mid-afternoon on 27th November, having sailed 12,527 miles in 81 days and came 9th in the IOR division.

After competing in the notoriously windy Sydney - Hobart race, *Seltrust Endeavour* set sail for home by entering The Spice Race, which was from Jakarta, Indonesia, to Rotterdam which had been sponsored by Nedloid, a large shipping and finance group. There is no space and certainly no log to tell of this race, but after the Cape Town stopover, and halfway to the Cape Verde Islands *Seltrust Endeavour*'s rudder dropped off. The official R.O.R.C. jury one - a spinnaker pole with a bucket on the end - was rigged. Many of us, who have been obliged to know about it, have wondered whether it would ever work, but it did. Jono Callow vouched for this, but said that *Seltrust Endeavour*'s rig almost made it unnecessary. They had managed to save the rudder and when they arrived at the Cape Verde's a tug lifted the stern out and welded the rudder back on again.

Some months later Selection Trust awarded Mike Dunham a special prize for outstanding seamanship. In 1981 Mike was talking to Alan Green, Director of Racing at the R.O.R.C. and said he'd like to hand over his prize to the R.O.R.C. to award annually for outstanding seamanship, such as John Chittenden's incredible rescue of two of his crew who were washed overboard from *Creighton's Naturally* at night in the Southern Ocean during the 1989 Whitbread race. In 1993 it was awarded jointly to the 10 skippers of The British Steel Challenge.

Laurel Holland

Laurel Holland has raced and cruised approximately 20,000 miles both with her ex-husband Ron Holland, the designer of many Swans and now of luxury motor cruisers, and with the late Rob James, the very popular and much respected multi-hull racer who died tragically after falling overboard in the Salcombe estuary. In addition to the Southern Ocean Racing Conference events, Laurel did the 1981 Trans-Atlantic Two-Star in *Kriter Lady*, a three-masted Freedom-type monohull. What follows is her account of the 1986 Two-Star in the 45ft catamaran *Sebago*, which was sponsored by the well-known American deck-shoe company.

The 1986 Two-Star Trans-Atlantic Race

"Joan, Joan, the mast's coming down," I hollered to Joan Greene, my co-helmswoman and an ocean-racing veteran who was down below. A squall had hit us with driving icy rain and sustained winds of 45 knots plus. "Nonsense," Joan shouted, "it's bullet-proof." But a few seconds later down came the 60ft foil-shaped mast with the two-reefed 155 square ft mainsail. I screamed again to Joan as the boat, which had been doing 15 knots, stopped abruptly and began to wallow in the confused seas. I'd been flung from the weather hull into the netting. As I was scrambling back into the cockpit Joan popped her head up.
    It was about 1500 on 31st March. Joan Greene and I had left Dartmouth early that morning on what was meant to be our 500-mile qualifying passage for the 1986 Two-Star. The mast had fallen over like an oak tree and it hit the leeward dagger-board housing. It took us two hours to tidy up the mast,

sails and rigging so the boat didn't suffer any further damage. There was a hole in the boat's float which was taking in water. What was worrying me was that we were right in the shipping lanes and it would soon be dark. Several ships saw the incident and stood by for a time, but they carried on when we didn't radio for assistance. Our VHF was of course out of action as it was under the water, and our emergency aerial, which every boat is required to carry, for some reason didn't work.

Eventually a ship which was not flying any flag approached close to inspect the two red hulls wrapped in a cocoon of sails, wire and rope. We weren't too keen as we were preoccupied with our survival. We were anxious that she might run us over. She came so close that she hit us, which frightened the life out of us. Her captain decided to put a man aboard to see if we needed any help. We couldn't understand what language he was speaking - although it gradually dawned on us he was Russian - he obviously knew about small boats and was able to deal with our immediate needs. He signalled to his Captain for a tow-line, and helped us climb up the ladder which had been thrown down.

Shivering with cold, we were taken inside and the sailor started stripping off our layers of clothes, Strobe lights, whistles, Mustos and everything . We both had three layers of everything so we looked very fat and because we were so tired looked terrible. We suddenly realised that they thought we were men. The captain came in just as I was down to my last layer of thermal long underwear and feeling a little awkward. A broad smile came over his face and he left the room and the sailor who'd come aboard obviously got quite a shock. They took away all our clothes after inspecting them - perhaps to see if there was any spy equipment - and within minutes a Russian woman appeared and gave me a sleeveless cotton smock to wear over my thermals. The real trouble was that we couldn't communicate, and I wanted to go to the loo. Eventually I ran out and after a long search found the crew's heads only to be interrupted by a Russian sailor who I think was as embarrassed and surprised as I was.

I found Joan in the radio room. Owing to the language problem it took ages for us to get onto Niton Radio, Isle of Wight, and tell them to put out a 'Securité' (VHF language for a navigational hazard) giving *Sebago*'s position - so that she wouldn't be run down - and to organise a tow to within reach of Dartmouth. Eventually the Russian radio officer got onto the right channel and explained what had happened. In spite of the swell we got back onto *Sebago* and the Russian ship towed us slowly towards England. She couldn't come within the three-mile limit so we were towed to Torquay by a fishing boat. We were met by British Intelligence officers and asked for details of the Russian ship's radio equipment as they thought she must be a spy ship, but there was nothing we could tell them. Although we'd got our clothes back fairly dry we were cold after the long tow and were glad to get back to our favourite cafe in Dartmouth, twenty four hours after we had left it and have a hot breakfast.

Sebago was designed and built by Walter Greene, Joan's husband, in 1983 for the 1984 One-Star, the Quebec-St Malo race and the 1985 Round Britain Race, all of which he was either first in his class or was placed. The problems we had later on in the trans-Atlantic race with the the shroud and then the forestay implied that Walter's three races may have weakened the whole rig. The mast had gone over the side because the starboard running backstay had parted at the top. Forty-eight hours after being back in Dartmouth, Walter organised a lorry-load of Sika spruce and Douglas fir to Andrian Thompson's yard at Totnes at the top of the river Dart. After several weeks the new mast was made and the boat repaired.

We qualified five days before the start, so we had five nights at the Trans-Atlantic Cafe, next to Millbay docks in Plymouth. Warmth and keeping dry for most multi-hull sailors seems to start and end at cafes like the Trans-Atlantic. They also offer the best atmosphere in which to dream about fast sailing and are the best places to listen to boat builders and designers and to talk about hulls, rigs, solar panels and self-steering systems. Once at sea it's all very different.

When the race actually started on 8th June it seemed like the beginning of a holiday, but teething problems soon developed and continued for days with the new mainsail battens and furling system. The battens kept shooting out so that we had to drill holes in them and tie them in. At times we were doing twenty five knots and one hull would come out of the water, but to work on the battens we had to slow down. Joan got very depressed which was unlike her. Conditions weren't good for such work. The wind was dead on the nose all the time and blowing hard. We bore away to work on the battens to avoid plunging into the waves which would be dangerous, even though we were of course clipped on. From my log I see it was on June 11th that we tacked away from the rhumb line course, and Ann Fraser, a Club member, passed us in her Contessa 32 *Gollywobbler*. She was laughing like mad and looked very cheerful, as indeed she had cause to be, passing a multihull so soon. It was pretty terrible being passed by a monohull which was already pointing nice and high for Newport, while we were were sailing away from it.

We tacked again when all the work was done and were doing about 10 knots on a course now fairly high of the rhumb line. I knew I was a born optimist in spite of seeing such small monohulls beating us - Willy Carr was another one who had passed us laughing louder than his foghorn - still hoping that at some stage the wind would back allowing us to surge forward. Joan had started to think about Newport and the Goat Island Marina and the nearby cafe. She'd suddenly realised that being a vegetarian I hadn't provisioned *Sebago* with any meat. We had sandwiches for three days and after that we ate like rabbits: cereals, nuts, fruit out of tins, Mars bars. We couldn't heat anything because of the motion and because there was so little room. We had to crawl into the hull and only had two cups of coffee during the whole passage.

We did two hours on and two off. In the cockpit we were totally exposed to continuous spray from over the bows as well as up through the netting. When steering we had to brace ourselves with our feet to stop ourselves sliding off the boat. All the circulation went out of our feet and eventually our sponsor's shoes and equally seaboots, which got full up with water, resulted in us getting something like hypothermia in our feet. It took six months for the blood to be restored properly and it was a very painful process. The main trouble about multihulls is the wear and tear on the human body which is very difficult to overcome. We wore goggles against the constant spray, but found that salt-laden eye-pieces caused sores, so we had to put up with our bare faces being doused continually with sea water. By the end of the race we'd got boils all over our bodies.

When I was in my bunk - recently vacated by Joan because we always lived in the weather hull - it was like being in a lift because of the motion. The noise of the boat's passage through the water and when the waves hit the hull was unbelievable; it was when I didn't hear the waves that I was worried because that meant the weather hull was out of the water and the lee hull was dug in; I could see the part of the cross beam which was inside the hull twisting under the strain. We never took our clothes off during the entire twenty four-day passage. It would have been too dangerous in case one was needed on deck, or worse still if the boat capsized. So to try to thaw out I climbed fully dressed into my sleeping bag and then into a sailbag, which absorbed the water that dripped from the deckhead the whole time.In spite of the noise and general discomfort I slept deeply and had vivid dreams. They were all about the same thing: about getting into a warm environment. I think they helped me to keep going and to realise that some day it would all be over.

It was on 16th June that the next disaster happened. During the night I had heard a funny noise near where the cap shroud was bottle-screwed to the chainplate on the side of the hull. I told Joan and she thought I was imagining things. We had 'a difference of opinion' and she went on watch and I came back on deck. The sun was just coming up when Joan saw a crack in the cap shroud bottle-screw and put the helm over before it broke completely. We were now going in the wrong direction and did so for twelve hours while we fixed up a jury rig. There was still two inches of play, but we slowly tested the rig and gathered speed in the right direction for two days, but then the forestay parted from boat and mast. A 60ft 'wing' mast - tapered and on ball bearings - leaning aft at 30 degrees is a sight you don't forget. We jury-rigged with the last running backstay and used the main-sheet blocks and every available working line to get sufficient purchase to heave the mast back to something like its proper position. It took a long time and we were absolutely exhausted. One thing was for sure. The rigging was even more weary than we were.

Eventually we put four reefs back into the main to slow *Sebago* down as we were travelling to weather at 10 knots in the fog across the Grand Banks on port tack. It was still blowing hard. We'd decided to make for St John's, Newfoundland, our closest and safest destination but we could only make it on port tack, otherwise the mast would fall down. If the wind veered we would have to sail the boat backwards. Equally, having a wing mast, if we sailed too high the boat would self-tack and then the mast would come down again. During the night Joan showed great courage because she didn't wake me although a fishing trawler loomed up through the fog and she had to steer the boat dangerously high in order to miss it by a few feet. Then there was the added worry of icebergs or 'growlers' - the small ones which have split off from the monsters; so from then on we did one hour on and one hour off for the remaining week.

It was an anxious time and we had to be very careful with the waves and their effect on the mast. Joan got very depressed, but I just laughed. If I hadn't done I would have ended up crying.We were in fog for seven days and as we approached St John's the wind veered so we were driven eastwards. In spite of the fog we knew we weren't far from land as we had picked up the local radio. Eventually we came out of the fog and saw some high cliffs, but quite a long way off. We called up The Mounties, on our VHF and they came out in a small naval ship which after a number of unsuccessful attempts passed us a tow. I was up for'ard and had to get this warp aboard. It was not only very heavy, but because they hadn't let enough line out it was doubly difficult, particularly when it came to tying a bowline.

Unfortunately they did not understand our problems when it came to the actual tow. They said they could not do this at less than six knots and the towing warp was not long enough to take the weight of *Sebago*, so that a lot of the time they virtually pulled the boat through the water. We had no option. It would be dark soon; we had no engine and to approach a leeshore in *Sebago's* condition would have been foolhardy. On port tack we would have been driven slowly eastwards and back out into the Atlantic. Once the tow had begun it was touch and go whether the mast would come down. To help the mast, we tried to keep the load on the port side. I remember that it was during the tow that I saw my first puffin and some Arctic type of dolphins which provided some light relief.

It was 2000 by the time we got in to what was a tricky harbour entrance and were safely tied up. But the damaged state of *Sebago* and our own distress - we were very cold as it had been blowing hard until we got into the lee of the cliffs - meant nothing to the Immigration officials. What is certain is that we looked awful. The officials insisted on coming aboard and searching the boat because they had some idea we were drug dealing. Having crawled right for'ard they thought they had struck gold because they discovered our escape provisions in a grab bag near the escape hatch. Inside they found a lot of packages wrapped in white packaging and cellotaped, which were of course flares and emergency food. They then found the liferaft. One of them started playing with the red toggle which inflated the raft if it was pulled. 'If you go on playing with that cord, I'm getting out of here,' I told the officer. 'If you pull it, you'll inflate the liferaft and be crushed to death.'

Eventually they signed our passports and entry papers and we were free to go ashore. By the time we found an hotel it was midnight and we were given some tomato sandwiches which were curling up at the sides. We had a gin and tonic and it went right to our heads - and then in spite of it being 2.30 a.m. some guys came in and we had another. Unknown to us Walter, Joan's husband, was trying to get into our hotel, but they have a law in Newfoundland which forbids entry to men asking for a certain woman, even if he's her husband! Eventually we got to bed and out of our wet clothes. We were so tired, and rocking about from the boat that we were completely disorientated; after being one hour on and one hour off it was difficult to sleep, in spite of being so tired. However we were only too thankful to get into a dry bed.

Walter, sailing another boat, had arrived in Newport a week before, and from there had been watching our progress via the Argos satellite machine every boat was equipped with. He finally got permission to enter our hotel mid-morning and congratulated us on saving the mast. I had to get some clothes, so having a credit card went into a French boutique and bought half the shop. I then went to a hairdresser and said: "Make me blonde." A week later we were all back at Yarmouth, Maine, and visited the *Sebago* factory. The logo for the firm is a little old man sewing shoes - a cozy and secure image of someone with warm hands and a glowing face. The logo was sewn on all our foul weather gear. 'Where is that little man?' I muttered to myself. We then went down to the waterfront to the closest warm and dry cafe. I don't think I'd do it again.

Tony Blofeld should also be mentioned as he did the original Two-Star trans-Atlantic in 1981 and also that in 1986, but I havn't been able to make contact with him.

Peter Hopps

Until Vivien Cherry returned in May last year from skippering *Coopers and Lybrand* in the British Steel Challenge round the world 'the wrong way,' there was no doubt that Peter Hopps was the Club's most prestigious ocean going Corinthian. I doubt if either cares much about such titles, and anyhow we will come to Vivien's magnificent and unique achievement in due course. The fact remains that Peter has been indulging in what some people may regard as the ultimate in masochistic sports for longer than any other Club member; in fact he introduced Vivien to the rigours of short-handed racing when she crewed for him in the 1985 Round Britain Race.

Apart from the 1979 Fastnet, Peter has done six trans-Atlantics.These include the 1988 Carlsberg in his trimaran *Triple Fantasy*; crewing in the 1990 Two-Star in the monohull *Ntombifuti* which came first in her class and the Round Britain in both 1985 and 1989 in *Triple-Fantasy*. In the summer of 1990 he received the ultimate accolade from the French when he was nominated top British offshore sailor by the Federation Internationale de la Course Open Offshore (Tracey Edwards the gallant skipper of *Maiden* in the 1989 Whitbread came second) and twenty-third offshore sailor in the world.This was probably because of his outstanding seamanship and astro-navigational skills, let alone pilotage, which he showed on those races. In 1992 in the 55ft *Enif* he did a fast crossing from Newport, Rhode Island, to the Lizard, taking only twelve and a half days in all. Here is his account of the 1989 Round Britain Race when he was crewed by James Chrismas.

The 1989 Round Britain Race

My start for the 1989 Round Britain race was one of the worst I've ever made. I don't know why I made such a mess of it, but it had absolutely nothing to do with our activities the previous night, which involved drinking a night club dry of their brandy, low-flying hand-bags and a famous nose-bleed! Anyhow we recovered from the situation by hitching a ride on our support boat's wake which dragged us up to the front of our class.

We were sailing in Class VI for boats from 30 - 35ft and as my boat *Triple Fantasy* had won this class in the race four years before, we were expecting to do well. However there would be some stiff competition: there was *Fiery Cross*, built in 1988 a very powerful boat designed and built by Merfyn

Owen for Rupert Kidd; then there was *A Capella*, which had beaten *Triple Fantasy* into 2nd place in the 1982 race and was famous for winning the first Route du Rhum Race in 1977; and *Two Hoots*, a Shittleworth designed catamaran, which looked very comfortable, but had a reputation for being a very fast boat.

The course is clockwise round Britain and Ireland, starting and finishing in Plymouth with four stopovers of 48 hours at Crosshaven, Cork; Barra, Outer Hebrides; Lerwick, Shetland Islands and Lowestoft. The stopovers are for rest and recuperation, but you normally end up leaving them more tired than when you arrived. With the wind forecast to be north-easterly, 4-5, we were looking forward to a nice fast easy sail to Crosshaven, two hundred and thirty miles away. We passed the Bishop Rock at 0330 Monday morning, having started on Sunday, and by mid-morning were enjoying a pleasant reach across the Irish Sea, expecting to finish sometime that evening. I should have known better.

I've now sailed across the Irish Sea several times and have not yet had a good passage; there's either too much wind, as on a famous occasion in 1979, or too little, as in a race in 1982, when having taken two days longer than expected we finished in Crosshaven with the only food remaining being a tub of margarine and two pints of water. In 1986 it ended up being one of the windless variety, and having rowed, sailed and drifted, we eventually crossed the line at 0350 on Tuesday. We were 14th overall, and 3rd in our class behind *Two Hoots* and *Fiery Cross*; somewhat disappointing. We revived ourselves with an excellent breakfast and several pints of Murphys at the Royal Cork Yacht Club, the oldest yacht club in the world.

Wednesday was golf day. Roy Hart, owner of the Barracuda 45 *Moonboots*, in Class 1V, and I had decided the previous year that it would be a good idea to play golf at the stopovers and have a Round Britain Golf Challenge - in conjunction with the race. Roy recruited Bob Fisher to join the party and brought along his crew, one Robin Knox-Johnston, and off we set for the Monkston Golf Club. After a very enjoyable round, we repaired to Coggan's Bar in Carrigaline for a few pints of Murphy's and formed the Offshore Golfing Society. (The proprietor of the hostelry, Finbarr Coggan, was elected Life President, on the grounds that he had set foot on neither golf course nor a yacht, but ran a very good pub).

The start for the next leg was at 0350 on Thursday morning; a nice run in sunny weather to the Fastnet Rock followed by a reach up the west coast of Ireland. We were enjoying ourselves sailing along at about 8-10 knots. James will now tell you a bit about how we kept body and soul together. 'Peter and I fed very well during the race in spite of our limited facilities. There was a one burner camping gas stove suspended on a plywood shelf and cooking utensils consisted of one saucepan, one frying pan and one kettle. We had a full cooked breakfast - bacon, eggs, sausages, baked beans, tomatoes - I usually had a slice of fried bread to soak up the surplus fat - good and healthy. The only exception was in very bad weather when we had porridge and honey.

To keep things on the stove Peter had rigged up a couple of wire strops to the shelf which could be shackled to the saucepan handles or kettle. The frying pan had to be held. Drying up, drying one's hands preparatory to lighting (or even smoking) a cigarette, drying off one's oilies before doing chartwork, and keeping Peter's glasses dry was all done with a chamois leather. The other essential item of boat equipment was a large pack of baby wipes to help freshen oneself up when caked with salt. Washing up was done in salt water with a generous slug of washing-up liquid, using 'the other bucket.' The bucket was also home for the saucepan. We only took four cans of beer and a small bottle of whisky and I don't remember drinking any of it or missing it while racing. We made up for our abstention when we went ashore.

Lunch was a salad sandwich with cheese or one of the various pre-packed sliced meats, and supper was stew or steak and kidney pudding with potatoes and peas or some other (usually tinned) vegetables. In between times there was a constant supply of tea (if you ever go sailing with Peter you will know what I mean), coffee, cup-a-soups, Bovril for Peter and Marmite for me - neither of us can stand the other's version of malt extract - and Club chocolate biscuits, Hob Nobs, fun size Mars Bars and a large supply of good quality plain chocolate for emergency energy.'

In mid-afternoon things started to go wrong. First the log broke. As we had no Decca and were relying on traditional navigational methods this was going to be something of a hindrance. At about 1900 the main halyard broke. We re-hoisted the main on the topping lift, but feeling cautious put one reef in. With a fairly light breeze (10-12 knots) this really slowed us down. After about twelve hours we got bored with caution and shook out the reef. By Friday afternoon, the wind had moved round to WNW Force 4 and we were charging along at 12 knots under full main and No 1 genoa. At 1700 we saw a boat ahead, passing her at about 1800; she was *Vidam*, a 38 foot trimaran in the class above us, so we were pleased to be catching up.

By 2200 we were abeam of Eagle Island off the north-west tip of Ireland. The wind deserted us for a while, but returned after about five hours from the south-west and increased during Saturday, blowing 35 knots by lunchtime. For those who haven't tried it, sailing a trimaran in windy conditions is a very wet activity. Beating to weather in a gale or near gale is nasty: bashing one wave after another, with water seemingly everywhere. On a small boat like *Triple Fantasy*, it is advisable not to go too fast, 8-10 knots is O.K., otherwise you'll tend to take off over a wave and crash into the next one!

Once you come off the wind a bit onto a reach, things get much worse. Instead of doing 8-10 knots, you'll be doing 15 or more, scooping up solid water which gets dumped in the cockpit all over the poor helmsman. But it's very exhilirating; subject to wave conditions running in heavy weather can be brilliant. On the leg up to Barra, we were running in 35 plus knots of wind with full main and spinnaker; we averaged about 20 knots, so the apparent wind was only 15-20 knots. You must be careful to avoid digging the bow in, otherwise you might trip up. *Triple Fantasy* is very good in this respect, and has never given cause for concern.

The run up to Barra was excellent sailing; we passed *Two Hoots* during the early afternoon, but I was aware of a slight navigational problem looming. It's approximately two hundred miles from Eagle Island, our last fix, to Barra Head. Without a log, we had no real idea how far we had gone, as it's difficult to judge the speed of a trimaran going fast and visibility was about 1·5 to 3 miles; we could easily sail past Barra Head without realising it. Although it was mainly overcast, the sun did occasionally break through the clouds, and occasionally the visibility increased, and when the two things happened together I was able to get a sunsight with the sextant. We sighted Barra Head at 1700 and crossed the line at 1930. We'd picked up to 9th overall and 2nd in our class behind *Fiery Cross*, who'd finished about 1330. Sunday in Barra was wet and horrible so we spent most of the day in the bar. On Monday we were invited to the traditional cocktail party in the castle. As there is no golf course on Barra the best we could do was to drive off the battlements into the sea.

The race started again at 1930 under spinnaker, rounded

Barra Head and set off for the Island of St Kilda. We passed St Kilda at 0830 on Tuesday and set course for Muckle Flugga. The wind was north-west about twenty five knots, so we were close-hauled, but going nicely, although it was very cold. The wind increased during Wednesday to 45 knots. During this leg James cooked some tinned haggis which we'd found in one of the shops in Barra. That was excellent, but towards the end of that leg it was so rough that he couldn't cook. James's description being a comparative newcomer to trimarans was interesting: 'We were working one hour on deck and one hour off, during which time we had to bail out (15 min), navigate (five to ten mins) and try to sleep. I lay as far for'ard as possible with my feet on the cooker in order to avoid the puddle at the aft end of the bunk. We kept a good supply of Mars bars, plain chocolate and tea, cup-a-soup or bitter lemon (very refreshing) flowing in order to stave off the cold and tiredness.'

We rounded Muckle Flugga with two reefs in the main and a reefed headsail. We shook out the reefs in the jib and shot off towards Lerwick, covering sixty miles in three hours. We finished at 0530 on Thursday, still 9th overall, but we'd taken over five hours out of *Fiery Cross*'s lead; they were now only 50 minutes ahead. For good measure it started to snow just after our arrival.

James told me afterwards that his most vivid memories of the race were visual: the fantastic scenery; the birds, although he was disappointed that he only saw one puffin and the awe-inspiring size of the waves round the top of the Shetland Islands. He subsequently learned from the lighthouse keeper that at the time of their rounding they were 25 ft mean wave height with the wind increasing from Force 8 to 10. 'That was when Peter suggested that we didn't seem to be going very fast and we shook out the reef in the No 2 jib and debated shaking out the second reef in the main. We didn't in the end because we reckoned it would take too long to put it back again for the beat to the finish at Lerwick.'

One of the features of the Lerwick stopover is the hospitality of the locals. Each crew is assigned to a family to be looked after. Our host was Bill Smith, who arrived at 0830, very apologetic for not being there to meet us when we came in. On seeing our four bin liners full of washing. he said: 'Ah good, you know the score; if that's everything let's go.' Back at his house he introduced us to his wife, who enquired 'Have you any washing you need doing?' Four bin liners later her smile was still intact: 'Is that everything?' she asked, if a little nervously. 'Yes,' I replied. You could detect a sense of relief in her expression. After we'd had a bath, we were given breakfast: bacon, eggs, sausages, mushrooms - the works. We sat down to eat and told our hosts about our progress in the race so far. Well I did. James just ate, and for the only time ever before or since finished before me Those of you who know us will find this hard to believe, but it's true. I think the poor boy must have been hungry.

We spent the rest of the day fixing the boat. We'd broken the main halyard and had a new one made up in Lerwick.We fitted it, replaced a shroud which was fraying and fixed a few other things which needed doing. On Friday we played the second round of the golf contest. As we were due to leave at 0530 the next morning we decided that we should be in bed by 2230. James went out to dinner and got back about midnight, while I got hijacked and ended up drinking whisky on board another boat until about 0130.

Consequently we were a little late over the line. However with the wind in the east at about 20 knots we made good progress, covering the first hundred miles in eight hours. We had discovered that the log was completely bust. I'd had a replacement part sent up to Lerwick, and had fitted it, but now absolutely nothing on it worked. This was annoying, as the landfall at Lowestoft is potentially the most difficult of the whole race. Still at this stage it didn't really matter much, so we just kept going. The wind died and fog came down. The fog cleared after a day or so and we were relieved to get a few sunsights to find our position. The wind remained light for the rest of the leg; in fact we didn't change sail at all between Sunday night and when we finished at 0730 on Tuesday morning. We had passed *Fiery Cross* and were now leading our class by about fifty minutes.

As we'd had so little wind during the leg, there was virtually nothing to be fixed on the boat, and we were both well rested. There didn't seem much to do other than drink and have a good time! Sadly, another consequence of the light wind was that Roy Hart didn't get to Lowestoft until after we left, so we were unable to play the final round of the golf competition.

Having taken the lead in the class, we got serious and actually started on time. We had a pleasant reach down to the North Foreland, and worked our way through the Dover Straights.By 2230 on Thursday we were off Dungeness, running under full main and spinnaker. However lightning could be seen to the south-west, so we dropped the spinnaker and sailed goose-winged. We were soon hit by a wind-shift of 180 degrees. By 0600 on Friday, the wind had settled to south-west, about 12 knots, but foggy. We groped our way round St Catherine's Point, then Portland Bill at about 2030. The next headland, and the last, was Start Point, and we got there early Saturday in visibility of about 30 yards. The wind now virtually deserted us, and after more rowing we eventually crossed the line at Plymouth at 1148 Saturday morning. We were disappointed to find *Fiery Cross* already there.

We'd finished 2nd in our class and 8th overall. We had a

lot to be satisfied about; we'd sailed through every weather condition imaginable and had had a good tussle with *Fiery Cross*. Also we'd managed to get round without the use of any modern navigational aids - not even a log for most of the way.

Ann Fraser

Ann Fraser is one of the Club's most intrepid ocean-going Corinthians. She has raced and cruised thousands of miles: the Round Britain Race twice, in 1982 and 1985. The 1986 Two-Star trans-Atlantic - when she passed Laurel Holland - arriving in Newport after thirty four days. Her account of this in the news letter makes grim reading and the Club awarded her the The Harbourmaster's Trophy for Seamanship. This was an award donated by David Widdowson in 1983 in memory of Peter Roberts and Gil Winfield. Laurel Holland was the next winner.

In 1988 Ann competed in the Ocean Cruising Club Pursuit Race to the Azores and stayed for the Sea Week Racing. She was either forced through crew problems to a make a fairly traumatic single-handed return trip to the U.K. which she described once again in the news letter. Ann has also cruised with and without the family in the Caribbean and then further east to Cuba and also to Gambia - for reasons only she can explain; many members may have read her account in *Yachting Monthly*.

What follows is a different aspect of long-range racing or cruising from that described in this chapter so far. There are times when frustration over a lack of crew or the wrong crew, engine and battery problems, let alone rigging failures face every skipper when he's far from home. It is then that he or she can feel very much alone.Ann seems to have had more than her fair share of these aggravations from all accounts.

Darkness Is No Friend

"If I were you," said Willy, sweat dripping off his nose as he struggled with *Gollywobbler*'s engine in 100 degree heat, "I'd head for the Cape Verdes first, rather than Antigua - it's easier for crew to fly home from there." We were sitting in the cockpit. The boat was moored in a remote island in Guinea-Bissau, the old Portuguese West Africa, and had been waiting the arrival of new crew from England with a replacement gearbox, following a mishap with an anchor-buoy line round the propeller in the Gambia river.

Willy's doubts - and mine - were about the untried and untested crew: Maurizio, a cheerful competent Italian, was no worry, but his wife Lesley, was inexperienced and apprehensive and - fatal mistake - had been persuaded into the venture by her husband. They had survived the trying flight out via Gambia, bush taxis, a river crossing and a final two-mile trek on a donkey with the gearbox as well as their baggage. But how would they take to the Atlantic?

Willy had left me in the safe hands, he said, of an oil-rig support vessel to deal with the sick engine. This was a false hope, as she disappeared out to sea next day. A frantic hunt round Bissau Harbour threw up a contact with a French mechanic working for the American Embassy. His contribution was to O.K. the alignment, but say to Maurizio in my absence: "You've got water in your lubricating oil - change it!" My query was: "what's water doing there?" Then memories of a blown cylinder head gasket in an ancient car flew to mind. Changing oil and a trial run confirmed my worst fears and made finding a mechanic in Praia, Santiago, a priority.

One day offshore and headed for Santiago, southernmost of the Cape Verde Islands, in a rolling Atlantic beam sea, whipped up by the trade-winds, Lesley succumbed to seasickness and could not be winkled out of her bunk for three days. I was feeling a bit green myself - and even Maurizio held off cooking prawns and paella for a day, but my forebodings about Lesley's ability to cope with a trans-Atlantic crossing were soon to be fulfilled.

Unfortunately we arrived on Christmas Eve, not the best time to find a contact made through the U.S. Naval Attache in Bissau, who had told me that the American Embassy had a yacht and the Ambassador was a keen sailor. Boxing Day found me sipping coffee with the Ambassador, a charming man who offered me the use of his mechanic. Sadly the Ambassador's car problems took priority and another mechanic from the town was routed out and inspected the engine. The boat was anchored in the middle of the harbour in the full force of the north-east Trades, often Force 6-7. He used my on-board spares to replace the head gasket but a subsequent trial run showed up a massive oil leak of approximately a litre an hour from a missing and unobtainable oil seal.

Meanwhile Lesley and Maurizio were sampling the delights of the open market and Lesley returned having been unwisely unable to resist the chestnut-brown clusters of grilled sausages, which she offered me and which I politely refused. My caution was justified; during the night noises from the heads indicated that Lesley had succumbed again and was in a bad way. Off to the U.S. Embassy again, this time to find a doctor from the local hospital, who turned out to be a competent Egyptian who diagnosed dysentery and insisted on Lesley being admitted to hospital pronto and put on a 'drip.'

By this time it was obvious that Lesley would not be fit to cross the Atlantic and she and Maurizio flew home. With no crew available, I was faced with single-handing to the Caribbean, where my cousin was due at the end of January. I was grateful for having made my solo passage back from the

Azores the previous year, against such an eventuality. Some Belgian friends in the harbour, Albert and Genevieve Bechet, who were on their way to Antigua in their 37ft yacht, *Henny*, suggested we sail in company. So taking twenty five litres of oil with me - and having hoisted twin furling headsails with the help of another Belgian singlehander - we were waved off with cries of good luck.

We had a lovely sail past the volcanic peak of Fogo Island and then we were out into the Atlantic with 2,200 miles to go to English Harbour, Antigua. It felt good to be sailing solo again, taking sunsights, working out how to do things best to save trouble and energy and planning watches and sleep times. *Henny* was two to three miles abeam, sometimes disappearing in the big swell, but a comforting sight. They had both furling headsails and mainsail to make things easier, but my slab-reefing and twin furling headsails worked well and I could reef and unreef in the dark and go on a reach if necessary. We were both aware of the difficulty of maintaining contact over a long passage, but before leaving we had a briefing session to work out radio schedules and emergency procedures.

The first night out brought more problems. The masthead light drained the service battery within three hours (I discovered later the T.W.C. booster regulator was not working). With no navigation lights, *Henny* could not see my position and there was an ever-present fear of collision in the big seas and the darkness. So the battery had to be charged three times a night; an exhausting procedure in a rolling boat involving draining the mixture of oil and sea water in the drip-tray into an old squash bottle, to avoid it soaking the starter motor and topping up with fresh oil before restarting the engine. Once I was so tired, I poured the oil into the wrong hole and too late realised the drip-tray was full again.

For three nights I wrestled with the ever more recalcitrant

engine and the problem of how to keep some kind of navigation light up: the Chinese made hurricane light went out at once; Henry could not see the low-placed stern-light, nor was I visible on their radar. I would watch *Henny*'s lights sometimes getting too close, requiring avoidance action, and calling whoever was on watch on the V.H.F. - "*Henny - Henny - Gollywobbler* - can you see me?" Then Albert's or Genevieve's comforting reply: "Oui Ann, ça va."

Exhausted, I found I was too strung up to sleep well during the day and got progressively more tired. On the third night, Albert suggested tentatively I might be better on my own, since I could then dispense with navigation lights. This made sense and with mixed feelings I watched their sternlight disappear. 'Oh well,' I thought, 'I really am on my own now.' With no navigation lights, the possibility of being run down in the dark as I had nearly been in the fog coming back from the Azores was a bit daunting. 'Better have a couple of G and T's and some sleep.'

Staggering up on deck two hours later to look for ships, I saw a light ahead, which even without my contact lenses looked like *Henny*'s sternlight. I was puzzled. They should have been miles off. It was like a vision - 'Lead kindly light' or some such message which I interpreted as meaning that I should follow. Hastily unreefing my headsails, I pursued the light, remembering that we had a radio contact for midnight. Bang on time, Albert's voice came through suggesting that I should sail astern of them at night and in the morning I'd have only two or three miles to catch up. It was difficult to refuse such a generous offer.

The eventual solution to the light problem was an anchor light hung on the backstay, which cast a ghostly bluish light over the cockpit, but was visible to *Henny* and didn't kill the battery. From then on we devised a three-watch system, in which the on-watch boat sailed without navigation lights and V.H.F. 'off,' keeping alert for dangers or the other boat getting too close. The off-watch boat maintained navigation lights (in my case the anchor light) with open radio, so that she could be called at any minute to alter course, speed or reef for approaching squalls. We would then reverse the procedure, allowing me to get three hours' sleep between midnight and 3 a.m. and would then take the 3 a.m. till dawn watch. In this way we all got adequate sleep and kept station two or three miles apart.

During the day we came up close and exchanged waves and on one occasion *Henny* trailed a crusty, newly-baked loaf astern for me, sealed in a tupperware box on a long line. We arrived at our waypoint off Antigua 17·5 days after leaving the Cape Verdes and hove to in the darkness to await daylight, because it was blowing hard. It had been a fast passage, with the winds seldom below Force 4-5 and often 6-7. Having identified the Pillars of Hercules at the entrance to English Harbour, I went to start the engine. It had a final Parthian shot for me - the gear lever button was jammed in the disengaged position and WD40 wouldn't release it. Therefore no engine. So out I had to sail again to hoist the main and beat back past the coral reef into the overcrowded harbour. Nerves jangling, I dropped the anchor in the nearest hole I could find, right next to *Henny*, who produced a celebratory rum, the first of many.

Vivien Cherry

Vivien Cherry, as I have already said, was introduced to offshore racing in 1985 when she crewed Peter Hopps in the Round Britain Race. After that there was no stopping her. In 1986 she did the *Yachting Monthly* Triangle with Peter Hopps.

In 1988 she did the Carlsberg Trans-Atlantic in *Panicker*. In 1989 she skippered her Sigma 33, *Andromeda*, in the Fastnet with a number of Club members: Fiona Saunders-Watson, Martin Dixon and Julian Pearson - very good up-for'ard but not quite so good at the wheel as he's virtually blind without glasses. Jonathan Clark and Peter Hopps were also in the race on different boats. I was skippering *Freelance*. There was 35 knots of wind going up to the Rock and we were taking seas over the bows, but it wasn't a 'bad' Fastnet. However all my crew let alone myself felt pretty tired at the end of it. So much so that combined with a skinful of Guinness I hardly recognised Peter sufficiently to say 'Hello' a few hours after getting into Plymouth.

In 1990 Vivien went to Tasmania to take part in the Australian Three Peaks race and in 1992 she was asked by Chay Blyth to skipper *Coopers and Lybrand* in the British Steel Challenge. You don't have to have read her book, written in conjunction with Keith Wheatley, to realise what a psychological challenge and achievement, as well as physical feat of endurance let alone seamanship, it was to skipper the virtually amateur crew of *Coopers and Lybrand* 'the wrong way round' the world and to finish 4th, nine minutes ahead of *Hofbrau* after just over 28,000 miles. I am grateful to Vivien for permission to use the following extracts from her book.

Trials of the Southern Ocean

'Looking back at my diary entry for 15 December, a fortnight after we had passed Cape Horn, I find: 'WHAT A DAY, WHAT A DAY,' written in stark capitals across the top of the page. It began with the worst storm that we'd so far encountered aboard *Coopers and Lybrand*. Our instruments were unstable so we couldn't record all the weather data, but other boats reported we seemed likely to have had wind speeds of 65 to 70 knots - force 10, gusting 11. There was so much spray flying that half the time we couldn't see the waves, but I estimate that they were perhaps 35 feet high.

At this point we had dropped the mainsail as even with three reefs we were overpowered. and we were sailing just under staysail. We were already two and half crew down: Phil was completely confined to his bunk with severe seasickness, Robert was still out of action with cracked ribs having been thrown against his bunk rail much earlier in the leg. His ribs were not making the improvement we hoped, but being a particularly stubborn Scotsman, Robert had been unwilling to take the role of an invalid and stay below for a while on light duties. Apart from pain killers, there was no treatment we could offer on board apart from not loading the injury, which meant avoiding winching or any physical work. Titch had also taken a fall below deck and knocked his ribcage. We didn't know whether it was bad bruising or worse but he was taking painkillers and finding it difficult to undertake any deck work.

I'd taken a decision during the night that we were going to need the storm trysail because the bad weather looked set to last for at least another twenty four hours. Having put the trysail up once in the Solent, even though it had been 30 knots and a very flat sea, we knew it was going to be very awkward and require assistance from nearly all the crew. The trysail was laid out ready in the companionway and stopped with cotton to prevent it breaking out and flogging whilst being hoisted. I'd been planning the next day's manoeuvre and was hanging up my 'foulie' jacket hoping to get two hours' rest before daylight and the task we had ahead when I heard the scream of 'man overboard' from on deck.

That cry cut through everything. For a fraction of a second I could not move. Then everything happened very fast. By the time I had hit the MOB button on the G.P.S. (which gives an instant record of our exact position at the time of the incident), Matt had already gone for the engine and had got it started whilst Sam rushed to wake everyone up. This annoyed me at the time because I felt that crowds of people were the last thing we needed. I realised later, that she had done the right thing because if Brian had been lost we would have needed all the crew on deck to search for him. Brian had been washed through the guardrails but had managed to loop his arm round a rail so that only his legs, up to about his knees, were actually trailing in the water. He was also clipped on with his safety harness.

The watch on deck consisted of John and Titch with David helming. John and Titch physically hauled Brian back on board. We got him down below, believing that he would be fairly shocked - in actual fact he had felt quite secure with his harness and knowing that he had a strong hold on the stanchion. The two crew on deck, John and Titch, were possibly more stunned because they had seen the big wave sweep him overboard.... I had mentally gone overboard with Brian at that first call and my heart rate took about two hours to calm down. I took over Robert's watch for breakfast time and later at 0600, we started to put the storm trysail up. To do so we needed three watches on deck just to get the slides into the main track.

The trysail was made of thick 12-ounce sailcloth. It was very new and very stiff. It had slides just like the mainsail and they needed to go up the same track as the main. The trickiest job belonged to the person standing on the boom feeding the trysail slides into the gate and the track. He had to do the operation one-handed because the other arm was wrapped around the mast to hold on. Two or three feet below, a second person stood on the mast winch, helping to get the lead straight as the slides went up into the track. As this was going on the halyard had to be taken up at precisely the right moment. Communications were obviously vital, but even when we shouted the wind would just whip the words away.

Matt and Arnie took turns feeding in the slides because of the sheer difficulties both of working at full stretch and being cold and tired. I think the closest comparison would be if you imagine wallpapering a ceiling, working with your hands above your head, with the ladder moving and icy water being thrown at you every five seconds. Arnie was a real gem; he thrived on situations like this. He appeared not be afraid of anything and was a great asset to the *Coopers* crew.

It took about an hour just to get the slides into the track. Few people, except those who push themselves to the limit at weight-training, would understand the pain of screaming muscles involved in this strenuous exercise. The cotton stops on the trysail parted because they were rotten before it was completely hoisted and it began to break out early, which further complicated the operation. The only injuries occurred when Matt fell approximately six feet from the mast; his size 11 boot kicked me in the face and he landed coccyx first on the staysail car. I suffered the worst nosebleed of my life - blood everywhere - and my first thought was 'what would I look like with a broken nose?' Luckily it wasn't as bad as that, but Matt couldn't sit down and I couldn't blow my nose.

By the time the trysail was sheeted to the boom and pulling, the exercise had taken one and a half hours. We took down the storm staysail after the watch change so we had a fresh crew; Neil, Geraint and Richard were on the foredeck. We hove-to and, with the staysail aback, dropped the sail. This took a long time due to damaged hanks which were worn, bent or broken. We were now truly battened down and going along at about seven knots with the sea still very big and confused. No matter how you try to avoid the big waves, there is always one with your name on it. You can see it coming with the top about to break, and all you can do is shut your eyes, hold onto the wheel, shout something to warn others and get very, very wet. After the water has washed along the deck and into the cockpit it takes another thirty seconds for it to drain away. The boat usually lands with a thud and a crash which shakes the rig, finishing off with a little shake at the top. It's very like watching a dog after a swim: it shakes itself starting at its nose and finishes with its tail.

The next item on my personal agenda was to get some sleep. My last rest had been a couple of hours after dinner the previous night, some fourteen hours ago. However sleeping under these conditions at sea was virtually impossible. Also lying in your bunk below proved to be as dangerous as being topsides. It was as the yacht fell off one of the big waves and crash-landed that Geraint did the same thing from his bunk. He was in the top bunk on the windward side when the lee cloth gave way. The knot on the end of the retaining rope had come undone and Geraint was violently thrown out. He hit the upright opposite, about two feet away, before landing on the floor still in his sleeping bag. Geraint was obviously in pain and John thought there was a possibility of head injuries. Brian and Sam, the two medics, checked him over as best they could and made him more comfortable with extra sleeping bags and pillows around; we also put the heating on. The injury was most likely to be either a dislocated or broken collar bone.

I quickly sent off faxes to those boats carrying doctors asking for advice; three of the boats came back with a radio call within ten minutes. What a great fleet! The injury was finally diagnosed as a broken collarbone. Having given him pain-killers we moved Geraint to a sitting position during a tack - the tack being necessary to avoid going downwind of a large iceberg. What a day!....

Christmas Day saw us lying fourth in the race. It was certainly a day to remember - in the middle of the ocean, in a Force 7, with snow showers. The leaders were three hundred miles ahead; *Nuclear Electric* followed by *Commercial Union* with *Hofbrau* in third place. In spite of the gap we caught up *Hofbrau* by over eight hours to enter Hobart fourth.... We were there six weeks. Nearly every boat needed repairs to masts, rigging, keels, skegs and sails; and I had a highly successful operation to my knee cartilege which had been giving me a lot of trouble. There was also some marvellous hospitality and when the fleet set out on the third leg of the race; the 6,800-miles through the Southern Ocean to Cape Town, there were spectator boats everywhere like in the Solent....

After six weeks of comparatively reasonable weather we began to meet something different. Depression after depression followed through with very little or no respite, bringing constant gale force winds. This is what we had all expected of the Southern Ocean; gales on the nose most of the time. A steady 40 knots wind has replaced 35 knots as the commonplace stiff sailing breeze. It was also very dark, very cold and the wind chill factor at 40 knots and air temperature at 4 degrees C must have taken the temperature down to about minus 30 degrees C. Later on a weather system topped even these winds by blowing up to 60 knots.

So far we have avoided any damage in this latest storm, but earlier we had a saga of steering faults. The wheel spindle locking pin sheered and the wheel started pulling out from the pedestal. Two hours steering a 67 ft yacht with an emergency tiller, in 40 knots is certainly an experience I do not want to repeat.

These constant gales gave the crew and yacht a terrible battering. Wind-powered spray viciously stung any unprotected skin and the crashing waves continually scrubbed the decks clean of detritus (usually human entangled with ropes) then washed out the cockpit. The boat recovers, shakes, picks up speed and surges forward, trembling with anticipation knowing that with the next wave the cycle starts again. The crew on deck were unrecognisable with faces hidden behind hats, hoods, scarves and goggles. Only in the doghouse did they emerge, faces glowing red with excitement and fear to tell of the last enormous wave. The maximum gusts of 65 knots had us holding on tight. The helmsman, with eyes shut, waited for the gust to end - the lulls at only 45 knots are a gentle respite and almost enjoyable sailing. How relative values have changed - never before have I said that sailing in 45 knots is enjoyable; what madness was this?

The Southern Ocean Club has been formed for those daft enough to go there. Bruised and battered the fourteen new members of the S.O.C. have been well and truly baptised after the last twelve days.The waves found more and more novel ways of outwitting the helm. There was the straight-on 'biggy' that had no back to it. The yacht was first airborne then crashed bellyflop style. Then there were the mountain-climbing ones - a big one concealing an even bigger one behind. Unlucky the driver when these waves coincided and the top broke over us. With each of these waves the helmsman either shut his eyes to avoid the smarting spray or ducked behind the wheel, knowing full well that the motion would whip the wheel out of his or her hands if you hadn't let go first....

It wasn't long before the depressions were rolling through again and it was time to be on deck and change the staysail for the storm staysail and tack.We hove-to to make the change and Mike Bass, our new single-legger from *British Steel*, lost his temper when the clew fitting caught his chin as it went down below. I called him back to the cockpit and had a discussion with him regarding this burst of uncontrolled anger, which had been a danger to the other four people on the foredeck. Anger makes you go blind and deaf, although the adrenalin keeps flowing giving lots of strength. It must be controlled, otherwise it can possibly harm other people on the boat. Once when I was helming and caught a gust which threw me at the wheel; the wheel spokes caught the top of my kneecap, which was very painful. Being very angry and then frustrated with myself, I stayed at the wheel for twenty minutes until my mood had abated. It was my bad knee, but it turned out to be nothing serious, just bruised.

The consistently bad weather had its impact on us - we were all getting very tired and mood swings came and went quite quickly. On waking up to go on watch people had to be told things two or three times to make them really understand. Tolerance levels were noticeably reduced. Sammy was struggling; she felt there was an over-protective attitude towards her which showed when she was not allowed to helm at times. This affected her so much that she felt she had to prove her own abilities each time on every watch to different people. Sam actually does have a feel for helming but, being quite small, doesn't always have the strength to do it for long.

By now, because I would have expected that the crew would have known their own and each others' abilities a lot better, I found it curious that they didn't always pick this up; was I expecting too much from people or do I just think in a different way? I was also surprised that the desire to learn about the weather had not developed more amongst the crew. I wonder if this is a social reflection that many people nowadays expect to be taught rather than self-teach.

Everything is wet; the sodden sailors drip in the doghouse; the washing up water leaps around the galley; hatches leak and the mast gate pours water in. Wherever the smallest pinprick is the ocean will find it. All through the gales we keep sailing our best, gaining a mile or two on our closest rivals and sometimes losing some. Spirits are high, even if people are tired, cross at times, and wet. If willpower could win this race we would already be in Cape Town. The dreams of the tropics get stronger as our track is now slightly northward and the distance to go less than 1,800 miles.'

Coopers and Lybrand was fourth into Cape Town, fourth into Hobart, and as I said at the beginning were fourth at the finish at Southampton after a nail-biting battle against *Hofbrau* - short-tacking and covering her all the way from Portland Bill to the Needles and through the Solent. What a way to complete a round the world race.

Tony Short
J.O.G. Racing Offshore

You don't have to be in the Roaring Forties or off the Newfoundland Banks to be wet, cold and tired: you can experience all those sensations and more in the English Channel. In the Atlantic or the Southern Ocean there's nothing to hit except the possible whale, iceberg or container that's been washed off the deck of some ship. But you've got to be very unlucky to do so. In the Channel or North Sea the weather can be vile at any time of the year and you have the shipping lanes to contend with as well. Both are particularly relevant if you're racing a 27ft long 'H' boat without an engine. That's what Tony Short has been doing the last twelve years, although after four years he did get a Seagull. His first boat was *Zadig*, but in 1988 he bought *Hesperus*.

Tony joined the Club in the early '50's and sailed Fireflies, before crewing Tony Newman in Fourteens for a bit. He later bought one for himself. In 1981 he decided to go offshore, although he hadn't had much experience and does not appear to have known a great deal about navigation. I asked him: "Why did you do it?" "Well," Tony replied, "I had a great yen to sail across the Channel. Uffa sailed to Le Havre in *Avenger*, so I thought I'd have a go in a slightly bigger boat, and have been doing roughly 2,000 miles a year ever since."

'H' boats are made in Finland in the Gulf of Bothnia like Swans, and nine thousand of them have been built since 1968. They have a 250sq ft main, a small jib and draw 4ft 6ins. "The're rather like a Folkboat," said Tony, but I suspect lighter, judging by some his spinnaker runs. He seems to have raced to practically every port on France's Channel coast - Fecamp, Trouville, Deauville, St Vaast, Cherbourg and also round to St Malo and Lezardrieux in Brittany, apart from a cruise down the Chenal du Four to Camaret. He's recently bought a small GPS, but for many years had nothing but a compass and a log he hung over the side. I presume he'd read about tidal vectors.

'On one passage to Deauville,' he told me, 'just when we were crossing the shipping lanes I fell asleep, to be wakened suddenly by a continuous row of lights from our port bow right round to our starboard beam. Ahead someone was flashing 'dot,dot,dash' on an Aldis light, which I knew to be 'U' in Morse code meaning 'you are running into danger.' We were inside the tow rope of two tugs towing an oil rig up-channel, and went about smartly. On another Deauville race we returned in a stiff blow with two reefs in and our landfall was a row of street lights by which I hoped I'd be able to read the street signs! We had no idea where we where. Eventually what seemed like years later I recognised the place as Selsey and we were off The Bill, having missed the Owers light completely with the wind, rain and the heel of the boat.

Sometimes we raced only two up and did quite well, but it's very tiring. Alcohol should be avoided. Returning from a race to Trouville we arrived at Spithead at dawn. I'd sailed all night, having only a lad who had done very little sailing and was not a lot of use as crew. I was cold and wet and took a nip of whisky and found myself hallucinating all the way to the moorings at Burseldon. The sea was lit up with flaming flares, transparent boats sailed past and the piles were in triplicate. A very unpleasant experience; it was more fatigue, than drink.'

Tony's fastest race was from Cowes to Brighton - fifty two miles in six hours 10 minutes. 'My crew, Julian Cochran was very experienced and would not let me take the spinnaker down. We did a similar spinnaker run from E.C.2. buoy, mid-Channel, to Weymouth when we averaged eight knots. Lydia Jackson and Martin Dixon were on board. Lydia and Sally Dixon (that was) joined me in 1985/86, and we sailed together until Sally went in for bigger things. We came back from Weymouth in a Force 8 gale.

Our racing has improved over the years in both Categories 3 and 4 Offshore. Having a regular crew like John Naylor and Sally and or Lydia helped enormously. In the 1989 J.O.G. race from Cowes to Poole via the Forts we came 1st in our class and 1st overall; on which occasion both Sally and Lydia were with me. The following year in the Good Friday J.O.G. race to Cherbourg we came 1st in our class and 3rd overall with Sally and John Naylor as crew. However we've always done badly in the 'H' Boat Nationals.The 'H' Boat Association have a world championship each year restricted to seventy starters, and three of us, all owners, crewed *Hesperus* in the 1990 championship based on Holbaek, Denmark, without coming to blows. We weren't quite last and were very well looked after by the Danes. Wet, cold, tired, lost, sunny, foggy, windy, bored, frightened, excited, and gratified, we have had a very full twelve years.'

Long-Range Offshore Cruising

Those of us in this category creep onto the end of Peter Hopps's list. We don't pretend to be as brave, mad or in most cases as young as those who have preceded us. We all admire and some of us envy the Hopps's, Hollands, Fraser's and Cherry's of this world, but after a certain age for some of us it wouldn't be sensible, although Sally and Lydia seem to be made of sterner stuff. That doesn't mean we can't take our boats through a gale or two, but not necessarily all the way to Newport or on the Round Britain Race.

Sailing anyhow is meant to be fun and so none of us has to make excuses for long-range offshore cruising. In any case it always demands a considerable amount of planning and quite often a lot more navigational care than crashing around the Atlantic. Gastronomically enjoyable as they are, cross-Channel trips to such places as St Vaast la Houge are not what I'm talking about. Long-range offshore sailing involves more seatime and adventure. For instance over three seasons recently Chris Buckley has taken *Wandering Moon*, his Fulmar 32, to the west coast of Scotland, south-west Ireland and the fjords of Norway - 'magnificent sailing but rocks everywhere.' They are all beautiful cruising grounds, but as always with the sea each area must be treated with respect. More recently of course Christopher and Sally have sailed into the Mediterranean and I think intend to sail further east this year.

This section should really have started with Simon 'Killer' Cawthorne who joined the Club in 1973. For some years he sailed Lasers, but for quite a number of years now he has been a professional skipper on among other boats *Highland Fling*, a Swan 53. We raced against each other in the Swan Regatta at Porto Cervo, Sardinia, when I was on my way through the Mediterranean in 1990 and in the 1992 Antigua Week.

Long before this in 1981 he raced across the Atlantic with Peter Hopps in a Moody 33 in the Caribbean Race.Organised by the R.O.R.C. this is from Cowes to Las Palmas, where there is a stopover, and then on to Antigua. 'We carried the spinnaker all the way through the Bay of Biscay,' Peter Hopps told me, 'doing two hundred miles in one day. The skipper was petrified.' I'm not surprised. In 1991 'Killer' was once again going westwards across the Atlantic, and among his crew was Bill Matcham, who has become a keel boat owner. I should have mentioned Francis Brown earlier because he cruised to Brittany and other places before going out to Singapore.

The last name to appear on Peter's list is 'John Herbert - a promising novice' - cheeky so-and-so. I think he said that because he helped me with my 'astro' homework. I shall not say much about my twenty-month 18,000-mile cruise except to recommend it. One proviso - it's not such a strain if you do it slowly like Chris and Sally. Secondly you need not only a good boat, but 'a good mix' as a crew if contemplating going as far as I went. If you aren't lucky enough to have a wife or an established partner, who likes sailing, don't get involved in the equivalent of a cruise-liner or skiing holiday romance. A boat is too small for that kind of thing, although Peter Hopps, as you would expect, told me of the Club member who was caught 'in flagrante delicto' with his skipper's daughter while on the Fastnet Race - but fortunately not by the skipper.

Be prepared for lots of wind in the Aegean, which will be 'on the nose' when you come back. The Meltemi often gets up to gale force from the north or north-west just about lunchtime. But the islands are lovely and so are parts of Turkey. Dubrovnik when I saw it was unforgettable, but I fear no more.We must have been one of the last foreign boats there before the fighting. There were no tourists; the cafes empty and the locals very friendly but frightened.

Elba, from where Napoleon made a dramatic escape, is worth visiting, after Bonnifacio in Corsica. The Atlantic, via the Canaries and the south-east Trades is a 'doddle' - even with Julian Pearson, Martin Dixon and my youngest son intoxicated during their watches not by drink but by *Freelance* surfing at times while under spinnaker. (I took it down just in time before the halyard chafed through.) If you can afford it some day charter, with others, a boat in the Caribbean. It's wonderful, but watch out for the reefs. Better, I think, than the Med, although chartering there is worthwhile and cheaper.

After the rather boring 2000-mile haul from the Virgin Islands, which are a must, entering New York on a summer's day with a good breeze blowing and the Manhattan skyline in the background was unforgettable. Then north to Newport, and all those extraordinary 'Great Gatsby' houses; Martha's Vineyard, then north again to Maine, which is something very special. Finally across to Halifax, Nova Scotia, to pick up my trans-Atlantic crew, and home with the north-west Trades - so simple. However there were a hundred and nine people to organise but it was all worthwhile. It seems a strange note on which to end the Centenary History of a riverside sailing club.

Our Club has spawned some of the finest dinghy helmsmen in the country, but it's somewhat paradoxical that the maximum enthusiasm today appears to be for offshore sailing, in spite of the cost. This is fine in it's way, but not really healthy for the future of the Club which first and foremost must be a river sailing club, with non-sailing members providing help, encouragement and in many cases valuable experience from their professional fields.

There are many reasons why certain classes of boats have died or gone elsewhere, and why turnouts are poor. They have all been discussed endlessly: they include reservoir sailing clubs, the ownership of cars which may lure sailors to non-tidal waters or even to the sea, the popularity of wind-surfing and spending more time with the family. None of us can do anything about any of these factors least of all the tide which regrettably prevents the Club allowing beginners, whatever their age, out sailing without a rescue boat being constantly in attendance. This does not make Robbie's instruction and Beginners Sailing easy to organise, but the sessions are yielding some results. Therefore let us resolve to support in every way we can the training of those new members who don't yet know how to sail, but who want to sail on the river. A welcome by-product of the navigation classes has been a number of new full members. We need these new members, not only financially, but to bring more vitality to the Club and make its future secure. And that surely is what we all want.

Appendix A

Racing at London Corinthian
by
Paul Williamson

We are very fortunate in having Race Records for most of our Club's history, in four specially printed volumes and eight ledgers, giving a unique and marvellous picture of our activities. The entries vary from the beautiful copperplate of the early years, through careful, cultivated handwriting of the '40's, '50's, and '60's, to near illegibility at later times and even illiteracy. The main gaps are pre-March 1902, and October 1909 to March 1935 (the greatest loss), and some other shorter ones. Since early 1991 no one could be found to keep up the detailed record, despite the single-handed efforts for some time of the Rear-Commodore, Paul Truitt, and the practice lapsed three years short of our Centenary - a sign of the times? As well as organising admirably all the past records of the sailing side, Paul Truitt has kept careful summaries since then. There is therefore a large amount of material to read and assimilate. In the space available I can only give an outline of the general picture; the rise and fall of our sailing classes, some of the outstanding names at various periods and quotations from the 'Remarks' space, which was kept up (entertainingly) for many years. So please forgive me for lapsing into note form at times.

1902-09: The early years, 1902-09, are fascinating of course, when we raced from the old Club, downstream of the pier, where Furnivall Gardens are now. There seemed to be about eighteen boats mentioned in the handicapping lists, turnouts ranging from an average of four to five, up to nine or ten occasionally, and a combined fleet of eighteen-twenty four on our already regular visits from Ranelagh Sailing Club. The boats were all different, of course, and raced with time allowances varying from scratch to twenty five minutes, the allowances being regularly adjusted during the season. Can you imagine the veiled acrimony surrounding the estimation of these handicaps by the Sailing Committee? And indeed the notes on the Sailing Committee records of 1935 onwards were continually referring to efforts to devise an improved form of handicapping, and complaints about the results.

Broadly speaking after 1902-09, when turnouts varied from four to ten, our turnouts rose to splendid peaks, even in Club races, of thirty, forty and even a record fifty nine, in the '50's and '60's, before declining through the '70's,'80's and '90's to our present often sad state of 'no quorum' in any class, or just three or four for a trophy race - and those from three or four times as many boats kept here than in the early 20th century days. Judging from photos of the time they varied from heavy dinghies to half-decked keeled gaff-rigged day-boats, kept on 'legs' off the Club.

In those days we had sixteen - twenty races a year, in a season from late March to early November. Comments on the starts, whether they were close or not were common, like 'a pretty little start.' Owners were generally referred to as 'Mr.' (though there were also regular lady helms). There are a couple of entries around 1907 of 'Disqualified for having a Paid Hand on board.' There were quite a few protests and a lot of disqualifications, mostly for fouling another boat, or often a mark or mark-boat - so they weren't all Gentlemen and 'Gave Up' (Retired) as soon as they had broken a Rule, as was established by the 1940's.

There are a number of entries of a 'Record time for the Course,' i.e. Club buoy to Barnes and back, so they must have been very set positions. The time was 57 mins 4 secs for twice round, and this would be nearly bridge to bridge. There was also the occasional attempt at rule-bending, a boat in 1904 being disqualified for kedging, not just out of danger, but 'further than required' in a light weather race. Capsizes were rare of course and provided comments like 'received plenty of assistance from Club members and towed to moorings waterlogged. There was also much reefing and shaking out of reefs, and masts, tillers and rudders 'carried away' - much more romantic than 'broke.'

Some quotes from 1902: 'The strong wind carried them up to Barnes in slashing style.' 'It has come to my knowledge that some of the above boats fouled one another at the upper mark - signed Rear-Commodore.' *'Iris* carried away her rudder during a slammer of wind....' *'Tercel* marched over the course in fine style....' In '06 there was a Special Race, where competitors had to start and finish moored fore and aft off the Club with sails down, and on one occasion in later years pass between *The Stork* training ship and Upper Mall, and then between the Eyot and Chiswick Mall, both going to and coming from a mark beyond the Eyot and the bank, twice round - very tricky now with far more manoeuvrable dinghies, but then.... ! Remember there was much more working boat traffic then, and there are entries about boats 'hampered by tugboat' or 'barge' and much later, after World War II, 'mark boat carried away by a string of barges.' Almost all the courses were to Barnes (long) at least once, whatever the wind conditions, and occasionally in later years, a short - to 'Thorneycrofts' or 'Chiswick,' a mark beyond the Eyot. Two last quotes from this period - 'Owing to accident, race postponed,' and *'Iris* sent crew ashore on 2nd round' - a marital disagreement, to lighten ship or to get some beer? She counted as a finisher - Oh for more details!

1935: Sadly we have no details of the period from 1909

to 1935, including World War I, but from now on we had twenty five to thirty boats racing, including three Fourteens. The prominent sailing members then were: P.Chandler, E. Mitchell, F.Royde, Miss Vaughan, G. Harris, W. Anderson, A.P.Herbert, George Bull and E.R.'Bob' Salt. All raced off individual handicaps, varied by their position in each race, and turnouts ranged from four to ten. The West London Hospital Cup had twenty one entries and The Shackleton, the Open for Fourteens, twenty including Peter Scott, and was won by Percy Chandler, a Club member, in *Ace*, crewed by Jack Holt, as the author has already mentioned. The season ran from May to October that year with twenty one races of all types.

1936: Thirty-four races in all, average starters in Club races about nine from a fleet of twenty eight. Hammersmith Bridge to Greenwich Race, fastest time 2 hrs, 27 mins, 35 secs; slowest 3hrs,18 mins. Up to nineteen entries in Trophy races; 'Doreen Cup won by Miss Vaughan, first lady in history of Club to do so.' 'Brent Sailing Club having lost their water at the Welsh Harp, and have proved themselves good sportsmen and company.' On the suggestion of Dr. Olaf Bradbury the first winter season was launched; seventeen races, starters ranging from four to twelve.

1937: '*Boss*, a new 16-foot racer launched,' the first of the London Corinthian One Designs, of which only three were built because of World War II, the longest lasting being LC/3 *Dart*, belonging to Ted King-Morgan. Three ladies racing regularly, including Miss. A.W. Procter, who proved to be one of our keenest members, starting in Handicap, then in Fourteen, a Swordfish and finally an Enterprise.

'Sailing Rules to be more strictly enforced in future - members are getting lax in some matters.' Shackleton won by E.Bruce Wolfe, after his third in 1936 - the start of a marvellous record. Many Club races lasted only forty minutes or less, as courses seemed not to be tailored to the wind conditions. Winter racing continued successfully, twenty two boats turning out in a sixteen race series. Very icy conditions at times; bilge and sheets frozen solid - and this was in pre-wet suit days, and little personal and boat buoyancy.

1938: Thirty-five races of all kinds in the summer, averaging ten plus entries, and up to thirty two in Club Trophy races. Shackleton won by Bruce Wolfe again, from twenty nine. Experiment of course on occasions, boats could either do one Long or two Shorts. London River Race, Hammersmith, Greenwich; and Tower Bridge, Woolwich and back to Greenwich. Some things don't change - there were collisions with scullers and many complaints of driftwood. A turnout of seven at an August Bank Holiday was regarded as 'poor,' out of twenty three boats taking part in the series. Winter started with fifteen to seventeen, including Tom Fielding for the first time in a National Twelve.

1939: 'Several spectacular Chinese gybes....' a pre-kicking strap comment. Several references to The Brewery and Windless Corner. A number of protests each season. Bruce Wolfe only 2nd of twenty two in Shackleton. Turnouts a little down on winter, around ten. Joe Bloor first recorded. 'War being declared on Sunday, 3rd September 1939, at 11.15a.m., the sailing must at least for the time being, suffer.' November - 'The war has seriously interfered with the finish of the season.' There were no races from 2nd September until 29th October, the first of a seven race winter series, three to seven starters.

1940: For the summer season engraved silver spoons were given as prizes for first and second (including crews) in each Club race, and entries were up to nine. 13th July: 'Order came that all boats had to be removed from the moorings, and sailing not to be allowed on the river.' But sailing was allowed again from August. 17th August: 'Race abandoned as all but two boats sank when placed in the water' - presumably they had 'opened up' while ashore.'After 7th September, Hitler's Blitz started in earnest and racing seemed to stop. Early in October a bomb fell in the river and damaged some of the boats, and so ever since no official races have been held, but a few members have gone cruising now and then. Those sailing members who remain are bravely trying to carry on despite old Hitler.'

1941: The next entry is 25th May, and normal racing was resumed, with four to eleven entries. Miss Hobling, another long-term enthusiast, made her appearance. Ranelagh Sailing Club visited at the suggestion of Jack Holt, the race being won by Beecher Moore out of ten.

1942: Winter turnouts were a little down, but another visit from R.S.C. included Ian Proctor, in a National Twelve. Book tokens now being awarded for Club races. Open and Trophy races produced up to twenty three starters and Club races up to eleven, so racing was very healthy again. In September, at the suggestion of A.P. Herbert, a pursuit race was held for the first time, the twelve boats divided into four starts according to potential speed.

1943: Some Pool races were held, with prizes of 7/-, 5/- and 3/- on occasions. Turnouts holding up well, and Misses K. Hobling and A.W.Procter out in almost every race. First appearance of Michael Gilkes.

1944-45: Club races continued to attract up to ten or more, out of twenty boats listed with handicaps, the first four in each race having them adjusted. United Hospitals Sailing Club had sailed with us since the beginning of the war, as they weren't able to sail at Burnham on Crouch for security reasons. The record book is damaged by damp because it was left out after the flying bomb fell in June, blowing away most of the top storey of the Club. Curiously no mention was made in the Race Record book about this. There is a gap between November 1945 and July 1946.

1946: Some of the most regular sailors were Olaf Bradbury, T.A. Charlesworth, P.W. Clement, H.G. Bassett, E. King-Morgan, G. Bull, R. Jorgensen, A. Storm Roberts and Misses Hobling and Procter. Five to ten entries generally, several Fourteens, a couple of National Twelves, L.C.S.C. One Designs and Handicap.

1947: Bruce Wolfe won the Shackleton. The Fourteens started racing as a scratch class within the Club class, but including LC/3 *Dart*, sometimes with their own longer course. Incomplete results around here until winter. 26th October - the familiar entry 'R.O. - E.R. Salt.' First two Fireflies appeared, (212) and (213), *Judy* and *Pennyroyal*, owned by H.J. Palmer and P.D. Banbury. Excellent winter turnouts of ten to fifteen; Fourteens, five to seven; Fireflies, two to three, Handicap, four to five. W.H. Barr a regular.

1948: Ranelagh April visit produced twenty seven starters, Jack Holt winning in a National Twelve, most of their fleet being Merlin Rockets, designed and built by Jack. Team racing in Fourteens and Fireflies v the R.O.R.C.; the Club lost badly. John Herbert and Don Storrar started racing Fourteens. Bruce Wolfe missed the Shackleton (twenty starters), but Pamela Wolfe was second. 'There is no petrol allowed for private cars, so no boats have been bought on trailers.' Tamesis towed six boats down.

L.C.S.C. Trophy - fifteen starters - 'John Herbert ran ashore on Eyot, shoved off without crew, but returned and picked her up....' (Always the gentleman....) Anthony Lousada shared *Dark Wind* with him. Trophy races up to eighteen, Club seventeen. The West London Hospital Cup had thirty one starters, including two from Strand on the Green Sailing Club for the first time and ten from Twickenham Sailing Club. In the July visit of Ranelagh, Fourteens and Merlin Rockets raced off scratch, National Twelves and Fireflies were allowed ten and 'slower boats' individually. A 'Charlesworth' was set sometimes, i.e. Barnes, Thorneycroft, Barnes finish in a NW breeze. Seventeen starters for the Greenwich race. The winter season of sixteen races had up to eighteen entries, mostly Fourteens, three to four Fireflies, a few Handicap and the first Swordfish - so healthy turnouts. The summer season scheduled thirty seven races of all sorts - c.f. today about thirty winter and fifty summer.

1949: 'Nine a small turnout.' Charles Currey visited in a new Fairey moulded Fourteen, but Bruce Wolfe won again in the Shackleton (twenty one starters) - 'quite a good entry....' In June Miss Hobling, now regularly in a Firefly, won from eighteen in the Greenwich race - towed back by the President, A.P.H. in *Water Gipsy*. Dickie Dixon and L. Wood doing well in Fourteens, along with T.A. Charlesworth, E.L. Farnsworth and M.J. Gilkes. An Open for National 18's produced eight entries, one from the Club. twenty-twenty five entries in Club races was common, summer and winter.

1950: From the summer season the Fourteens - L.C/3 and the Swordfish raced as a class, followed by the Fireflies, then Handicap, now called the Open Class. Fourteens and Fireflies continued to have individual handicaps for parallel series running concurrently. Turnouts were around eight, four and five respectively. The first Jos Collins Memorial Trophy for Fourteens was won by E. Bruce Wolfe, who was second to C.B. Lapthorne in the Shackleton. The first Morton Stephenson Firefly Tankard Open had fourteen entries and was won by Alan Vines, one of the Vines dynasty. John Clarke, who did much for the Club over the years, was racing *Kestrel* in the Open Class, as was Molly Eady in *Allegro*, and Philip Withers Green in *Sandpiper* - our Commodore during the great move to Linden House, and donor of the Trophy. In the 'All-In' races the Fourteens gave the Fireflies 12 per cent and Handicap 18 per cent, which was added to their class handicaps (glad I wasn't working things out in those days). By autumn the three classes were getting turnouts of up to eleven, nine and eight respectively.

1951: Two Club races were cancelled in February - 'wild and bitter weather' or 'cold blasts, very wet.' The winter winners in the Fourteens were: Joe Bloor, Michael Gilkes, Don Storrar, and P.C. Dickie Dixon; Fireflies: Dr. P. Clements and David Edwards; Open Class: Molly Eady and John Clarke - nearly all remembered still by some of the oldest members - let alone David Edwards, still racing. Gavin Robertson, Peter Calder, Arthur Tarrant, and Simeon Bull were there by summer if not before. The Ranelagh visit had forty seven entries, the Fourteens' Opens (both won by Bruce Wolfe) seventeen, the first Nina Wood Firefly Team race three teams of three, and sixteen for their individual Open. Ordinary races ranged up to twenty four entries. Winifred Procter had now moved to a Swordfish, and later Miss Hobling did too. 15th July: 'launch would not start and upstream buoy not laid out.' From the winter season the Swordfish and LC/3 had a separate start.

1952: Typical winter race had four to five Fourteens, four Swordfish, eight Fireflies and five Open. 31st March 'racing cancelled owing to bad weather - snow.' The Ranelagh visit produced fifty four starters - those were the days! The Fourteen Opens were down to eleven, but both were won as usual.... May - 'as an experiment the Fireflies were sailed single-handed. Most helmsmen agreed this was an enjoyable and invaluable experience, and that other single-handed races should be arranged.' A long range forerunner of the O.K.s and Lasers perhaps? In June the Pool of London Race was for the first time from below Hammersmith Bridge to Cherry Garden Pier, opposite Wapping Old Stairs, and another race back - fourteen entries. The 'Hospitals Week-End' had twenty six entries, including six from Strand on the Green, but none from

Twickenham nor Tamesis by now. The Fourteens and Swordfish had a number of races cancelled for lack of entries, and returned to racing together as a class in winter - up to ten Swordfish then and fourteen Fireflies. First team race in Fireflies between boats kept at Wally See's moorings and the Club, for a cup presented by the late Mr. Walter See. 28th December - 'race cancelled owing to fog.'

1953: 3rd January '*Mosca* retired with a large hole.... having been hit by a racing eight.' First Tilney Tankard for Swordfish - eight entries. Three winter races were cancelled - 'Strong gale,' 'Floods,' 'Blizzard.' April - Trent Cup for Fourteens. Two-day, two-boat team race, eleven teams and normal Fourteen Open the following weekend - quite a festival. Bruce-Wolfe didn't quite win, but was well up, with Bruce Banks, Stewart Morris, C.B. Lapthorne and 'our' Michael Gilkes. Mike Cook, of Upper Thames Sailing Club, later to join us in the Fireflies, did well, as did Bruce Fraser. May - five of the Open Class apparently raced to Strand on the Green Round the Island, elapsed time 2 hrs 20 mins. Summer turnouts still excellent, often twenty plus. Trophy race for Open Class had eight entries. September - '*Tigger* disqualified through not paying Entrance fee to O.O.D.' Nina Wood Firefly Team Trophy had sixteen teams of two, won by the Club, Jane Bluff and David Edwards, and the Morton Stephenson won by Wally Maddison of Tamesis, and also a winter member of the Club from 1933. In the winter season we had up to thirty three entries, including seventeen Fireflies.

1954: February. 'the motor launch broke down.' The Fourteens' Opens won by Stewart Morris, Bruce Wolfe and Bruce Banks in first three as usual. Firefly Team Racing v a number of mainly Thames Area Clubs featured from now on. Cherry Garden Pier Race - fifteen entries, summer series around fifteen. June - first appearance of John Underwood in a

Fourteen, a crafty sailor still remembered with exasperated affection by many. October - first Team Race v Norwich Frostbite Sailing Club, four a side in Fireflies with all but one capsizing.

1955: Winter season - Fourteens up to seven, Swordfish six, Fireflies thirteen, but the Open Class suddenly down to two or three. Prominent in their classes: Fourteens, Michael Gilkes, Joe Bloor; Swordfish, Peter Curry, Peter Strauss and Tom Fielding; Fireflies, David Edwards, Dickie Dixon, Peter Bloor, Walter Saxelby, Robert Bull, Wally Maddison and Gavin Robertson. Misses Hobling and Procter still regulars in Swordfish. Both Fourteen Opens won by Bruce Wolfe. In May Chris Buckley won his first two races in Fireflies after warming up with seven of thirty two starters in the Lady Bull Bowl. Ranelagh visit had forty six entries. Summer Club races producing up to fifteen Fourteen/Swordfish and nine Fireflies. Philip Whitlow prominent in Fourteens and Tony Newman and Lawrence Grand arrived, also Patrick Troughton, that excellent actor and second 'Dr. Who.' Big turnouts for Firefly Opens and the Club thrashed the Castaways Sailing Club 1, 2, and 3 to 4, 5 and 6! Seventeen in an ordinary Firefly Club race. 27th December: 'a black day, heavy rain, wind rising to gale force during the first lap. No rescue launch available and so many boats capsized that those surviving had to abandon the race to act as life-boats.' Fifteen starters.

1956: Club races now called Points Races, though Handicap and Scratch series still being run in tandem in both classes. Tilney Tankard produced eight Swordfish. 'the motor boat was not operating, so a squally race was declared void, due to capsizes etc.' Stewart Morris won the Fourteen Opens, Bruce Wolfe second, Brian Lapthorn third. 'Short-wave radio was used to link the Club, the rescue-boat and two shore-stations during these races.' 2nd June - Pool race: 'Miss Procter completed the course, whilst Mr. Underwood took an involuntary swim,' but won his next race at Ranelagh from thirty six entries. 'Hospitals' weekend - the first appearance of Paul Williamson, sailing with Strand on the Green Sailing Club in a Heron. He came third out of twenty with Bruce Fraser. Arthur Tarrant first of thirty six in Firefly Open. Trophy races had entries up to eighteen per class, with eighteen Fireflies for a points race on one occasion. Jeremy Pudney was prominent in the Fireflies, also Chris Buckley, Wally Maddison, Dickie Dixon and Robert Bull. The pattern of large winter turnouts and fairly large in the summer was now well established.

1957: John Underwood continued a pattern of disqualifications on protests, retirements, and wins, which was to last for years. Thirty for Lady Bull's Bowl, eleven Swordfish for Tilney Tankard. In the Fourteen Opens, with Bruce Fraser absent, Bobby Pegna won both from fourteen and sixteen. The name Kemlo, sailing with Strand on the Green, first appeared in our results. Team racing in Fireflies flourishing and popular Opens. Other regulars in Fireflies: Tony Jenkins, Hugh Davies, Peter Calder, Len Fay and John Jupe.

1958: Wally See Trophy flourishing, and most turnouts generally, except Open Class. 'No race for Fireflies (all away pot-hunting).' Fourteens' Opens - Bruce Wolfe back and won both. Pool of London - ten entries - 'The Club launch leaked excessively.' Tilney Tankard - twelve Swordfish. Jimmy Bridge-Butler down as O.O.D. West London Hospital - 'This was well handicapped on the Portsmouth method' - at last! Peter Hinton, soon to be one of our best helmsman, appears in his Firefly *Fuego*. Cyril Goulborne was also prominent. Mike Cook used terylene sails on his Firefly, with a personal handicap adjustment, of course.

1959: Individual handicaps within a class came to an end. Club trophies drawings between four and thirty one. A windy

Fourteen Open produces a win for John Herbert in the Jos Collins, with Bruce Wolfe second but he won The Shackleton the next day. Molly Eady in *Allegro* prominent when the Handicap/Open Class was out, Tom Fielding now in a Swordfish, but on 19th July he appeared in the first Enterprise (2842) though one had appeared earlier, possibly a visitor, in the L.C.S.C. Trophy. - thirty nine entries. Courses were variations of Barnes, Chiswick, (or Lep), Bemax, and Club or Home. Bill White arrived in the second Enterprise. Peter Roberts was a regular in a Firefly, a great Club character and long-time launch driver and Harbour Master.

1960: The Enterprises had their own Class start in the Winter Series, with ten boats in the Club. Sixteen Fourteens and Swordfish raced and thirty one Fireflies. Winter winners were: Fourteens, John Herbert and Anthony Lousada, E.H. Edwards and Peter Strauss; Fireflies, Cyril Goulborn, Peter Hinton and Chris Buckley all very close; and Enterprises, Joe Bloor, Tom Fielding and Geoffrey Freestone. The Firefly Open attracted forty seven, won by Mike Cook and up to twenty one in Firefly points races. In winter Philip Rayner was a regular in Fireflies and Jeremy Pudney was doing well. Mike Collyer, in his Firefly *The Heap* won from twenty in a Club Trophy race. Chris Buckley beat Bruce Wolfe into second place in both Fourteen Opens. Hugh Kemlo appeared in Fireflies.

1961: Miss Procter and Cyril Goulborn now in Enterprises. The Swordfish has suddenly declined to only the occasional one. Bill Simpson in the Enterprises and Miranda Seal in the Fireflies. Summer winners: Fourteens - Chris Buckley. Tony Newman, John Underwood; Fireflies: - Peter Hinton, Dickie Dixon, Gavin Robertson; Enterprises: Joe Bloor, S.L. Fowler, Tom Fielding. John Herbert, Arthur Prince, Dr. Paul Smart and Jack Sheills prominent also in the Fourteens. The first Enterprise Open weekend had eighteen entries, wins for Peter Bloor and

Cyril Goulborn. October: 'Fog - not many competitors' - actually thirteen in three classes, so normal turnouts very healthy. In winter: Simeon Bull, Paul Smart and John Herbert lead the Fourteens; Jeremy Vines, Peter Hinton, Jeremy Pudney the Fireflies; Paul Williamson, Bill Simpson, Joe Bloor the Enterprises.

1962: Up to thirty entries in the Fourteen Opens, the Jos Collins being won by Simeon Bull and The Shackleton by Stewart Morris - Bruce Wolfe second. The Firefly Opens attracted sixteen teams, Strand on the Green (Hugh Kemlo and Paul Williamson) and thirty two individuals. Thirty-two also for the first Linden House Trophy to which we had moved. No Handicap nor Swordfish now, and frustratingly, no record of courses, until late 1974, when our present numbered buoys were in operation. Winter Points had up to thirty two entries in three classes.

1963: Spring and summer entries generally rather down, sometimes no Fireflies. Bruce Wolfe won both Fourteen Opens. A Jumelage team race between the Club, Boulogne-Billancourt and Zaandam, near Amsterdam, was won by the Club. The Enterprise Opens had many more visitors, up to thirty one entries, including John Underwood, now in *Popetty*. Fifty entries for the King-Morgan with Ranelagh, but summer Points rather volatile, the Enterprises being the most consistent. L.C.S.C. Trophy in September, one O.K., Alan Whitehead appeared. Summer Points winners: Fourteens - Jack Shiells; Fireflies - Peter Hinton; Enterprises - Bill Simpson. Up to forty two entries in winter series, generally Enterprises, Fourteens and Fireflies respectively in size of turnout.

1964: Chris Buckley and Hugh Kemlo now prominent in Enterprises. Fireflies getting between twenty five to thirty for their four Open races. Summer leaders: Fourteens: M. King, Jeremy Pudney and Tony Newman; Enterprises - Chris Buckley,

Paul Williamson and Bill Simpson. Fireflies: Peter Hinton, John Jupe, C. Jones. Enterprise turnouts remained around ten, often no Fourteens or Fireflies or only four to five. 'R.N.L.I. to be re-sailed, mark laid too late (sic)!' O.K. 625, Simon Bullimore entered twice, and on 7th November first O.K. race in separate start - Eddie Kirkwood-Lowe, Martyn Wheatley and Jimmy Bridge-Butler. Last appearance of Winifred Procter, keenly racing here since 1937.

1965: Winter '64-'65, up to about eight Fourteens, twenty three Enterprises, eight Fireflies and eight O.K.s in Points races, and sometimes more in Trophy races. Winter results: Fourteens: - Tony Newman, Simeon Bull, Jeremy Vines. Enterprises: Paul Williamson, Hugh Kemlo, Bill Simpson. Fireflies: John Hart, David Edwards, E. Welch. O.K.s: Simon Bullimore, Martyn Wheatley, Eddie Kirkwood-Lowe. Fourteen Opens: Jeremy Vines and Bruce Wolfe first and second of twenty five. Summer Points holding up fairly well, although rarely any Fourteens. Gavin Robertson now in an Enterprise, Paul Williamson and Chris Buckley in O.K.s. Wally See Cup now four-sided race in Enterprises and won by Fireflies. King Morgan Trophy with Ranelagh 'only' twenty three entries. Firefly *Pansy* now sailed by Miranda Kemlo. Firefly Opens good, if a little down. Elsie Bloor doing more than her share of O.O.D. First O.K. Opens, up to twenty entries, won twice by Chris Buckley. Forty five in the Linden House Trophy, won by Hugh Kemlo in Enterprise *Skim* (so what's new?).

1966: After vanishing for the summer the Fourteens returned in strength for the winter of '66-'67, and turnouts were up to thirty eight in four classes, forty eight for the Dark Wind Trophy and thirty seven for the Enterprise Opens, Tom Hill and John Underwood winning - only five visitors. In the Fourteen Opens James Vernon won from Jeremy Pudney and Bruce Wolfe the first day, and Mike Peacock from Jeremy Pudney and

Stewart Morris the second day - twenty eight starters. Royal Thames Yacht Club Trophy for Fireflies, five of twenty one finished - 'wind Force 6, gusting 10!' - Jeremy Vines the winner. Team races in Fireflies still frequent and mostly successful. Summer Points - rarely any Fourteens, often no Fireflies, Enterprises up to fifteen or so, O.K.s six or seven. Good O.K. Open, won by Chris Buckley in *Twinkle-Tyme II*. Huge turnout, forty two for Firefly Opens, many visitors. Fourteens returned for the Winter, level pegging with the Fireflies and O.K.s, with Enterprises consistently the strongest class - up to twenty in Points races. On 11th December, on a Trophy day sixteen Fourteens, twenty one Enterprises, thirteen Fireflies and nine O.K.s were out - fifty nine in all, the highest ever turnout recorded.

1967: January - fifty eight starters on one Trophy race day; forty four in Dark Wind Trophy. Thirty or so in Points races; the Winter Series '66-'67 was probably the high water mark of the Club. Winter winners from all these, P. Lee and Simeon Bull from twenty two Fourteens; Hugh Kemlo and Bill Simpson from thirty four Enterprises; Keith Goulborn and Tony Weller from eighteen Fireflies, and Robin Dent and Jimmy Bridge-Butler from nineteen O.K.s. The Fourteens rarely appeared in the summer season; the Enterprises - five to sixteen, the Fireflies and O.K.s varying between none and eight. Bruce Wolfe was second in both Fourteen Opens from twenty nine. O.K. Opens - fourteen to twenty. Good Points turnouts in winter, up to about forty.

1968: Enterprise Open up to thirty entries; Firefly Opens, thirteen to seventeen; Fourteen Opens, twenty four to twenty seven, both won by Bruce Wolfe; O.K.Opens fourteen to eighteen; Firefly autumn Opens - ten teams and twenty seven individuals - won by P. Milanese. Summer Points - consistent Enterprises, rarely any Fourteens, Fireflies and O.K.s between three and six when they were out. Pool of London - eleven. Hospital weekend - twenty nine and thirty seven; King Morgan - thirty two, so summer Points, but not Trophy races, had declined. Gilbert and Una-Jane Winfield appeared in *Mirrors*.

1969: Winter Points healthy, twenty to twenty five out often. Enterprise Opens up to thirty seven, won by Phil Crebbin and Hugh Kemlo. Fourteen Opens, twenty five entries. Shackleton won by Keith Goulborn, a recent afficianado to the Fourteen fleet and the first time he showed he could beat the best, including Bruce-Wolfe who was fifth. Billy Graham had won the Jos Collins. Summer Points very variable as in 1968. Another Jumelage - this time at Hammersmith; the Club beat France and Holland. O.K. Opens, nineteen and twenty five. Team racing in Fireflies still fairly frequent. Tony Robinson and Liz Cratchley prominent in Firefly *Faun*. Excellent Firefly Open entry, won by Peter Hinton, now also at Laleham Sailing Club. Class turnouts improved in winter as usual.

1970: Hugh Kemlo won one of the Enterprise Opens, from twenty seven, after a winter in Fourteens. Winter winners: Fourteens: Keith Goulborn from twenty three; Enterprises - Clive Norris from thirty: Fireflies - probably Tony Weller, but a full record is missing; O.K.s: J. Edward from sixteen. Keith Goulborn and Ian Cox won the Fourteen Opens, twenty one out, but no Bruce Wolfe. Keith also won both spring Firefly Opens. Summer Points volatile, only Enterprise fleet at all consistent, a few Fourteens out sometimes (Bill Simpson now with them) and generally only three or four Fireflies and O.K.s. Winners: Fourteens: - Hugh Kemlo; Enterprises: - John Underwood: - Fireflies: Tony Robinson; O.K.s: J. Edward. We now scheduled around forty six summer races and thirty seven winter. Up to forty three in O.K. Opens, both won by H. Sweetman with J. Edward and Paul Williamson getting seconds. Firefly Opens down a little and winter turnouts generally better than summer.

1971: Records on wind conditions and courses kept again. Enterprise Opens up to seventeen entries. Summer Points up to fifteen to twenty out in all four classes. Winner of Fourteen Opens was James Vernon (Bruce Wolfe hadn't entered) and winning time was 2hrs 39mins. O.K. Open up to thirty one entries, one of a number plagued by very light conditions, which eventually put off visitors. Firefly Open - ten teams and twenty eight individuals.

1972: Winter turnouts strong in Fourteens and Enterprises, but Fireflies and O.K.s often only two to four. Fourteen Opens won by Hugh Kemlo and Keith Goulborn, from twenty one. No records kept from 11th March 1972 to 4th March 1973. Nine Hornets raced one weekend as visitors, persuaded I suspect by Bob Fisher.

1973: Robin Johnson, Robin Dent, John Hart, Ray Rouse, Alex Edwards fairly regular in Fourteens; Tom Trevelyan and Chris Crosland in O.K.s; John Kaye, Bill Buckley, John Start, Gerry Speidel, Nigel Hensman and David Edwards in Enterprises. Only six for Pool of London race. Summer average turnout around eleven. O.K. Opens - twenty two; Firefly - seven teams, fifteen individuals, but Fourteen Opens up to twenty seven, Hugh Kemlo and Jeremy Pudney in first two. Two Lasers *Down Under* and *Meltemi* appeared with their owners Katie Clemson and David Widdowson.

1974: January - Lasers had four starts to themselves, including Bob Fisher and two for Hornets. Enterprise Open - thirteen and seventeen. Winter Series turnouts: Fourteens - four; Enterprises - five; O.K.s - four; Fireflies - three. Winners P. Hallett, John Underwood, Paul Williamson and Tony Robinson. Summer Points sometimes down to just three boats out. Firefly Opens - seven teams and ten individuals, O.K.s - eighteen, with Robin Kemp winning both races. From the winter the Handicap class consisted of Lasers and any other class with two or less entries. October - 'P. Hinton, three stitches in head from boom.' Out of twenty four or twenty five possible Winter Points races the Fourteens sailed in nine, Enterprises twenty five, O.K.s eight and Fireflies eighteen and the average turnout for all Club races was fourteen. Lady Bull's Bowl, sailed in September, saw the last race recorded for Tom Fielding, an active supporter since 1938.

1975: Enterprise Open won by Hugh Kemlo and John Underwood from twelve and fourteen, virtually no visitors. Fourteen Opens won by Hugh Kemlo from up to twenty starters - O.O.D. was Tom Fielding. R.T.Y.C. Pursuit Race only eleven entries, King Morgan twenty six, Hospitals Weekend twenty three. Pool of London 'blustery weather - no entries.' Firefly Opens three teams, eleven individuals. Leading crews: - Jamie Docker, Simon Cawthorne, Yvonne Hugh-Smith, joined in the winter by Mark Hinton and Chris McLaughlin. O.K. Opens down to eight to nine starters - very light winds again. National Albacores visited for one weekend.

1976: Winter Points, hitherto our high spot produced quorums of: seventeen out of twenty nine races for the Fourteens; twenty nine out of thirty one for the Enterprises; four out of twenty nine for the O.K./ Lasers and two out of thirty one for the Fireflies. Simon Cawthorne, Elaine Simpson and Victoria Andrews lead the crews. 28th March - first Laser Open produced twenty entries. Bob Salt as Senior Race Officer officiated throughout much of 1976-77. Excellent turnout of thirty five for King Morgan. Fourteen Opens won by Ray Rouse, a new name to watch out for, from twelve and fifteen. Generally a poor summer for turnouts. John Underwood won the evening series (organised and run by him). The Pool of London-Tower Bridge Race was combined with Ranelagh, starting from Putney. The Lasers had two Opens, nineteen entries, both won by C.

Udo, whose Dutch sailing club nobody could ever spell. Trophy races in November still produced ten Fourteens, nine Enterprises and nine combined O.K.s and Lasers. An Albacore meeting had no entries.

1977: Occasionally the Handicap fleet of O.K.s, Lasers and Fireflies out-numbered the consistent Enterprise fleet in winter. A Laser Open and the Fourteen Opens had around twelve entries. August - Bruce Fraser protested the O.O.D., and won. Owen Cracknell won the summer Fourteen Points; David Beaney appeared in Enterprises. Simon Bombarda was a leading crew and John Roberson and Simon Cawthorne tied in the combined O.K-Laser-Firefly fleet. Much better turnout in winter with up to thirty eight in Club Trophies and forty four for Points.

1978: Lawrence Grand, Hugh Kemlo and R. Singleton won the three classes. Philip Rayner well up in a Laser. The Fourteen Opens had splendid turnouts of twenty three and twenty six, both won by Keith Goulborn. Pool of London Race had seventeen starters, organised from Gil Winfield's Thames barge yacht *Seagull*. Up to thirty on Hospitals week-end, won by Will Henderson in National Twelve from Strand on the Green. Paul Williamson now in Lasers, as were Hugh Kemlo and Paul Hillman, ex-Ranelagh. Two experiments - Early and Late Points series for Enterprises and two days of Match racing.

1979: Winter series winners: Fourteens, Tony Robinson; Enterprises, Bill Buckley, Handicap, Hugh Kemlo. Keith Goulborn won both Fourteen Opens from twenty. In the summer series entries improved with up to twenty two; Fourteen, Enterprise, Laser and O.K. Opens attracting between twelve and twenty seven.

1980: Winter turnout volatile but mainly good; season subdivided into early and late series. Total of eleven Fourteens out; fifteen Enterprises; eighteen Lasers; seven O.K.s, but no

Fireflies! New all-in Handicap series in August and September started. 'Stand-in' Race Officers very frequent, often Evelyn Rayner or Sailing Committee Rep. Twenty seven in Linden House Trophy; twenty six for Christmas Punch Bowl. Sally Dixon and David C. Edwards leading crews.

1981: Up to thirty two out on Club Trophy days. Only ten and fifteen for Fourteen Opens, no visitors, won by Hugh Kemlo. May - 'buoys supplied and laid by Gavin Robertson, launch out of action.' Hospitals' weekend: twenty two and thirty seven starters. Enterprise winners: Gavin Robertson, Jerry Alexander. Handicap: Paul Hillman, Robin Johnson. Crews: Samantha Dixon, Gabriel Kemlo. Very few race officers turning up, with Evelyn Rayner very often deputising. Linden House entries crashed to four, but *Dark Wind* seventeen.

1982: Fourteen Opens: eleven and thirteen, won by Hugh Kemlo. Peter Mack, Martin Dixon, Dick Bradburn, Andy Hewett, David Glover, Ann Petersen, J. Fawcett, Francis Brown, Stephen Aris, Gerry Roseingrave, Johnny Aung, Julian Pearson, and Alan Beaney, all additional regulars. Five to seven Lasers now having own class start. Enterprise Opens: twenty three starters, both won by Alan Beaney.

1983: Winter Points had reasonably healthy turnouts for Enterprises and Lasers. Very few Fourteens and none for Handicap. Nick Paine prominent in Lasers. No record of Jos Collins; and Shackleton had seven entries. Late summer All-In Series had a quorum in all races, averaging ten boats per race, mostly Lasers. Autumn Opens: Enterprises five; Lasers - fourteen, Ben Aris won both.

1984: Winter Points and 'Cinema Indoors Trophy.' No Shackleton, but eleven for Jos Collins and thirteen for the Horizon Trophy, the first John Underwood Memorial series of four races. This drew up to fifteen entries per day. 27th August - a friendly race to the pub at Mortlake, in the rescue boat to

Syon House and back, and race back to the Club. All participants invited by Sally Dixon to dinner.

1985: Winter All-In Trophies varied from nine to eighteen. Fourteen Opens (seven to eight starters) both won by Jeremy Sibthorpe. Prominent in Enterprises: Steve Grant, Bill Buckley, David Edwards; Lasers: Robin Johnson, Andy Hewett, Justin Scott and Nick Paine. Lark Open attracted eight entries. Summer Points averaged about ten boats in total. Carol Dunne, Kate Hammersley and Sally Dixon prominent as crews. Enterprises and Laser Opens now combined to give more of a regatta effect.

1986: Winter Points turnouts very variable: occasionally a few Fourteens; two to eight Enterprises: the same for Lasers. Winter crews: Ann Rennie and Carol Bennett prominent. Keith Goulborn won from eight in both Fourteen Opens. Lark Open attracted five. Councillor Smith's Trophy for under 23s had no entries and only five for the Mayor's Cup. Good entry for Enterprise and Laser Opens: between twelve and eighteen including some visitors. Simon Beeby and Mark Dowling appeared in Lasers. November; a visit from Seaview Sailing Club was won by the Club.

1987: Paul Truitt appeared in Enterprises and Dave Rennie joined the more familiar names in that class; also Huw Foulkes in Fourteens. Gabriel Kemlo won the Summer Points for Lasers, from Robin Johnson and Justin Scott. Councillor Bill Smith's Trophy replaced by the Bolwell Cup, for under 23s, won by Gabriel Kemlo from Fergus Kemlo. Entries well down on last summer's.

1988: Up to fourteen Fourteens for their Autumn Opens; Enterprise Opens five and six. Steve Grant, Chris Perkins, Alan Beaney, Bill Simpson, David Edwards still fairly regular. Faithful crews, Sally Dixon, Miranda Kemlo and Elaine Simpson.

1989: Fourteen Opens both won by Julian Pearson from eight and eleven. February - The Valentine Vendetta, five short races for Enterprises and Lasers brought out fifteen starters - devised by Simon Beeby.

1990: 'From 1st January, 1990, only Trophy Races, Open Meetings and Series Results will be recorded in this book.' End of History! But race entry sheets are kept where possible. Winners of the summer Points: Enterprises - Gavin Robertson, David Edwards, Bill Simpson; Lasers: Paul Williamson, J. Eckford, Hugh Kemlo (also 4th in Enterprises). Sally Dixon in the crews was followed by Lydia Jackson and Georgia Lepper. Better turnouts in the Linden House, Christmas Punch Bowl and Taurus (Hair of the Dog) Trophies - up to twelve.

1991: Two Laser 2 Opens had entries of three and four. The Dark Wind Trophy, with seven entries from Norwich Frostbite Sailing Club, surged to twenty three. Frank Bluff had eight Enterprises; Laser Flask, three; Nina Wood for Lasers, ten and Jos Collins, five.

1992: In the Winter Points twenty two Enterprises sailed at least once, averaging four to five a race, and of sixteen Lasers, three to four. In the summer the King Morgan again had only ten in combined fleet. Nine and fourteen in Hospitals weekend. In the summer Points series the Enterprises averaged two to six per race with the Lasers the same. The late summer Handicap drew three to nine entries and the Linden House five, all Enterprises.

1993: The Valentine Vendetta was popular again, with fifteen, but the Winter Points turnouts were very variable, from one to three a class, but up to ten in total. The Dark Wind Trophy was down to three entries, but the King Morgan up to twenty one and the L.C.S.C. Trophy fourteen.

General impressions and thoughts. We seem to have returned to the turnouts of the pre-war years, but from a much more numerous base. Our greatest turnouts were in the '60's, declining steadily to about 1988, since when we have continued to bump along the bottom. Reasons? Who knows, but possibly the responsibility of the Club building and the anonymous size of the Club has not helped, although Ranelagh Sailing Club has also crashed, but without a change in building. Strand on the Green Sailing Club often average more boats out than us nowadays, eight from twenty three active, out of thirty kept there. S.G.S.C. race only on Sundays, so it could be that the Club has too many races since there has been a decline in dinghy racing generally. If we knew the answer we could put it right.

Outstanding helmsmen: Bruce-Wolfe amongst many eminent Fourteen visitors. Jeremy Pudney, Keith Goulborn, Jeremy Sibthorpe and Julian Pearson in Fourteens. Peter Hinton, Chris Buckley and Hugh Kemlo able to win in any class they tried, but particularly Hugh, who has won virtually every Club Trophy, often many times, and probably turned out more often than anyone since his debut in 1960.

Other long-term features: Bob Salt, as a sailor and O.O.D.; Tom Fielding and Winifred Procter; and still faithfully racing in 1993, David Edwards (1949), Gavin Robertson (1950) and Bill and Elaine Simpson (1960). Finally the Enterprise Class, which has lasted best having seen off possible takeovers from the Lark and Laser 2.

Appendix B

Commodores of The London Corinthian Sailing Club

1894-1900 D.White	1947-1948 W.O.Bradbury
1901 A.Daubeny	1949-1951 F.W.Herbert
1902 A.J.H.Whittaker	1952-1955 TomFielding
1903-1905 R.P.Jacob	1956-1958 A.S.Roberts
1906 A.J.H.Whittaker	1959 C.E.C.King-Morgan
1907-1908 F.H.L.Houlditch	1960-1963 E. P.Withers-Green
1909-1911 E.G.Boutel	1964-1967 G.C.Buckley
1912-1913 W.R.Richardson	1968-1971 Simeon Bull
1914-1915 C.S.Villiers	1972 S.Simpson
1916-1921 T.C. Allengame	1973-1974 E.R.Salt
1922 M.H.Whyte	1975-1976 Sir Anthony Lousada
1923 W.Forster	1977-1978 Don Storrar
1924 W.E.Huckle	1979-1981 A.J.M.Robinson
1925 R. Tilbury	1982-1985 P.C.Rayner
1926 FrankCollis	1986-1988 Mrs. S. Dixon
1927 E.Salt	1989-1990 F.H.Brown
1928 W. E.Huckle	1991-1993 S. Beeby
1929-1930 G.W.Y.Swanson	1993-1994 A.J.M.Robinson
1931-1932 H.W.Mason	
1933-1946 Sir George Bull	

Appendix C
Financial Support for the Centenary History

The Centenary Committee is very grateful to the following for their help towards the cost of publishing this history of the Club.

NAME	YEAR of JOINING
George Harris	1927
Joseph Bloor	1939
Donald Storrar	1948
Kevin Maybury	1950
Gavin Robertson	1950
Joe and Mary Cronk	1950
Arthur Tarrant	1951
Michael Cook	1953
Christopher Buckley	1955
Sally Buckley	1955
Peter Scott	1956
Bill White	1956
Barbara Robinson	1957
Tom Hill	1959
Bill Simpson	1960
Alan Pedersen	1960
Caroline Bishop	1964
David Widdowson	1965
Tony Robinson	1968
Una-Jane Winfield	1968
John Roberson	1968
Philip McDanell	1971
Martin Dixon	1978
James Chrismas	1979

NAME	YEAR of JOINING
Denys Vipond	1979
Mr. & Mrs. P.P.M. Robin	1984
Nicholas Beck	1984
John Martin	1984
Simon Beeby	1986
Judith Healey	1986
Dawn Johnston	1986
Trevor Chapple	1990
Christopher Warrick	1990
Murray Bean	1992
Gillian Ross	1993
John Wilden	1993

Appendix D

Major Trophy Winners

I am sure members will understand that for reasons of space I must limit the names of members who have won Club trophies or distinguished themselves in Open Meetings at other clubs to the most important races in each class. This I think should be sufficient to do justice to the subject and those concerned. In any case as classes faded out and turnouts declined trophies were not only reallocated but the names of the winners became somewhat repetitive.

International Fourteens
Open Meetings

The Shackleton Trophy: Presented to the Club in 1934 by Lady Shackleton in memory of her late husband Sir Ernest Shackleton, the famous explorer. In between 1935 and 1960 the winner was generally E. Bruce Wolfe; others included Stewart Morris, Bruce Banks, C.B. Lapthorne or other visitors.

1935: *Ace* (228) P.L.Chandler; 1960: *Boanerges* (661) G.Buckley; 1969: *Shearwater* (683) K.M.Goulborn; 1971: *Coromandel* (808) R.Dent: 1972: *Dismay* (883) K.M.Goulborn; 1973: *Fortuosity* (930) H.Kemlo; 1974: *Windwhistler* (952) K.M.Goulborn; 1975: *Windwhistler* (952) K.M.Goulborn; 1976 *Seabeat* (1050) R. Rouse; 1980: *Windcheater* (1096) J.Pudney; 1981: *Bird of Dawning* (1095) H.Kemlo; 1982: *Bird of Dawning* (1095) H.Kemlo.

Jos Collins Trophy: Subscribed for by Club members in 1949 in memory of Jos Collins, a member from 1933 and Harbourmaster for many years. The trophy is in the form of a silver bailer:1959: *Water Music* (678) J.Herbert;1960: *Boanerges* (661) G.Buckley;1962:*Fleur de Lys* (715) S.Bull;1966: *Easy Beat* (768) J. Vernon; 1967:*Fanciful* (894) J.Pudney;1970: *Dismay* (883) K.Goulborn.

Club Trophy

President's Trophy: Presented by Sir Alan Herbert in 1948 for International Fourteen Foot and Swordfish dinghies. The trophy is a silver tray with a poem by A.P.H. on it. Simeon Bull won the first trophy outright as described in the text. A new silver tray was presented with a new poem. Some years after A.P.H.'s death in 1971, the name of the trophy was changed to The Sir Alan Herbert Trophy, Sir George Bull having become President. This is now being sailed for by helmsmen of 50 years or more and has reverted to the President's Trophy. As I have had that honour thrust upon me I suppose it's quite appropriate.

1948: *Ace* (345) W.Bradbury; 1949: *Nore* (?) L.Hellyer;1950 *Robin Hood* (531) F.Wells;1951: *Tarka* (547) T.Felton;1952 *Pheon* (590) A.Roberts; 1953: *Grey Goose* (15/17) F.Cator;1954: *Friar Tuck* (589) Dr. M.Gilkes;1955: *Lutine* (15/47) P.Curry; 1956-1958: *Serapis* (615) S.Bull;1959: *Fleur de Lys* (715) S.Bull;1960: *Fleur de Lys* (715) S.Bull; 1961: *Concerto* (706) Dr. P. Smart;1962: *Talaria* (804) J.Shelley; 1963: *Concerto* (706) Dr. Paul Smart; 1964: *Curlew* (757) A.W.Prince;1965: *Firebird* (748) J.M.Vines; 1966: *Pequod* (905) S.Bull;1967: *Fanciful* (894) J.Pudney; 1968: *Fanciful* (894) J.Pudney; 1969: *Windwhisper* (925) J.Pudney;1970: *Wasp* (791) H.Kemlo; 1971: *Dismay* (883) K.Goulborn;1972:

Fortuosity (930) H.Kemlo;1973: *Soliloquy* (961) C.Bullock; 1974-1977: *Windwhistler* (952) K.Goulborn;1978: *Gemini* (934) Dr.T. Trevelyan;1979-1984: *Bird of Dawning* (1095) H.Kemlo;1985: *Tartan Magic* (1090) N. Edwards; 1986: *Fortissimo* (1127) C.Kitson; 1987: *Bird of Dawning* (1095) H.Kemlo; 1988: *Fortissimo* (1127) C.Kitson; 1989-1990 not awarded; 1991: Mollie Johnson; *Laser* (123603) R. Johnson; 1992: Race abandoned; 1993: No race because of strong winds.

Prince of Wales Cup Race

Club members or ex-Club members in the first six

1967: 2nd *Fanciful* (894), J.Pudney; 1969: 5th *Windwhisper* (925) J.Pudney; 1970: 1st *Windwhistler* (952) J.Pudney; 6th *Seawife* (934) J.Geoffrey; 1971: 2nd *Windrustler* (962) J.Pudney; 5th *Dismay* (883) K.Goulborn;1972: 6th *Dismay* (883) K.Goulborn; 1973; 1st *Windchatter* (1000) J.Pudney; 3rd *Dismay* (883) K.Goulborn; 5th *Magnum Opus* (930) D. Owen; 1974: 1st *Maius Opus* (1030) D. Owen; 4th *Windchatter* (1000) J.Pudney; 6th *Windwhistler* (952) K.Goulborn; 1975: 2nd *Opus Maximum* (1044) D. Owen; 1976: 1st *Seabeat* (1050) R. Rouse; 1977: 3rd *Windwhistler* (952) K.Goulborn; 4th *Gemini (934)* Dr.T. Trevelyan; 1978: 2nd *Windwhistler* (952) K. Goulborn; 1979: 2nd *Windconqueror* (1066) J.Pudney; 5th *Bird of Dawning* (1095) H.Kemlo; 1980: 6th *Windclipper* (1118) J.Pudney;1981: 3rd *Windclipper* (1118) J.Pudney; 5th *Storm Beat* (1086) R.Rouse; 6th *Windwhistler* (952) K.Goulborn; 1984: 5th *Moody Blues* (1128) Dr.T.Trevelyan; 1986: 5th *Ramrod* (1179) J.Sibthorpe.

285

Winners of the Itchenor Gallon

1968: *Windwhisper* (925) J.Pudney; 1971: *Windrustler* (962) J.Pudney; 1972: *Windchatter* (1000) J.Pudney; 1973: *Dismay* (883) K.Goulborn; 1975: *Windchuckler* (1046) J.Pudney; 1977: *Windwhistler* (952) K.Goulborn;1978: *Stormbeat* (1086) R.Rouse; 1979: *Windwhistler* (952) K.Goulborn; 1981: *Windwhistler* (952) K.Goulborn; 1982: *Bird of Dawning* (1095) H.Kemlo.

Firefly Trophies
The Doreen ChallengeCup

Presented in 1905 by H. Crowley Jones and raced by the Handicap class originally. Allocated to Fireflies in 1949.

1949: *Fillister* (279) J.Bloor; 1950-1952: unrecorded; 1953: *Dainty* (462) J.Armitt; 1954: *Burrasca* (782) D.Edwards; 1955 -1956: *Driftwood* (1077) P.Dixon; 1957: *Domani* (1478) J.Jupe; 1958: *Ragamuffin* (809) D.Storrar; 1959-1961: *Fuego* (465) P.Hinton; 1962; *Drummond* (2282) H.Kemlo; 1963: *Fuego* (465) P.Hinton; 1964; *Windswept* (2846) P.Calder; 1965: *Bolero*: (1438) P.Hinton; 1966; unrecorded; 1967: *The Heap*: (556) M.Collyer; 1968: *Domani* (1478) J.Jupe; 1969: *Wee-Booty* (1673) K.Goulborn; 1970: unrecorded; 1971: *Burrasca* (782) D.Edwards: 1972: unrecorded; 1973: *Burrasca* (782) D.Edwards; 1974: *Nutters* (2198) R.Portway; 1975: *Burrasca* (782) D.Edwards; 1976: *Supermousse* (2663) P.Hinton; 1977; *Hub-Hub* (3331) R.Portway; 1978: Hub-Hub (3331) R.Portway; Re-allocated to Lasers in 1979 as an Open Meeting Trophy. 1979: *Ruime-Rakker* (52331);1980: *Tin-Tin-Two* (77937); 1981-1982: *Not Yet* (85187) R.Johnson; 1983: *J'Oublie* (77614)

H.Kemlo; 1984: *Ruined II* (107028) A.Hewett; 1985: *Mollie* (107024) R.Johnson; 1986-1987: Tin-Tin (113688) H.Kemlo; 1988 *Mollie* (123603) R.Johnson; 1989: *Chicago Sting* (52435) D.Glover; 1990-1991: *Touchwood* (73659) Una-Jane Winfield; 1992-1993: *Mollie* (123603) R.Johnson.

Royal Thames Yacht Club Cup

Presented by the R.T.Y.C. in 1955 to be sailed by Firefly dinghies in the winter season.

1956: *Phoenix* (1366) P.Lamey; 1957: *Formulus* (1398) J.Conway-Jones; 1958: *Harmatton* (1647) M.Allott & C.Andrews; 1959: *Leste* (1258) R.U.S.C.; 1960: *Wee Booty* (1673) C.Goulborn; 1961: *Harpy* (1809) B.Southcott; 1962: *Teremot II* (1480) J.Pudney; 1963: *Daisy* (963) J.Vines; 1964: *Swerve* (2912) M.Cook; 1965: *The Heap* (556) M.Collyer; 1966: *Daisy* (963) J.Vines; 1967: *The Heap* (556) M.Collyer; 1968: *Gemini Too* (2816) J.Tagg; 1969: *The Heap* (556) M.Collyer; 1970: *Nutters* (2198) K.Goulborn; 1971: *Pansy* (129) H.Kemlo; 1972-1973: not recorded. 1974: Trophy reallocated as an all-in pursuit race.

Morton Stephenson Firefly Tankard

Presented by Morton Stephenson in 1949 as an Open Event.

1949: *Nimbus* (316) Dr. M.Gilkes; 1950: *Firelite II* (571) A.Vines; 1951: *Glissade* (657) Dr. P.Clements; 1952: A.Cleminson; 1953: *Transient* (157) W.Maddison; 1954-1955: *Phoenix II* (1366) Sqd-Ldr P.Lamey; 1956: *Nomad* (297) A.Tarrant; 1957: *Wigwam* (1492) G.Buckley; 1958: *My Guinness* (358) P.Goodison; 1959-1960: *Vector* (627) M.Cooke; 1961: *Tenemot II* (1480) J.Pudney;

1962; *Blossom*: (1351) J.Pudney; 1963: *Fuego* (465) P.Hinton; 1964: *Mood Indigo* (1325) G.Taylor; 1965-1966: *Bumboat* (2902) D.Bacon; 1967-1968: *Spaghetti* (3146) P.Milanese; 1969: *Daisy* (693) J.Vines; 1970: *Pansy* (129) H.Kemlo; 1971: *Gay Abandon* (3262) T.Wright; 1972: not recorded. 1973: *Bolero* (1438) P.Hinton; 1974: *Nutters* (2198) R.Portway; 1975: *Fred* (916) R.Hasler.

Frank Livingstone Trophy.

An Open Event for Firefly dinghies
Presented by John and Frank Livingstone in 1957.

1959: *Harmatton* (1697) M.Allott & C.Andrews; 1960: *Wigwam* (1492) G.Buckley; 1960-1961: *The Heap* (2345) M.Collyer; 1962: *Teremott II* (1480) J.Pudney; 1963: *Fuego* (435) P.Hinton; 1964: *S S S Mug* (2787) R.Preedy; 1965-1966: *Bolero* (1438) P.Hinton; 1967: *Wee Booty* (1673) K.Goulborn; 1968-1969: *Daisy* (963) J.Vines; 1970: *Nutters* (2198) K.Goulborn. Discontinued.

Nina Wood Team Trophy

Presented by Laurie Wood in memory of his wife in 1950 for an inter-club team race.

1951: Miss J.Bluff & Dr. P. Clements, L.C.S.C.; 1952: unrecorded; 1953: Miss J.Bluff & D.Edwards, L.C.S.C.; 1954: W.Owers & D.Hicks, R.A.F. S.A.; 1955: L.Line & I. Spear., Royal Signals Sailing Club; 1956: W.H.S.A.; 1957: Thames United Sailing Club; 1958: G.Janssen & J.Dry, Laleham; 1959: J.Day & A.Janssen, Laleham Sailing Club; 1960: J. Day &

P.Brewer, L.C.S.C.; 1961: J.Vines & J.Dankley, Cambridge Cruising Club; 1962: H.Kemlo & P.Williamson, Strand on the Green; 1963: E.Reilly & D.White, Felixstowe Ferry; 1964: J.Vines & G.Buckley, Oxford and Cambridge Sailing Club; 1965: N.Hessig & P.Milanese, Bosham Sailing Club; 1966: M.Collyer & P.Hinton, L.C.S.C.; 1967: E.Reilly & D.White, Felixstowe Ferry; 1968: C.Hawkes & P.Ranoe, Bosham Sailing Club; 1969: P.Hinton & J.Tagg, Laleham Sailing Club; 1970: H.Kemlo & S.Vines, L.C.S.C.; 1971: P.Shaw & M.Curry, Itchenor Sailing Club; 1972: no records; 1973: H.Riddle & W.Edwards, L.C.S.C.; 1974: R.Portway & P.Hinton, Laleham Sailing Club; 1975: M.Hudson & S.Hinton, Laleham Sailing Club.

Swordfish Class
The Tilney Tankard

Presented by H.G.T.Bassett in 1953

1953-1954: *Grey Goose* (15/72) F.Cator; 1955: *Piscator* (15/25) E.Edwards: 1956: *Fantome* (15/67); 1957: *Audax* (15/66) K.Hobling; 1958-1960: *Mary Lou* (15/88).

The Enterprise Class
The Frank Bluff Trophy

Presented by Frank Bluff in 1938.
Allocated to Club Enterprise races in 1960.

1961: *Custy* (4713) S.Simpson; 1962: *Ratbag* (4713) J.Rawlinson; 1963-1964: *Shoshana* (7025) P.Williamson; 1965: *Skim* (1836) H.Kemlo; 1966 *Popetty* (7030) J. Underwood;1967: *Man of*

Berwick (10707) H.Kemlo; 1968: *Popetty* (7030) J.Underwood; 1969: Nordlys (13595) C.Norris; 1970: *Popetty* (7030) J.Underwood; 1971: *Molotov Cocktail* (14860) I.Templeman; 1972: unrecorded; 1973: *Polaris* (9552) C.Buckley; 1974: Popetty (7030) J.Underwood; 1975: *Skim* (1836) H.Kemlo; 1976: *Baguette* (2368) A.Bailey; 1977: *Sundown* (6344) P.Frost; 1978: Sizzling *Bacon* (15664) P.Montague; 1979: *Rolling Bones* (13599) P.Montague; 1980: Beans *Again* (19964) D.Beaney; 1981: Mustang *One* (17501) N.Edwards; 1982: *Zenobia* (18116) G.Robertson; 1983: *Bean Evil Again* (20323) A.Beaney; 1984: *Force Four* (19233) D.Edwards; 1985: *Moonriser* (19593) W.Buckley; 1986: *Or This One* (20647) David Glover; 1987: *Zenobia* (18116) G.Robertson; 1988: *Moonriser* (19593) W.Buckley; 1989: *Crisis* (6115) S.Beeby; 1990: *Dram* (20650) D.Rennie; 1991: *Magic Time Machine* (22124) Clive Norris; 1992: *Force Four* (19233) D.Edwards; 1993: *Zenobia* (18116) G.Robertson.

Open Enterprise Trophies

Eyot Challenge Cup. Presented by E.M. Van Moppes in 1938. Allocated to Enterprise dinghies in 1960.

1961: *Easterly* (3680) P.Bloor; 1962: *Orrid Ogre* (4287) C.Goulborn; 1963: *Roxanne* (1712) R.Hughes; 1964: no records; 1965: *Skim* (1836) H.Kemlo; 1966: *Emily* (7722) T.Hill; 1967: *Cho-Cho-San* (9785) W.Bauer; 1968: *R.Stevensons* (12929) T.Wade; 1969: *Cinzano* (8809) P.Crebbin; 1970: *Linden Lion* (15,000) H.Kemlo; 1971: *Molotov Cocktail* (14860) I.Templeman; 1972: no record; 1973: no record; 1974: *In Transit* (15146) F.Neale; 1975: *Skim* (1836) H.Kemlo; 1976 *Easterly* (3680) H.Kemlo; 1977: *Ho Ho* (9673) H.Kemlo; 1978: *The Bean Machine* (13857) D.Beaney; 1979-1981: *Beans Again* (19964) D.Beaney; 1982: *Bean Evil Again* (20323) A.Beaney;

1983: *Nailbiter* (19567) S.Grant; 1984: *Seawood* (20807) D. Manson; 1985: *Moonriser* (19593) W.Buckley; 1986-1987: *Take It For Granted* (21362) S.Grant; 1988: *Mr. C* (21795) S.Grant; 1989: *Moonriser* (19593) W.Buckley; 1990: *Skim* (1836) H.Kemlo; 1991: *Seawood* (20807) D.Manson; 1992: *Tiamat* (14822) Chris Perkins; 1993: *Zenobia* (18116) G.Robertson.

John Livingstone Trophy

Presented by John and Frank Livingstone in 1957

1961: *Orrid Ogre* (4287) C.Goulborn; 1962-1963: *Shoshana* (7025) P.Williamson; 1964-1965: no record; 1966: *Popetty* (7030) J.Underwood; 1967: *Man of Berwick* (10707) H.Kemlo; 1968 *Pilot* (1836) sailed by H.Kemlo; 1969: *Skim* (10707) H.Kemlo; 1970: *Enshallah* (11299) P.Charles; 1971: *The Fly One* (15234) R.Collins; 1972-1973: no records; 1974: *In Transit* (15146) F.Neale; 1975: *Popetty* (7030) J.Underwood; 1976: *Easterly* (3680) H.Kemlo; 1977: *Symbiosysis* (18179) R.Cambrook; 1978: *Skim* (16166) H.Kemlo; 1979 *Rolling Bones* (13599) P.Montague; 1980: *Beans Again* (19964) D.Beaney; 1981: *Moonriser* (19593) W.Buckley; 1982: *Bean Evil Again* (20323) A.Beaney; 1983: *Skim* (1836) H.Kemlo; 1984: *Bean Evil Again* (20323) A. Beaney; 1985: *Take It For Granted* (21362) S.Grant; 1986-1987: *Beans Mean Business* (21368) A.Beaney; 1988: *Bean Lucky* (21809) A.Beaney; 1989-1993: *Blanc Bean* (20234) D.Beaney.

The O.K. Class
Trophies for Open Meetings

The John Martin Trophy

Presented by John Martin in 1965

1965: *T in C* (458) G.Buckley;1966: *Tinkle-Tyme II* (940) G.Buckley;1967: *Panache* (793) P.Williamson; 1968: *T in C* (488) G.Buckley; 1969: *Jennie Bailey* (651) R.Digby;1970: *Poison Dwarf* (1289) H.Sweetman; 1971: *Humbug* (1193) C.Miller; 1972: *Mokturtle* (1207) J.Bickerton; 1973: *Cart in the West* (818) T.Darwin; 1974: *Half-Hearted* (1510) R.Kemp; 1975: *Spirit* (1721) M.Mence; 1976: *Daylight Come* (1774) A. McMichael;1977: *What's Up Doc?* (1759) C.Evison; 1978: *Banjo* (413) M.Brookes;1979: *More Ruddy Sauce* (1210) D.Matthew;1980: *How Now* (1933) T.Weeden;1981: *Blood Vessel* (1893) I.Godfrey;1982: *Va Polie* (1304) C.Selby.

The Bridge-Butler Trophy

Presented by James Bridge-Butler in 1965

1965: *T in C* (488) G.Buckley;1966: no record;1967: *T in C* (488) P.Hinton;1968: *Censored* (178) R.Wilde;1969: *Hoof-Hearted* (1117) R.Kemp;1970: *Poison Dwarf* (1289) H.Sweetman;1971: *Nichala* (954) N.Read Wilson;1972: *Fat Freddie* (865) H.Kemlo;1973-1974: *Half-Hearted* (1510) R.Kemp;1975: *Rodsok* (1683) R.Tidd;1976-1977: *What's Up Doc?* (1759) C.Evison;1978: *Django* (1738) R.Webb; 1979: *More Ruddy Sauce* (1210) D.Matthew; 1980: *Organised Chaos* (1153) D.Beaney; 1981: *Blood Vessel* (1893) I. Godfrey;1982: *Va Polie* (1304) D.Matthew.

The Laser Class Trophies

Apart from the Doreen Cup as from 1979

The Laser Flask

A Club Trophy presented by Simon Bombarda in 1978

1978: *Egg* (52340) S.Cawthorne;1979-1980:*White Owl* (75371) P.Hillman;1981: *RedShift* (61225) C.Koper;1982: *Not Yet* (85187)R.Johnson;1983-1984: *PaNick* (41334)N.Paine;1985:*Mollie* (107024) R.Johnson;1986: *Capt Haddock* (113688) H.Kemlo;1987-1988: *Mollie* (123603) R.Johnson;1989-1990: *Tin-Tin* (138269) H.Kemlo;1991: *Mollie* (123603) R.Johnson;1992-1993: *Tin-Tin* (138269) H.Kemlo.

The Copper Kettle

Presented by Ian Bruce in 1976 for an Open event

1976: *Pig* (21536)C.Udo; 1977:*Incitatus* (29138) A.Wilson;1978: *Incitatus* (29138) C.Udo;1979-1980: *Ruime Rukker* (52331) C.Udo;1981: no finisher; 1982: no name (57940) D.Beaney;1983: *Ben the Boy* (103342) Ben Aris; 1984: no name of boat or helmsman (8366); 1985: (120427) A.Stones; 1986: *Mollie* (123603) R.Johnson; 1987: no name (126339) J.Scott;1988: *Captain Haddock* (113688) H.Kemlo; 1989: no name (121666) S.Beeby;1990: *Tin-Tin* (138269) H.Kemlo;1991: *Touchwood II* (136614) Una-Jane Winfield;1992: no name (119289) M.Sancken;1993: *Tin-Tin* (138269) H.Kemlo.

The Nina Wood Trophy

Allocated to the Lasers as an Open event from 1979

1979: *Ruime Rukker* (52331) C.Udo; 1980: *Not Yet* (85187) R.Johnson; 1981: *Roxane* (75254) H. Kemlo; 1982: no name (73151) M.Sancken; 1983: *Ben the Boy* (103342) Ben Aris;1984: no name or number D.Halling: 1985: no name (120427) A.Stones; 1986: no name (113688) Iain McGregor; 1987: no name (88779) R.Whitton; 1988: *Mollie* (123603) R.Johnson; 1989 no name (133246) N.Paine; 1990: no name (119289) M.Sancken: 1991: no name nor number J.Houghton;1992-1993: *Tin-Tin* (138629) H.Kemlo.